UNRULY WORDS

UNRULY WORDS

A Study of Vague Language

Diana Raffman

OXFORD
UNIVERSITY PRESS

OXFORD
UNIVERSITY PRESS

Oxford University Press is a department of the University of Oxford.
It furthers the University's objective of excellence in research, scholarship,
and education by publishing worldwide.

Oxford   New York

Auckland   Cape Town   Dar es Salaam   Hong Kong   Karachi
Kuala Lumpur   Madrid   Melbourne   Mexico City   Nairobi
New Delhi   Shanghai   Taipei   Toronto

With offices in

Argentina   Austria   Brazil   Chile   Czech Republic   France   Greece
Guatemala   Hungary   Italy   Japan   Poland   Portugal   Singapore
South Korea   Switzerland   Thailand   Turkey   Ukraine   Vietnam

Oxford is a registered trademark of Oxford University Press
in the UK and certain other countries.

Published in the United States of America by
Oxford University Press
198 Madison Avenue, New York, NY 10016

Library of Congress Cataloging-in-Publication Data
Raffman, Diana.
Unruly words : a study of vague language / Diana Raffman.
pages cm
Includes bibliographical references and index.
ISBN 978-0-19-991510-1 (hardcover : alk. paper)   1. Semantics.   2. Vagueness
(Philosophy)   3. Borderline cases.   4. Language and languages—Philosophy.   I. Title.
P325.R26 2013
401.43—dc23
2013010506

1 3 5 7 9 8 6 4 2
Printed in the United States of America
on acid-free paper

In Memory of
Rita, Relly, Joe, Memère, Dorothy,
Robert, Mary, Ellie,
and Ruth

CONTENTS

CONTENTS

PREFACE

In my first work on vagueness (e.g., Raffman, 1994, 1996), I argued that linguistic vagueness was a form of contextual sensitivity and that certain psychological factors entered crucially into the contexts relative to which vague words are applied. I thought that insofar as language is vague, semantics could not be divorced from psychology in the way most philosophers of language have supposed. Those early papers received some attention but also met with skepticism. I was told that I didn't understand the difference between a semantic theory and a theory of use, or worse, that I wasn't doing philosophy: I was telling an interesting but merely psychological story.

I have since come to believe that vagueness has nothing essentially to do with context-sensitivity (though the two often appear together). The competent application of a vague word is variable, both inter- and intrasubjectively, in roughly the way I initially had in mind, but not because of any contextual sensitivity. In fact, I now think it is of the essence of vagueness that the competent application of a vague word varies even when the operative context is held fixed. And while the psychological factors I originally cited do play a role, I now see them as explaining certain features of the competent *use* of a vague word, as distinct from its semantics strictly speaking. (I have also learned that some linguists find a distinction between semantics and use nonsensical. I guess there is no pleasing all of the people all of the time.) On my present view, in the broadest terms, vagueness is a form of multiple reference, and the competent use of a vague word is characterized by arbitrary divergences among competent speakers' applications of it. In the pages that follow, I develop and defend this different, noncontextualist approach.

The list of people and institutions who helped me to write this book is too long to enumerate here. I will mention only some of them and hope that the others will accept my implicit thanks. I am grateful to Jonas Akerman, Nick Asher, Chris Barker, Simon Blackburn, Susanne Bobzien, Scott Brewer, Tyler Burge, Lynda Burns, Elizabeth Cohen, Daniel Dennett, James Davies, Imogen Dickie, Richard Dietz, Paul Egré, Daniel Farrell, Graeme Forbes, Patrick Greenough, Katherine Hawley, Benj Hellie, Terry Horgan, Don Hubin, Mari Riess Jones, Hans Kamp, Chris Kennedy, Bill Ladusaw, Eve LaPlante, Mike Martin, Mohan Matthen, Sebastiano Moruzzi, Jennifer Nagel, Caroline Palmer, George Pappas, Chris Potts, Geoff Pullum, Greg Ray, Giuseppina Ronzitti, Mark Sainsbury, Barbara Scholz, George Schumm, Phil Serchuk, Allan Silverman, Walter Sinnott-Armstrong, Barry Smith, Roy Sorensen, Jason Stanley, William Taschek, Sergio Tenenbaum, Neil Tennant, Michael Tye, Jonathan Vogel, Michael Watkins, Jefferson White, Tim Williamson, Jessica Wilson, Crispin Wright, Elia Zardini, and a very wise anonymous referee for Oxford University Press. Ruth Barcan Marcus advised and encouraged me from 1980 to the time of her death in 2012. My family and friends have put up with years of holiday breaks interrupted or obliterated altogether by my obsession with this material. They know who they are, and I hope they know how grateful I am.

What vagueness is.

I also received a lot of helpful feedback from audiences at Dartmouth College; Columbia University; the Institut Jean-Nicod; the Institute for Philosophy at the University of London; the North American Summer School for Logic, Language, and Information at Stanford; Northwestern University; The Ohio State University; the Society for Exact Philosophy; Tufts University; UCLA; UC Santa Cruz; the University of St Andrews; the University of Texas at Austin; the University of Toronto (especially the students in my two graduate seminars on vagueness); and Washington University in St Louis.

For funding and/or the use of facilities, I am indebted to the Arché Centre at the University of St Andrews, the Rockefeller Foundation Bellagio Center, The Ohio State University, the Social Sciences and Humanities Research Council of Canada, and the University of Toronto. OUP editor Peter Ohlin, associate editor Lucy Randall, and the production team were wonderful to work with.

My greatest debt is to Stewart Shapiro, Del Lindsey, and Angela Brown, my former colleagues at Ohio State University. Shapiro, author of an important book on vagueness (*Vagueness in Context*, Oxford University Press, 2007), has educated me and influenced my views at virtually every step of the way, and our conversations about vagueness over the years have been one of the great joys of my philosophical life. Psychologists Lindsey and Brown designed and, with me as gofer, ran an experiment to test a hypothesis of mine about how competent speakers apply vague words. I was exceptionally lucky to connect with these two fine scientists willing to spend their time and energy investigating questions that must have seemed to them bizarre at best. Philosophers rarely get the chance to test their empirical hypotheses, and I am deeply grateful to Lindsey and Brown for enabling me to do so. As will become clear in chapter 5, our experimental results form the evidential basis of the theory of vagueness presented in this book.

UNRULY WORDS

Chapter 1

Introduction and Fundamentals

Abraham stood yet before the LORD. And Abraham drew near, and said, Wilt thou also destroy the righteous with the wicked? Peradventure there be fifty righteous within the city: wilt thou also destroy and not spare the place for the fifty righteous that are therein? . . . . And the LORD said, If I find in Sodom fifty righteous within the city, then I will spare all the place for their sakes. And Abraham answered and said. . . . Peradventure there shall lack five of the fifty righteous: wilt thou destroy all the city for lack of five? And he said, If I find there forty and five, I will not destroy it. And he spake unto him yet again, and said, Peradventure there shall be forty found there. And he said, I will not do it for forty's sake. And he said unto him, Oh let not the LORD be angry, and I will speak: Peradventure there shall thirty be found there. And he said, I will not do it, if I find thirty there. And he said, Behold now, I have taken upon me to speak unto the LORD: Peradventure there shall be twenty found there. And he said, I will not destroy it for twenty's sake. And he said, Oh let not the LORD be angry, and I will speak yet but this once: Peradventure ten shall be found there. And he said, I will not destroy it for ten's sake. And the LORD went his way, as soon as he had left communing with Abraham.

Genesis 18: 22–33
King James Bible

Perhaps the only point on which all theorists of vagueness agree is that vagueness is a form of unclarity—specifically, an unclarity about the boundaries of things. In language, vagueness concerns the extent of a term's application: There is no clear or definite boundary between the items to which the term applies and the items to which it does not. Some philosophers (e.g., Tye 1996, Hawley 2002, Maddy 2007, Barnes 2010) think that objects in the mind-independent, language-independent world also can be vague: Where does the mountain end and the valley begin? But the primary locus of vagueness is natural language, and linguistic vagueness is what I will be talking about.

'Tall', 'blue', 'heap', 'rich', and 'old' are prime examples of vague words: No clear line divides the tall people from the above average, or the blue objects from the green, or the old people from the middle-aged. In contrast, people who are precisely 6 feet tall are clearly divided from people of any other height, and objects that reflect light of precisely 475 nanometers are clearly divided from objects of any other reflectance. Most theorists of vagueness take the unclarity to be semantic, meaning that vague words lack sharp boundaries of application (they have "blurred" or "fuzzy" boundaries), but some take the unclarity to be epistemic, meaning that vague words have sharp boundaries whose locations are unknowable. I will say more about these different interpretations shortly.

As we start out, it is helpful to note how vagueness differs from several other species of linguistic unclarity, including underspecificity, ambiguity, and certain forms of indeterminacy. If you ask me when the meeting starts and I reply, "Between nine and five," my reply is precise, hence not vague, but it is *underspecific* for the purpose at hand. *Ambiguity* is the possession of two or more meanings, no matter whether vague or precise. For example, the ambiguous word 'odd' can mean 'peculiar' (presumably vague) or 'not evenly divisible by 2' (presumably precise). The difference between vagueness and at least one species of *indeterminacy* is explained by Patrick Greenough:

> Suppose we stipulate that the open sentence '*x* is an oldster' is determinately true of every person sixty-eight years of age and over, determinately false of those persons sixty-five years of age and under, and neither determinately true nor determinately false of the remainder. If a speaker applies this term to persons who are between sixty-five and sixty-eight then we are entitled to say that they have done something not quite right and done something not quite wrong according to the dictates of the stipulation. But … '*x* is an oldster' … is *not* vague but rather, in some sense, semantically incomplete. This species of indeterminacy per se is not vagueness, since the term 'oldster' draws a perfectly sharp and clearly identifiable three-fold division across its associated dimension of comparison. (2003, 245)   *sharp division - not vague*

Vagueness differs also from the kind of indeterminacy found in, say, the claim that Sherlock Holmes liked arugula. (Conan Doyle didn't say.) In principle this kind of unclarity could be removed without changing the meanings of any of the words involved. (Conan Doyle could have said.)[1] In contrast, vagueness is supposed to be a permanent unclarity whose removal would risk changing the meaning— indeed would threaten the very communicative utility—of a vague word. Crispin Wright asks us to

> suppose it is possible [to sharpen 'heap']. Then what in the semantics of [the word] is already inconsistent with our so refining [it]? …. 'Heap' is *essentially* a coarse predicate, whose application is a matter of rough and ready judgement…. It would for example be absurd to force the question of the execution of the

command, 'Pour out a heap of sand here', to turn on a count of the grains. (1976, 333; emphasis added)

Some philosophers do conceive of vagueness as a form of indeterminacy, however. We will hear more about this idea.

Possession of unclear boundaries (semantic or epistemic) is often thought to be linked in some necessary way to two other linguistic phenomena: borderline cases and sorites paradoxes. Many theorists think that vagueness just consists in having borderline cases, where the latter are conceived as items to which it is unclear whether the word in question applies. More formally, borderline cases for a vague word 'Φ' are supposed to be *neither definitely (clearly) Φ nor definitely not-Φ*.[2] A cloth patch whose hue lies midway between a definite blue and a definite green may be neither definitely blue nor definitely not-blue, and a 65-year-old person may be neither definitely old nor definitely not-old. Christopher Kennedy and Louise McNally write that "the possibility of...'borderline cases' is one of the defining properties of vague predicates" (2005, 360), and Roy Sorensen notes "wide agreement that a term is vague to the extent that it has borderline cases" (2012).

Soriticality, the property of generating the notorious sorites paradox, is also often said to be criterial or constitutive of vagueness. For example, Otavio Bueno and Mark Colyvan claim that "a predicate is vague just in case it can be employed to generate a sorites argument" (2008, 5), and Wright asserts that "it would be inconsistent with elements already present in the semantics of [vague] predicates so to refine their senses that the sorites reasoning was blocked" (1976, 333). To see how the paradox gets going, suppose we are interested in the richness, measured by annual salary, of Americans aged forty to sixty in 2001. Then consider a series of salaries progressing from one that would make such an American clearly rich, say $200,000, to one that would make him clearly middle income, hence clearly not-rich,

contra Fine

4

say $50,000. (If you dislike these figures, feel free to substitute ones you prefer. The endpoints of the series need not be paradigm or prototypical cases—just clear or non-borderline ones.) Suppose further that each salary in the series is one dollar lower than its predecessor. Then it seems we can generate the following argument:

> $200,000 is a rich salary.
> For any number n, if $n is a rich salary, then $(n - 1) is a rich salary.
> Therefore $50,000 is a rich salary.

The premises seem true and the reasoning valid, yet we arrive at a contradiction: $50,000 both is and is not a rich salary.[3] Use of mathematical induction is not the culprit, for the absurd conclusion can be reached also by (among other things) a series of applications of *universal instantiation* and *modus ponens*:

> $200,000 is a rich salary.
> For any number n, if $n is a rich salary, then $(n - 1) is a rich salary.
> If $200,000 is a rich salary, then $199,999 is a rich salary.
> If $199,999 is a rich salary, then $199,998 is a rich salary.
> Etc.
> Therefore $50,000 is a rich salary.[4]

Soritical reasoning may be familiar from debates about abortion rights: Since a newborn infant is a person, and a human organism, say, one second younger than a person is also a person, it seems to follow that a conceptus is a person. The existence of the latter argument suggests that the word 'person' too is vague. (Of course, the conclusion that a conceptus is a person is not obviously absurd. Hence it is a matter of some urgency for defenders of abortion rights to figure out what is wrong with soritical reasoning generally.) Dorothy Edgington observes that

> the paradox is not just a philosopher's puzzle, but something which affects our lives. There's the 'mañana paradox': the unwelcome task which needs to be done, but it's always a matter of indifference whether it's done today or tomorrow; the dieter's paradox: I don't care at all about the difference to my weight one chocolate will make. (1997, 296)

Theoretical difficulties caused by the paradox and by vagueness generally are not confined to philosophy and linguistics. Among other things, vagueness poses significant problems in the law (e.g., Waldron 1994, Endicott 2000, 2011), and in one way or another soritical reasoning threatens the coherence of the preference and indifference relations in rational choice theory (e.g., Quinn 1990, Ackerman 1994, Voorhoeve and Binmore 2006, Tenenbaum and Raffman 2012).

The major premise of the paradox (or each conditional premise) expresses the intuition that vague words *tolerate* incremental changes on the dimensions decisive of their application. As Wright explains, "there is with respect to any vague predicate the notion of a positive degree of change...insufficient to alter the justice with which [the predicate] is applied" (1975, 229). The mystery of the paradox is that, since any two adjacent items in a sorites series are only incrementally different, either both satisfy the predicate in question or neither does; either both salaries are rich or neither is. But then how is a transition made from 'rich' to any other predicate ('middle income,' 'borderline rich,' 'not-rich,' etc.)? How can there be—as surely there must be—a last rich salary in this apparently seamless, boundaryless, series?[5]

On its face, the paradox seems to show that many of our ordinary words are incoherent: Their use leads to contradictions. On the other hand, ordinary speakers use vague words all the time without landing in absurdities like the one above; no competent speaker will keep applying 'rich' all the way down to $50,000. Indeed, far from paralyzing or incoherent, vagueness seems essential to our ability to communicate using natural language; vague words allow us to communicate easily, in a quick and casual way, without having to count grains of sand or dollars and cents of salary. These considerations suggest that the paradox is solvable, i.e., that it should be possible to discover what goes wrong in the paradoxical argument. Although several philosophers have argued that the sorites is incurable and vague words really are incoherent (e.g., Frege 1903, Dummett 1975), most have sought to exonerate vague language by clearing the puzzle away.

At a minimum, an adequate theory of vagueness needs to say exactly what vagueness is and what borderline cases are, and respond to the sorites paradox, and also make clear how these three phenomena—vagueness, borderline cases, and soriticality—are related. It has proven extremely difficult to do all of this; many attempts have been made. Since the project of this book is to provide such a theory, we need at the outset to have an idea of the major competing accounts that have been proposed and the kinds of difficulties they face. These other accounts have been amply reviewed and criticized elsewhere (e.g., Williamson 1994, Keefe and Smith 1999, Keefe 2000), so I will be brief.

1.1. WHIRLWIND TOUR OF COMPETING THEORIES OF VAGUENESS

Broadly speaking, we can distinguish four families of theories. Three of them take vagueness to be a semantic phenomenon, while the fourth construes it as epistemic.

(1) *Multivalued* approaches, including three-valued and degree theories, conceive of the blurred boundaries of vague words in terms of the

assignment of one or more values intermediate between true and false. According to three-valued theories, the sentence '$n is rich' is true of salaries that are definitely rich, false of salaries that are definitely not-rich, and *indefinite* of salaries that are borderline rich (viz., neither definitely rich nor definitely not-rich). Degree theories, which recognize infinitely many truth-values, hold that a borderline rich salary satisfies 'rich' to some degree intermediate between 0 and 1—say, 0.4 or 0.5.

Multivalued approaches offer a variety of solutions to the sorites paradox. For example, one three-valued account defines the conditional in such a way that the major premise is indefinite, hence untrue, because its instances are indefinite whenever the adjacent salaries at issue are borderline cases (e.g., Tye 1994). On this view the paradoxical argument is valid but unsound. According to one degree theory (e.g., Machina 1976), since each successive salary in the series satisfies 'rich' to a slightly lesser degree, each conditional premise is slightly less than true. However, the paradoxical argument is invalid because its conclusion, which is wholly false, is less true than its least true premise. Here *modus ponens* is less than fully valid. Another degree theory (e.g., Edgington 2001) has it that the paradoxical argument is valid because the 'unverity' of the conclusion is no greater than the sum of the unverities of the premises; essentially, the conclusion is no more false than all of the premises put together.[6]

(2) According to *supervaluationists* (e.g., Fine 1975, Keefe 2000), a sentence containing a vague term 'Φ' is true (false) just in case it is true (false) on every admissible way of making 'Φ' precise. More exactly: 'x is Φ' is true *simpliciter* or definitely true just in case it is true on every complete admissible precisification of 'Φ.'[7] Roughly, a (complete) precisification is a way of making a term's application precise or "sharp" by classifying any unclear items either as Φ or as not-Φ; and an admissible precisification is one that also satisfies certain intuitive constraints. For instance, any admissible precisification of 'tall' will classify basketball player Shaquille O'Neal as tall (for a

human being), and if it classifies a given person as tall, it will also classify any taller person as tall. On this view, the major premise of the sorites paradox is false (*simpliciter*, definitely): Every complete admissible precisification of vague predicate 'Φ' establishes a sharp boundary between the extensions of 'Φ' and 'not-Φ'; hence the major premise is false on every such precisification. Borderline cases belong to the extension of 'Φ' on some but not all of its admissible precisifications; hence x is a borderline case for 'Φ' just in case 'x is Φ' is neither definitely true nor definitely false. Although its semantics for vague words is gappy, supervaluationism is meant to preserve excluded middle: On each admissible precisification, every item either is Φ or is not-Φ—rich or not-rich, tall or not-tall—hence the sentence 'x is Φ or x is not Φ' is definitely true, even where x is a borderline case. Thus the theory is not truth-functional: A disjunction can be definitely true even though neither of its disjuncts is. Of the four families of theories, supervaluationism enjoys perhaps the greatest following.

(3) *Contextualist* theories of vagueness take many forms, but their fundamental idea seems to be that vagueness is a form of context-sensitivity. According to one contextualist approach, a vague term like 'rich' is sensitive to contexts defined in part by the shifting verbal dispositions of competent speakers (e.g., Raffman 1994, 1996, 2005b). The most fully developed contextualist theory (Shapiro 2007) holds that vague expressions are sensitive to conversational contexts. On this dynamical approach, competent speakers have discretion to apply or withhold a vague predicate in borderline cases, depending on their conversational goals; borderline cases are items with respect to which competent speakers can 'go either way,' as Shapiro puts it (2007, 10). When a speaker chooses to apply a vague term to a borderline item, and his interlocutors acquiesce in his usage, a new conversational context or 'score' is established and the extension of the term is adjusted to include the item in question. In both "individual" and "conversational" versions of contextualism,

the sorites paradox dissolves essentially because there is no single context relative to which every instance of the major premise is true.[8]

(4) The fourth family of theories, *epistemic* theories, construe vagueness as a form of ignorance (e.g., Sorensen 1988, Williamson 1994, Graff 2000). Here the major premise of the sorites is false because there is in fact a sharp (though unstable) boundary between the rich salaries and the not-rich; it's just that we cannot know where the boundary lies.[9] Being a borderline case consists in being neither knowably rich nor knowably not-rich. According to one prominent version of epistemicism (Williamson 1994), we can't know where the boundary lies because its location is a function—also unknowable, or at least unknown—of our competent applications of 'rich' over the entire history of its use, and of course we cannot survey that entire history. (The sharp boundary is unstable insofar as the usage of a vague word may change over time.) In other words, the epistemicist contends that 'rich' has unknowable sharp boundaries that are fixed by an unknown function of the unknowable history of its competent use. Our use of the predicate is successful because competence does not require knowledge of the boundary's location:Competent speakers are permitted to make (what are strictly speaking) errors in their classifications of borderline cases. A contextualist variant of epistemicism holds that vague words have unknowable sharp boundaries whose locations shift from context to context (Graff 2000). On this view the major premise of the paradox is false but it seems true because the sharp boundaries shift in such a way that they are never located where we are currently looking or judging. A claimed virtue of epistemic theories is their retention of bivalence as well as classical logic: Any salary either is rich or is not, and the sentence '$n is rich' either is true or is false, though we cannot always know which.

The preceding accounts have advanced our understanding of vagueness, to be sure, but each is problematic in one way or another.[10]

OK, defined by use. But we might know this [margin note]

For instance, the nonstandard conceptions of validity employed by multivalued theories, and indeed the very idea that truth comes in degrees, may seem unintuitive and/or ad hoc. The three-valued approach described above yields no tautologies. Also, a degree theory seems unmotivated in the case of a nongradable vague word like 'medium' (more on gradability shortly). Supervaluationism too has its shortcomings. In preserving excluded middle, the supervaluationist must say that a disjunction can be definitely true even if neither disjunct is definitely true; and it turns out that, when applied to sentences containing the definiteness operator, a number of classical inference rules including contraposition, conditional proof, and *reductio ad absurdum* no longer hold. Contextualist theories have come under fire for employing an ad hoc and unintuitive notion of a context, for applying only to a subset of vague words,[11] and for being improperly psychologistic. And the faith-based epistemic view multiplies mysteries.

Proponents of these theories have responded to many of the criticisms brought against them, and improvements have been made. But it remains the case that no theory of vagueness has yet won widespread acceptance. Part of the reason, I think, is that philosophers working on vagueness have taken for granted that a semantic theory—that is, a theory that regards vagueness as a semantic feature of language—cannot be classical.[12] In particular, they suppose that only an epistemic theory can preserve bivalence. Dominic Hyde writes that

> even if an epistemic analysis is possible, the indeterminacy surrounding the application of soritical terms is generally considered to be a semantic phenomenon. ... If seen in this way, classical semantics appears in need of revision, and with it classical logic. (2011)

Williamson says,

> Most work on vagueness has taken it for granted that [epistemicism is] absurd. It therefore rejects the...supposition that an utterance of 'TW is thin' [where TW is a borderline case] is either true or false. (1994, 185)

The assumption is that bivalence entails sharp boundaries. Sven Rosenkranz asserts that "if all borderline statements are either true or false, as epistemicists contend, then vague words have sharp boundaries" (2003, 449). According to Rosanna Keefe, "epistemic theorists retain a classical [semantics]. This commits them to sharp boundaries to the extensions of our predicates" (2000, 62).

The theory to be developed here overturns this assumption. It is semantic—vague words lack sharp boundaries of application—but classical. (Contra Williamson, one can find epistemicism absurd without rejecting bivalence.) It is also simpler than its competitors in several respects; for example, it has no need of a definiteness operator, and while it recognizes the existence of higher-order vagueness, it rules out the possibility of higher-order borderline cases. This semantic but classical approach comes into view when we ground our theorizing about vagueness as deeply as possible in commonsense intuition and our actual competent use of vague words. Insofar as the sorites paradox can be generated from simple, intuitive propositions and rules of inference, we may expect intuitive considerations to play a central role in its solution. I think commonsense is rich with insights about vague words and that some of these have been overlooked. I will retrieve as many of them as I can and put them to theoretical use.

First I want to make some observations about vague words that should be more or less neutral among the theories described above. Some of these points will be familiar; some will not.

1.2. INITIAL OBSERVATION 1: BLURRED BOUNDARIES, SHARP BOUNDARIES, AND STOPPING PLACES

The distinction between blurred and sharp boundaries of application has been understood in a variety of ways.[13] As we saw a moment ago, many theorists cast it in terms of bivalence. Gary Ebbs writes,

> A concept has sharp boundaries...just in case for all x, the term that expresses the concept is true of x or false of x. The law of excluded middle entails that for all x, x is bald or x is not bald; if all sentences in which the word 'bald' occurs are bivalent, then the concept bald has sharp boundaries. (2001, 306)[14]

Wright characterizes blurred boundaries in terms of soriticality:

> Lack of sharp boundaries *as such*...seem[s] to imply paradox. To say that F lacks sharp boundaries in a series of the germane kind is to say, it seems, that there is no element x, which is F but whose immediate successor, x', is not. That is a claim of the form,
>
> $$\sim(\exists x)(Fx \,\&\, \sim Fx')$$
>
> and is accordingly classically equivalent to the major premise [of the sorites paradox,]
>
> $$(x)\,(Fx \rightarrow Fx').\ (2007, 4)$$

The blurred/sharp distinction has also been analyzed in terms of a word's possession of borderline cases. Keefe writes,

> Clearly, having fuzzy boundaries is closely related to having borderline cases. More specifically, it is the *possibility* of borderline cases that counts for vagueness and fuzzy boundaries, for if all

actually borderline tall people were destroyed, 'tall' would still lack sharp boundaries. It might be argued that for there to be no sharp boundary between the *F*s and the not-*F*s just *is* for there to be a region of possible borderline cases of *F* (sometimes known as the penumbra). (2000, 7)

Michael Tye seems to think that a sharp boundary would be a unique, fixed division that enjoys consensus among competent speakers. He writes,

> It seems clear that competent language users will not agree upon precisely where the boundaries are to be drawn in the sequence between the true, the indefinite, and the false statements. Of course, this is not to say that such people will not specify precise points if they are *forced* to assign either 'true' or 'false' or 'neither' to each of the statements…one after another. Still it seems highly unlikely that even one and the same person will pick exactly the same points on different occasions. It is not true, then, that the transitions from true to indefinite statements and from indefinite to false statements are sharp. (1994, 199)

And of course, epistemicists think that sharp boundaries are (unstable) divisions that are hidden from competent speakers.

However sharp boundaries are understood, they must be distinguished from mere permissible stopping places in a sorites series. By 'permissible stopping place' I mean simply any place at which a competent speaker, classifying the items in a sorites series *seriatim*, could permissibly stop applying the predicate in question. For example, in our series of salaries from $200,000 (clearly rich) to $50,000 (clearly not-rich), a competent user of 'rich' may permissibly stop applying it at $145,999, or at $145,998, or at $140,000, or at $136,002, among many others, even relative to the single context of Americans aged forty to sixty in 2001.[15] All of these salaries and many others are permissible stopping places. As far as I know, no theorist of vagueness, including the epistemicist, thinks that the existence of permissible stopping places in a sorites series indicates the presence of sharp boundaries—not even given that stopping somewhere is a requirement of competence with the predicate.[16]

Perhaps if we identify some distinctive features of permissible stopping places we can understand sharp boundaries by contrast. The following seem like plausible candidates:

(i) Competent application of a vague word requires that users stop applying it before the end of a sorites series. Hence there must be some permissible stopping places.

(ii) Permissible stopping places are evident in the verbal behavior of competent users of a vague word. A competent user proceeding along a sorites series will in fact stop applying the word before reaching the last item.

(iii) However, no particular stopping place is required. Competent speakers are permitted to vary in their stopping places even relative to a single context. Different speakers, and the same speaker on different occasions, will stop at different places, even when contextual factors are held constant. (In chapter 5 I will provide some experimental confirmation of this variation; grant it for now.)

(iv) Accordingly, permissible stopping places are not legislative. Stopping at a particular place does not signify that other stopping places are incompetent or incorrect or even legitimately questionable. Multiple stopping places are equally permissible.

(v) Accordingly, any particular stopping place is arbitrary: One could always have stopped elsewhere. (Even the epistemicist will agree with this much.)

This is a big deal!

To say that a particular stopping place is arbitrary is not to say that it is irrational or unintelligible. Rationality does not always demand reasons. I will return to this point.

Our thought was that we might understand sharp boundaries by contrast with (mere) permissible stopping places. We will learn more about both notions as our theory of vagueness develops, but we can say straight off that sharp boundaries are not evident in the competent use of a vague word. Also, sharp boundaries (if such there be) are presumably legislative: If a speaker proceeding along a sorites series stops at a place other than the sharp boundary between the extension and anti-extension of the predicate, her stopping place is incorrect, strictly speaking.[17] The difference between sharp boundaries and mere stopping places will play a leading role in the theory of vagueness.

1.3. INITIAL OBSERVATION 2: VAGUENESS AND GRADABILITY

As we have seen, vagueness has been associated more or less closely with tolerance, borderline cases, soriticality, indeterminacy or indefiniteness, and ignorance, among other things, and I will say more about all of these. Vagueness has also been associated with gradability, about which I want to make a few early remarks.

In general a term is gradable just in case it permits comparisons. It does this by taking comparative and superlative forms and/or modifiers like 'more' and 'less' and/or intensifiers like 'very,' 'so,' and 'such.' The predicate 'tall' is gradable: One tree can be taller than another, and a building can be the tallest in the world; a person can be very tall, or too tall to play the leading role, or insufficiently tall to reach the cookie jar. In contrast, a person cannot be very 6 feet tall, or so next in line, or too dead. Kennedy explains that "gradable adjectives establish relations between objects and measures of the degree to which they possess some property" (2004, 1). One thing can "possess tallness" to a greater or lesser degree than another. Arguably, nouns and adverbs also can be gradable: Stravinsky was such a genius, and Federer plays tennis more skillfully than golf.

Some theorists take gradability to be characteristic or even constitutive of vagueness. For example, Kees van Deemter asserts that "vague descriptions are referring expressions that contain gradable adjectives" (2006, 1; see also Sassoon 2007 for discussion). Not all vague words are gradable, however.[18] For example, suppose that the height of the flame on a gas stovetop is controlled by turning a continuously adjustable knob. And suppose that three settings are marked around the knob—'low,' 'medium,' 'high.' Presumably the boundaries between the low flames and the medium, and between the medium flames and the high, are unclear in the way that indicates vagueness; the predicates 'low,' 'medium,' and 'high' are vague. 'High' and 'low' are also gradable: For any two nonidentical flames, one is higher and the other lower. There are highest and lowest flames, and a flame can be so high that it burns the sauce or too low to melt the butter. 'Medium,' on the other hand, doesn't seem gradable: We would not say, of two flames, that one is *more or less medium* than the other—closer to or farther from being medium, perhaps, but not more or less medium. Talk of a 'very medium' or 'insufficiently medium' or 'too medium' flame doesn't sound good either, unless you mean that the flame is very or insufficiently or too *close* to medium.[19] _ OK! Medium

The precise predicate '6 feet tall' helps to illustrate the difference between being Φ-er or *more* Φ, on the one hand, and being *closer to* Φ, on the other. In an obvious sense, a height of 5 feet is closer to a height of 6 feet than a height of 4 feet is, but 5 feet is not *more 6 feet* than 4 feet is. By the same token, it makes no sense to say that someone is very 6 feet tall, or not 6 feet tall enough to reach the cookie jar. Thus, although both the vague predicate 'medium' and the precise predicate '6 feet tall' are associated with a linear ordering of values on a decisive dimension of application, neither predicate is gradable. Mere affiliation with such an ordering does not guarantee either gradability or vagueness. (Unlike 'medium', the predicate '6 feet tall' is precise because there is no relevant unclarity about where its application begins and ends.)

Notice that despite being nongradable, 'medium' does seem to be soritical: If a given flame is medium, then another flame incrementally higher or lower is also medium. So gradability is not necessary for either vagueness or soriticality. The question of whether gradability is sufficient for either vagueness or soriticality is harder to answer; I will come back to it in chapter 4.

1.4. INITIAL OBSERVATION 3: VAGUENESS AND SORITICALITY

Vagueness is often defined in terms of soriticality, but this popular view doesn't stand up well under pressure. Most theorists of vagueness believe that the sorites paradox is a resolvable fallacy: The argument is defective, and we can figure out why. If that's right, then vagueness is not, after all, a source of paradox. Maybe someone will say that even after the defect in the sorites is discovered, the argument will still *appear* to consist in unimpeachable reasoning from true premises to a false conclusion and so will still be paradoxical.[20] But this is a strange view, for it makes vagueness a contingent psychological feature of language, dependent on how things appear to us. Furthermore—here I can judge only from my own case—once I had discovered (what I will argue is) the key to solving the puzzle, the major premise of the argument no longer appeared—no longer appears—true. I can now still see why the premise formerly seemed true, or why it may seem true to the uninitiated, but again, this is a dubious way to define vagueness—namely, as the property of generating an argument that previously appeared, or appears to the uninitiated, paradoxical.

Perhaps the thought is that vagueness consists in generating an argument of a certain form.[21] Maybe this is what Bueno and Colyvan intend when they say that "a predicate is vague just in case it can be employed to generate a sorites argument" (2012, 29). But what does 'can be employed' mean here? If a sorites argument is a fallacy, a vague predicate cannot be *correctly* employed in it. Is the criterion supposed to be that a vague predicate is a term that, when employed incorrectly, appears (to the uninitiated) to generate an argument of the relevant form?[22] Surely vagueness is a more substantial property than that. Soriticality is an illusory feature of words like 'tall' and 'rich'; their vagueness is real.

OK. If sorites can be de-paradoxed it can't be used to define vagueness.

1.5. INITIAL OBSERVATION 4: VAGUENESS AND CONTEXT-SENSITIVITY

Whatever the prospects for contextualist theories of vagueness, there is no denying the fact that most if not all vague words are contextually sensitive. A tree may be tall compared to aspens but not compared to redwoods; a country may be culturally rich but not financially so; a person's hair may be red in contrast to (as opposed to) brown but not in contrast to orange. If I tell you that someone or something is tall or rich or red, and you are not otherwise aware of the context in which I am speaking, you may not yet have enough information to assess the truth of my assertion. Hans Kamp writes,

> It is typical of a vague predicate that what objects it is true of depends on the context in which it is used. There are certain

adjectives in particular—such as e.g. large, or soft, or clever—about whose extensions we can say hardly anything in abstraction from any contextual setting; it is only with respect to a given context of use that we can meaningfully ask whether a certain object is large, and there are very few, if any, objects of which it is clear absolutely whether or not they are clever or soft. Different contexts resolve these questions in different ways; the same object may count as definitely clever in one context and yet as definitely not in another. (1981, 242)

not sufficient

Context-sensitivity is probably not sufficient for vagueness: The expressions 'the fastest speed' and 'the winning score' seem context-sensitive but not vague (cf. Robertson 2000). Whether context-sensitivity is necessary for vagueness is a harder question; I will return to it later. However that issue is resolved, vagueness and context-sensitivity are frequent if not constant companions, so we need to understand how they are related. This question will be the focus of chapter 3.

necessary ?

1.6. VAGUENESS AND RULE-FOLLOWING

The preceding are just some initial, more or less theory-neutral observations about vague words. It will be helpful to have them on the table as we construct our theory. A principal aim of this book is to sift carefully through the phenomena of vagueness, soriticality, borderlines, context-sensitivity, and the rest to determine how, if at all, they are related. We will find that although they often appear together, they are less closely connected, and sometimes less prevalent in natural language, than is commonly supposed.[23]

We will also learn that a certain traditional conception of linguistic competence is incorrect. This traditional view—Wright calls it the *governing view* (1987)—can be expressed as a pair of theses. The first is that language mastery is a fully rule-governed competence, and knowledge of the rules in question is implicit propositional knowledge (as opposed to some sort of mere "know how"). As Wright puts it, "linguistic competence is constituted by sensitivity to the dictates of internalized rules" (1987, 210). The second thesis is that the rules in question are discoverable by rational reflection, independently of any appeal to "external behavioural notions." Specifically, we can discover these rules by reflecting upon

> our conception of what *justifies* the application of a particular
> expression[,] our conception of what we should count as an ade-
> quate explanation of the sense of a particular expression[, and]
> the limitations imposed by our senses and memories on the kind
> of instruction which we can actually implement, [among other
> things]. (1975, 326–327)

Wright contends that the governing view is incoherent because, in the case of vague predicates, the rules served up by the reflective procedures it sanctions are inconsistent: One rule prescribes tolerant application of 'Φ,' while another prescribes application of 'not-Φ' to at least some items in a sorites series.[24] Together these rules generate the sorites paradox. Since our ordinary use of vague predicates is largely successful, Wright reasons, it cannot be guided by inconsistent rules (1975, 329). Therefore, if the use of vague words is in fact governed by rules, they are not rules of which we have implicit propositional knowledge or that we can discover by self-reflection. Wright resigns himself to the conclusion that mastery of a vague word is better understood "on the model of a practical skill, comparable to the ability to hit a good cross-court backhand or ride a bicycle" (1987, 239). In other words, mastery of a vague word is better understood as a kind of *knowledge how* than as *knowledge that*.

how to be
semantically
competent

Like Wright, I will argue that the governing view is flawed, but the flaws I see are different from, and less damaging than, the ones he cites. Contrary to the first thesis of the governing view, linguistic competence is not entirely governed by rules; at a certain point, the rules give out and competent linguistic practice must become arbitrary. That fact notwithstanding, most of our use of vague words *is* rule-governed, hence not arbitrary; the rules in question are consistent, and our knowledge of them can be understood as implicit propositional knowledge. Moreover, these rules are discoverable largely by the self-reflective procedures described in the second thesis. As we will see, what's to blame for the sorites paradox is not the governing view so much as an overly strong conception of tolerance.

1.7. TWO POLICIES AND A CAUTION

I adopt two policies in what follows. First, probably many parts of speech are vague, including verbs (e.g., 'run'), adverbs (e.g., 'quickly'), and quantifiers (e.g., 'most');[25] but predicates—adjectives and nouns that predicate properties of things, as in 'The patch is blue' and 'That collection of sand grains is a heap'—have been of greatest interest to philosophers, and I will talk mostly about those. (In deliberately sloppy fashion I will speak indifferently about vague predicates and vague words.) In fact, much of the time I will work just with some lexical, noncomparative adjectives and nouns—familiar examples like 'rich,' 'old,' 'blue,' and 'heap.' I believe that the theory developed in this book is applicable to all vague terms, but I will not try to show that in a systematic way here.

Second, thus far I have used the term 'tolerance' in the usual way, following Wright, to refer to a semantic property of applying across incremental change on a decisive dimension. However, I will not use the term again until the end of the book, late in chapter 5; until then

I will speak only of the soriticality of vague words (keeping in mind that, ultimately, soriticality is illusory). This is because I think that vague words are tolerant, but the usual way of understanding tolerance is mistaken; in particular, tolerance is not properly expressed by the major premise of the sorites paradox. In chapter 5 I will say what I think tolerance consists in. It turns out to be a feature of the competent use of a vague word, as distinct from the semantics strictly speaking.[26]

Lastly a caveat: It is not the job of a theory of vagueness to deliver a verdict as to the vagueness, precision, soriticality, and so forth of every word that comes along. Certain questions may need to be put to competent linguistic intuition before any theory can be applied. For example, is the word 'strawberry' vague? Depending on one's theory, answering this question may require first determining whether 'strawberry' has borderline cases, or whether competent speakers are permitted to vary arbitrarily in its application, or whether there can be two incrementally different plants such that one is a strawberry and the other is not. As far as I can see, the latter questions need not, and often cannot, be answered by a theory of vagueness. Rather, they must be answered by competent, perhaps even expert, linguistic intuition.[27] (Maybe the botanists will have to be consulted.) We will see examples of this.

1.8. SELECTIVE REVIEW

Because my approach to vagueness departs substantially from the well-known treatments outlined above, and because coming to grips with an unfamiliar approach to a familiar topic is never easy, I will close each chapter with a review of certain key points. Such a review is needed least in this first chapter, so I will be brief. Let me reemphasize the following points:

(1) The widespread assumption that a semantic theory of vagueness cannot preserve bivalence is incorrect. The theory to be developed here is both semantic and bivalent. (It is *not* contextualist.)

(2) If the sorites paradox is solvable, a definition of vagueness in terms of soriticality cannot be correct.

(3) There are multiple equally permissible stopping places in a sorites series. (Chapter 5 will provide experimental evidence to support this claim.)

(4) Because there are multiple permissible stopping places, any particular stopping place is arbitrary and nonlegislative. One could always have stopped elsewhere.

(5) Some vague words, like 'medium' for example, are not gradable. Hence vagueness cannot be defined in terms of gradability.

1.9. LOOKING AHEAD

I said that an adequate theory of vagueness must resolve the sorites paradox, supply proper analyses of 'borderline case' and of 'vague' itself, and also show how vagueness, borderlines, and soriticality are related. Because my analysis of 'borderline case' introduces some machinery that I will need to use throughout the rest of the book, I will begin there.

Chapter 2

The In's and Out's of
Borderline Cases

"In this business you either
sink or swim or you don't."
David Snell (journalist)[1]

2.1. LAY OF THE LAND

Borderline cases for a predicate 'Φ' are items whose satisfaction of 'Φ' is in some sense unclear or problematic: It may be unclear whether a 63-year-old person is old, or unclear whether a 5-foot 11-inch man is tall. Lynda Burns cites a widespread view as holding that borderline cases "are not definitely within the positive or negative extension of the predicate.... Borderline cases are seen as falling within a gap between the cases of definite application of the predicate and cases of definite application of its negation" (1995, 30). Michael Tye writes that the "concept of a borderline case is the concept of a case that is neither definitely in nor definitely out" (1994b, 18).

The standard philosophical analysis defines borderline cases for a predicate 'Φ' as items that are *neither definitely (clearly) Φ nor definitely (clearly) not-Φ*. A borderline case for 'Φ' is then also a borderline case for 'not-Φ': Being borderline not-Φ consists in being neither definitely not-Φ nor definitely not-not-Φ, which is equivalent to being borderline Φ. On a semantic construal of the definiteness operator, if an item is neither definitely Φ nor definitely not-Φ, the sentences 'x is Φ' and 'x is not-Φ' are not true; they are also not false and so are neither true nor false. We have heard about some of the nonclassical semantics that have been recruited to capture the meanings of sentences that are neither true nor false, using devices such as supervaluations, indefinite or indeterminate values, and degrees of truth.[2]

As I explained in chapter 1, theorists of vagueness have assumed that a semantic theory cannot be classical—in particular, that it cannot preserve bivalence. Such a view is inevitable if borderline cases are conceived, as on the standard analysis, in terms of the opposition between a predicate and its *negation*. However, I will argue that if we give up this conception, we can formulate an intuitively plausible semantic analysis of borderline cases that fits comfortably with a classical logic and semantics. On the resulting view—I call it the *incompatibilist analysis*—borderline cases for a predicate 'Φ' are not-Φ, the sentence 'x is not-Φ' is true, and the sentence 'x is Φ' is false. I am not in general opposed to the employment of nonclassical systems; I think that a given domain of discourse should be assigned whatever logic and semantics suit it best. But I also think that the logic and semantics best suited to vague words are classical.

2.2. THE STANDARD ANALYSIS

First let me explain some terminology. To avoid scope ambiguities, I will hyphenate the standard analysis and say that borderline cases are neither-definitely-Φ-nor-definitely-not-Φ. Also, I will slide indifferently between formal and material modes of expression. For example, I will say both that 'x is (definitely) Φ' is true and that x is (definitely) Φ, and both that x is a borderline case for the predicate 'Φ' (or for the category Φ) and that x is borderline Φ. There are contexts, some having to do with vagueness, in which this casual way of talking might be problematic, but it won't cause trouble here. In particular, when I speak in the material mode I do not mean to endorse any particular metaphysics of categories or kinds or properties.

As is already apparent, the incompatibilist analysis will be inconsistent with all versions of the standard analysis of borderline cases. Among other things, the incompatibilist denies, whereas the standard analysis entails, that borderline cases for 'Φ' are borderline cases for 'not-Φ.' Nevertheless, the incompatibilist analysis may be best understood as a descendant of the semantic versions of the standard analysis. I want to begin, then, by setting out the basic tenets of this family of views.

If I understand correctly, proponents of the standard analysis conceive of borderline cases in terms of a certain kind of ordering. They suppose that for any predicate 'Φ' having borderline cases, there is some linear ordering of items (values) on a dimension decisive of the application of 'Φ', progressing from an item that is definitely Φ to an item that is definitely not-Φ. Call such an ordering a *Φ-ordering*. A blue-ordering that defines borderline cases for 'blue' will be a linear ordering of values on the dimension of hue; a tall-ordering that defines borderline cases for 'tall' will be an ordering of values on the dimension of spatial height; and so on.[3] Strictly speaking, in order to define borderline cases, a Φ-ordering must be a linear ordering of at least three values on a decisive dimension: definitely Φ, definitely not-Φ, and a value between the two that cannot be classified either as definitely Φ or as definitely not-Φ. By its nature a borderline case is supposed to be less Φ than a Φ item and more Φ than a not-Φ item, on a single (decisive) dimension. (Where 'Φ' is not gradable, a borderline case is *further from* Φ than a Φ item and *closer to* Φ than a not-Φ item.) Of course, most of the vague words we will discuss, like 'blue,' 'rich,' and 'old,' are associated with Φ-orderings containing many more than three values—maybe indefinitely many.

not the final account

A predicate 'Φ' whose extension is only partially ordered can have borderline cases insofar as there can be a Φ item, a not-Φ item, and an item that lies between those two on a decisive dimension but cannot be classified either as definitely Φ or as definitely not-Φ. For instance, the extension of the vague predicate 'big' is only partially ordered: Some big things are such that there is no fact of the matter as to whether they are equally big or one is bigger than the other, even with respect to a given context. They are big "in different ways": One is tall, another wide, another long, another voluminous, and so on. Nevertheless, borderline cases for 'big' can be defined on the individual, linearly ordered dimensions of height, width, length, and volume, and items that are incomparable may be borderline—neither-definitely-big-nor-definitely-not-big—on different dimensions. 'Bald' is another multidimensional predicate that has borderline cases—both the number and location (and maybe also the thickness) of hairs on the head are decisive (Burns 1986)—although its extension is only partially ordered.

Sometimes, in addition, there is unclarity as to which dimensions are decisive of the application of a vague term. This species of unclarity, often referred to as 'multidimensional vagueness,' is importantly different from soritical vagueness.[4] 'Nice,' applied to people, provides a good illustration. We may suppose that values on the dimensions of altruism and thoughtfulness are decisive, at least in part, of whether a person is nice. But what about being a good listener, or being reliable? Do the latter dimensions matter to whether you are nice? And if they do, how do they interact with altruism and thoughtfulness? These questions don't seem to have clear answers. Certainly borderline cases for 'nice'—neither-definitely-nice-nor-definitely-not-nice—can be defined on the individual dimensions of altruism (measured in, say, percentage of one's income donated to charity) and thoughtfulness (measured in, say, frequency with which one sends flowers to sick friends). But one might think that certain other instances of

and data-bility/

28

unclarity with respect to niceness are counterexamples to the idea that borderline cases are defined in terms of linear orderings. For example, one might think that someone who donates large sums to charity and regularly sends flowers to sick friends, but also monopolizes conversations and often misses appointments, is a borderline case of a nice person because it's not clear whether these two flaws are decisive or even relevant. Yet no linear ordering seems to be implicated.

My intuition is that if we call the altruistic monopolizer a borderline case of niceness, then we are using the term 'borderline' with a sense different from the soritical one. In particular, the unclarity at issue, as to whether being a good listener and being reliable are decisive, is unclarity not just with respect to whether he is nice, but with respect to whether he is definitely nice; this species of unclarity leaves it open that he is definitely nice and that he is definitely not-nice. For instance, if being a good listener is not decisive, the monopolizer may be definitely nice;[5] and if it is indeterminate whether being a good listener is decisive, it may be indeterminate whether the monopolizer is definitely nice. In contrast, being borderline nice in the soritical sense is inconsistent with being definitely nice: If a person is borderline nice in the soritical sense, then he is not definitely nice. I think that if we call the altruisitic monopolizer a borderline case of niceness, we mean *simply* that there is no fact of the matter as to whether he is nice, that it's indeterminate whether he is nice, in a sense that is more like semantic incompleteness than like soritical vagueness (cf. p. 3). (As will emerge, on my view it is incorrect to say, of a soritical borderline case for 'Φ,' that there is no fact of the matter as to whether it is Φ.) I will say more about the difference between soritical and multidimensional vagueness in chapter 4 (section 4.4). For now, my point is that, for the reasons just cited, the case of the altruistic monopolizer does not threaten the definition of soritical borderlines in terms of linear orderings on decisive dimensions.

[handwritten margin note: this analysis doesn't make any sense. Either it's unclear or it is decisive!]

[handwritten note at bottom: meh...]

Before we go further, it will be helpful to have at hand two contrasting examples of the kind of Φ-ordering that will be relevant to our discussion. First, let's continue to work with 'rich' relative to the salaries of Americans ages forty to sixty in 2001. Our rich-ordering contains annual salaries proceeding from $200,000, which would make such an American definitely rich, down to $50,000, which would make him definitely middle income, hence definitely not-rich. Suppose also that a salary of $125,000 can competently be classified as a borderline case, that is, as failing to be definitely classifiable either with the rich endpoint $200,000 or with the not-rich endpoint $50,000. (As always, if you dislike these figures, feel free to substitute ones you prefer.) I am going to assume that this rich-ordering is *replete*—in other words, that it contains all possible salaries that can be linearly ordered between $200,000 and $50,000. Nothing essential to my view depends on this assumption; but for reasons that will emerge, my view must be able to accommodate a replete ordering, and given its treatment of replete orderings, its treatment of nonreplete orderings will follow easily.[6]

Our second example will be a blue-ordering of patches progressing from one that is definitely blue to one that is definitely green, hence definitely not-blue. Some of the patches roughly midway in hue space between definite blue and definite green can competently be classified as borderline, that is, as failing to be either definitely blue or definitely not-blue. Again I will assume that this ordering is replete: It contains all possible hues that can be linearly ordered between definite blue and definite green. For ease of discussion, let us suppose that the hues of the patches map one-to-one into the real numbers in the interval $(1, 30)$, so that the first, definitely blue patch is assigned to 1 and the last, definitely green patch is assigned to 30. Suppose also that the patch assigned to 15 can competently be classified as borderline. (Figure 5.6 on p. 148 gives an idea of what some of these patches might look like.)

Plainly, the character of the definitely not-Φ items in a Φ-ordering that defines borderline cases for 'Φ' must be such as to support a distinction between being definitely not-Φ and being borderline not-Φ. More to the point, their character as not-Φ must be such as to comport with the claim that borderline cases for 'Φ' are *not*-definitely-not-Φ. The character (number of dollars) of the definitely not-rich salaries in our rich-ordering from $200,000 to $50,000 must be such as to comport with the claim that $125,000 is not-definitely-not-rich, and the character (hue) of the definitely not-blue patches in our blue-ordering from #1 to #30 must be such as to comport with the claim that patch #15 is not-definitely-not-blue. What does this mean about their character? To pose the question in a more challenging way: Why must we say that a borderline case for 'Φ' is not-definitely-not-Φ, rather than (definitely) not-Φ? Or, why must the sentence 'x is Φ' be neither true nor false in a borderline case, rather than simply false?

Proponents of the standard analysis have offered a variety of answers to these questions. I cannot canvass all of them here, but I want to mention four that are representative and, in my view, among the most cogent.

(1) "[A] borderline case of the predicate *F* is equally a border-line case of not-*F*: it is unclear whether or not the candidate is *F*. This symmetry prevents us from simply counting a borderline *F* as not-*F*" (Keefe and Smith 1997, 7). Call this the 'argument from symmetry.'

(2) If borderline cases were not-Φ, then their status with respect to 'Φ' (and 'not-Φ') would not be indeterminate (indefinite, unclear, uncertain). There would be a "fact of the matter": Borderline cases are not-Φ. Such a result runs counter to the very nature of borderline cases. Call this the 'argument from indeterminacy.'

(3) Even if we could say that borderline cases for 'Φ' are not-Φ, this would only postpone the inevitable. For then new, higher-order borderline cases would arise between the Φ items and the not-Φ (borderline) items in a Φ-ordering that defines borderline cases for 'Φ,' and these new borderline cases would have to be neither-definitely-Φ-nor-definitely-not-Φ. Thus we would arrive at the standard analysis at one remove, as it were. Russell writes,

> Someone might seek to obtain precision in the use of words by saying that no word is to be applied in the penumbra, but unfortunately the penumbra itself is not accurately definable, and all the vaguenesses which apply to the primary use of words apply also when we try to fix a limit to their indubitable applicability. (1923, 87)

Call this the 'argument from higher-order borderline cases.'

(4) In judging a borderline case, we are apprised of all the relevant facts; in other words, nothing is hidden from us. Yet we can't tell that 'x is Φ' is true, and we can't tell that 'x is Φ' is false. Therefore the sentence must be neither true nor false, since if it were true we could tell that it was true and if it were false we could tell that it was false. Call this the 'argument from accessibility,' the idea being that since no relevant facts are hidden, the truth-value of 'x is Φ,' if it had one, would always be accessible to competent users of the predicate.

I should note that advocates of the standard analysis with a three-valued semantics do typically acknowledge an attenuated sense in which a borderline Φ is not-Φ—in other words, a sense in which 'x is not-Φ' is true in a borderline case. The sense in question is a so-called *weak* sense of the negation (also known as exclusion negation), where 'not' takes 'false' and the third value to 'true,' and takes 'true' to 'false.' However, the standard analysis employs a *strong* reading of the negation (also known as choice negation), where 'not' takes 'false' to 'true,' and 'true' to 'false,' and leaves the third value alone; and so the sentences 'x is Φ' and 'x is not-Φ' are neither true nor false in a borderline case.

In what follows I will urge that by making certain adjustments to the standard analysis, we can define borderline cases plausibly as not-Φ, where the negation is classical. We will then be in a position to respond to the arguments from symmetry, indeterminacy, higher-order borderline cases, and accessibility.

2.3. THE INCOMPATIBILIST ANALYSIS

In fact, the view I am going to propose is often evident in writings by proponents of the standard analysis. Consider the following passages, for example:

> Vagueness is [a matter of] lacking 'sharp boundaries,' of dividing logical space as a blurred shadow divides the background on which it is reflected.... [This] figure equally exemplifies the idea of the borderline case, a region falling neither in light nor shadow. (Wright 1976, 226)

> The vagueness of a vague predicate is ineradicable. Thus 'hill' is a vague predicate, in that there is no definite line between hills and mountains. But we could not eliminate this vagueness by introducing a new predicate, say 'eminence,' to apply to those things which are neither definitely hills nor definitely mountains, since there would still remain things which were neither definitely

hills nor definitely eminences, and so *ad infinitum*. (Dummett 1978, 182)

[The] concept of a borderline case is the concept of a case that is neither definitely in nor definitely out. (Tye 1994b, 18)

It may seem that *strawberry* draws boundaries, since there are no borderline cases. But this is just an accident. There could very well be, and no doubt with the advent of genetic engineering soon will be, a series of plants between strawberries and raspberries, many of them borderline for both concepts. (Sainsbury 1997, 264)

[Some theorists] represent the sense of a predicate like 'green' or 'child' by its effecting a division of categorially appropriate objects into three sets. This is supposed to do justice to the actuality or possibility of borderline cases: surfaces intermediate between blue and green, people intermediate between childhood and adulthood. (Sainsbury 1991, 168–9)

And here, since it provides fodder for my view, is a definition from the *Merriam-Webster Dictionary* (2013):

> **Bor•der•line**…1a: being in an intermediate position or state: not fully classifiable as one thing or its opposite [e.g.,] a *borderline* state between waking and sleeping.

Notice that none of these passages characterizes borderline cases as neither-definitely-Φ-nor-definitely-not-Φ; specifically, none of them characterizes borderline cases in terms of an opposition between contradictories. Rather, they characterize borderlines in terms of an opposition between what I'll call *incompatible* predicates, like 'raspberry' and 'strawberry,' 'hills' and 'eminences,' 'light' and 'shadow,' 'in' and 'out,' 'waking' and 'sleeping.' (More about incompatibility in a minute.) Notice also that defenders of the standard analysis often slide between talk of contradictories and talk of incompatibles when discussing borderline cases. For instance:

> [According to the epistemicist,] there is no genuine indeterminacy, no region of borderline cases between the blue and the nonblue, the bald and the nonbald, the small and the large. (Wright 1995, 133–134)

> There is a variability about the application and nonapplication of [a vague] predicate to [a borderline case]: sometimes a certain shade is described as blue while others will describe the unchanged shade, seen in the same light, as green rather than blue. Someone may be described as bald in one context and as not bald in another, though they have the same number of hairs. (Burns 1995, 30)

> [A] borderline case is an object that is neither definitely F nor definitely not F...Tarmin may have enough canine characteristics to ensure that she is definitely either a dog or a wolf, without being either definitely a dog or definitely a wolf. (McGee and McLaughlin 1994, 210)

To develop the view I have in mind, I need first to say more about the relation of incompatibility. As I will use the term, incompatible predicates 'Φ' and 'Φ*' are contrary predicates such that some linear ordering of values, on a dimension decisive of the application of both 'Φ' and 'Φ*', is both a Φ-ordering and, conversely, a Φ*-ordering. (Call such an ordering a *Φ/Φ* ordering*.) Contraries are predicates that cannot both be true, but can both be false, of the same thing. Intuitively, incompatibles are contraries that form a family: 'tall,' 'average,' and 'short' are incompatibles on the dimension of height; 'rich,' 'middle income,' and 'poor' are incompatibles on the dimension of, for example, number of dollars of salary; 'blue,' 'red,' and 'green' are incompatibles on the dimension of hue; and so forth.

Now of course, even if borderline cases *can* be defined in terms of an opposition between incompatible predicates (this has not yet been shown), not all pairs of incompatibles share borderline cases. 'Rich' and 'destitute' are incompatibles, but nothing is borderline between being rich and being destitute; similarly 'red' and 'green.' Just which pairs in a family of incompatibles share borderline cases seems an open question, and intuitions will diverge: Does 'large' share borderline cases with 'small?' 'rich' with 'poor?' 'tall' with 'short?' However one resolves these questions, the point is that in order to share borderline cases, two incompatibles must be sufficiently close together within their family. Let us say that they must be *proximate* incompatibles.

I need then to say what it is for incompatible predicates to be proximate, in a way that allows for intuitive divergence of the sort just mentioned.[7] Proximity can be understood in terms of a predicate's permissible variability of application. As I observed in chapter 1, competent users of a vague word are permitted to vary in their applications of it, both inter- and intra-subjectively, even relative to a single context. For example, in our rich-ordering of salaries from $200,000 to $50,000, I might classify $125,000 as borderline rich while you classify it as rich, and you might classify it as rich on one occasion and as middle income on another. I might say that patch #15 in our blue-ordering is blue on one occasion and borderline on another. We speakers are well aware that such variation is permissible; as Wright observes, 'we do not, in general, expect agreement among otherwise competent judges' in such cases (1994, 138). Hence when we classify items like $125,000 and patch #15, we do so knowing that our classifications are largely *arbitrary*, that is, knowing that we could as competently have made different classifications. If on a given occasion I judge that $125,000 is borderline, I do not think you incompetent

[margin handwritten note: Incompatibles sharing a border make for border-line cases.]

or otherwise mistaken if you say it is rich, and vice versa. And if I judged yesterday that $125,000 is borderline but judge today that it is rich, I do not suppose that I am *correcting* my earlier judgment. Yesterday $125,000 seemed borderline; today it seems rich. (The 'seeming' needn't be phenomenological: $125,000 impresses me, or strikes me, as borderline or as rich.) The upshot is that some of the salaries in our rich/middle income ordering can competently be classified as rich (hence not-middle-income), as middle income (hence not-rich), and as borderline—whatever 'borderline' means.

The phenomenon of permissible variation in our applications of a vague predicate plays a central role in the theory of vagueness. We will explore it in depth in Chapter 4, and Chapter 5 will present the results of an experiment confirming that such variation does occur. At present the phenomenon is important because it enables a plausible analysis of proximity. We can say that incompatible predicates 'Φ' and 'Φ*' are proximate just in case there are items in a replete Φ/Φ* ordering that can competently be classified as Φ and competently be classified as Φ* (relative to a given single context). For example, 'blue' and 'green' are proximate because there are items in a blue/green ordering that can competently be classified as blue and competently be classified as green. Different competent speakers and the same competent speaker on different occasions are permitted to classify these items differently. 'Red' and 'green,' on the other hand, are not proximate: There is no hue in a red/green ordering that can competently be classified as red and as green. Similarly, 'rich' and 'middle income' are proximate, but 'rich' and 'destitute' are not. This way of defining proximity allows for intuitive divergence of the sort we were talking about, since competent speakers will diverge as to whether there are salaries in a rich/poor ordering that can competently be called 'rich' and competently be called 'poor', or heights in a tall/short ordering that can competently be called 'tall' and competently be called 'short.'

[handwritten marginalia: "This is what's doing all the work."]

[handwritten marginalia: "Have you never seen tomatoes ripen?"]

With the relation of proximity in hand, I propose, as a first approximation, that borderline cases for a predicate 'Φ' are items that belong to a Φ/Φ* ordering but are neither definitely Φ nor definitely Φ*, where 'Φ*' is a proximate incompatible of 'Φ.' Borderline cases for 'rich' are items that belong to a rich/rich* ordering but are neither definitely rich nor definitely rich*; borderline cases for 'blue' are items that belong to a blue/blue* ordering but are neither definitely blue nor definitely blue*; and so forth.[8] Or perhaps it is clearer to define first the notion of a *Φ[Φ*] borderline case*: For any proximate incompatible predicates 'Φ' and 'Φ*,' x is a Φ[Φ*] borderline case if and only if x belongs to a Φ/Φ* ordering but is neither definitely Φ nor definitely Φ*. Then x is a borderline case for 'Φ' *simpliciter* if and only if there is some proximate incompatible predicate 'Φ*' such that x is a Φ[Φ*] borderline case.

I said 'as a first approximation.' When borderline cases are defined in terms of an opposition between incompatibles, the definiteness operator is otiose insofar as it had been introduced to avoid flat-out contradiction. So our revision of the standard analysis can simplify and say that Φ[Φ*] borderline cases belong to a Φ/Φ* ordering but are neither Φ nor Φ*. Our proposal then is this:

(i)   For any proximate incompatible predicates 'Φ' and 'Φ*,' x is a Φ[Φ*] borderline case if and only if x belongs to a Φ/Φ* ordering but is neither Φ nor Φ*.

(ii) For any predicate 'Φ,' x is a borderline case for 'Φ' if and only if there is some proximate incompatible predicate 'Φ*' such that x is a Φ[Φ*] borderline case.

Call this the *incompatibilist analysis* of borderline cases. The incompatibilist analysis allows us to apply a classical logic and semantics to borderline sentences: If x is a borderline case for 'Φ,' the sentence 'x is not-Φ' is true and the sentence 'x is Φ' is false. If $125,000 is a borderline case for 'rich,' the sentence '$125,000 is not-rich' is true and the sentence '$125,000 is rich' is false; if patch #15 is a borderline case for 'blue,' then '#15 is not-blue' is true and '#15 is blue' is false. In a Φ/Φ^* ordering that defines borderline cases for 'Φ,' the not-Φ items include both the Φ^* items *and the borderline cases.*

Perhaps defenders of the standard analysis will object that natural language may not contain enough incompatible predicates to express every possible borderline category for a vague word and so the contradictory 'not-Φ' is required if we want to talk about borderline cases for 'Φ' in general. However, the most that could be claimed is that natural language may not contain enough *lexical* incompatibles to express every kind of borderline status. But why should the incompatibles have to be lexical? The contradictories 'not-Φ' and 'non-Φ' and 'not-a-Φ' aren't lexical. For example, suppose that 'heap' doesn't have enough lexical incompatibles to define all of the possible kinds of borderline heaps: 'neither a heap nor a handful,' 'neither a heap nor a few,' 'neither a heap nor a column,' 'neither a heap nor a pyramid,' and any other lexical incompatibles we can think of are not adequate to capture every kind of borderline heap. In that case, we can use a predicate such as 'neither a heap nor a flat expanse,' or 'neither a heap nor a flat expanse as opposed to a heap,' or 'neither a heap nor a mere small collection of grains,' or 'neither a heap nor a cube-shaped collection of grains,' and so on.

To approach the point from a different vantage, consider that in order to identify any borderline case for 'Φ,' we have to know the operative proximate incompatible. For example, in a blue-ordering of hues going from blue to not-blue, which ones are the borderline cases for 'blue?' We have no idea until we're told the operative incompatible—'green?' 'blue green?' 'violet?' 'red?' (Indeed, we can't even say which hues are the *blue* ones until we know the operative incompatible.) Similarly, which salaries are the borderline cases in an ordering from a rich salary to a not-rich one? We cannot begin to identify them until we know the operative incompatible: 'middle income?' 'upper middle income?' 'lower middle income?' Which are the borderline heaps in an ordering from a heap to a non-heap? To frame the point epistemically, if all we know about an ordering is that it proceeds from a heap to a non-heap, we cannot know which items in it are the borderline cases. We need first to know the operative incompatible— a column of grains? a handful? a cube? These examples suggest, if not prove, that any borderline case for 'Φ' requires an incompatible 'Φ^*' for its identification. If that is true, then the standard analysis is at best unnecessary.

An anonymous referee for Oxford University Press correctly points out that in order to function as an incompatible of 'Φ,' a predicate must have an established "range of competent and incompetent uses." Is it plausible that nonlexical incompatibles like the ones just suggested could possess such ranges? I think so.[9] In circumstances where an incompatible like 'flat expanse of grains' is introduced, we are wanting to name a certain class of (borderline) cases. And presumably we don't need or want a name for such a class unless we have already picked it out, already conceived of it as an extant, or at least possible, type of case. And to conceive of something as a borderline case is, at a minimum, to conceive of it as failing to belong, or failing to clearly belong, to either of two opposed categories or kinds. Which two categories? Well, a vague category Φ—here, heap—for which we already have a name, and some opposed category C. To conceive of something as borderline Φ is to conceive of it as failing to be Φ and failing to be C. But then if we are already conceiving of an item as failing to be C, the category C is already associated with a range of competent and incompetent classifications. In effect, the category C is already in use, and what remains is just the trivial task of naming it, calling it 'C'—here: 'flat expanse of grains.' Whether 'C' is lexical or not is immaterial.

Four points need emphasis. First, there is nothing epistemic about the incompatibilist analysis. As on the standard analysis, borderline cases arise from semantic features of the predicates involved. They arise because there are items in a Φ/Φ^* ordering that can fail to belong to the extension of either predicate. One could say that $\Phi[\Phi^*]$ borderline cases "fall within the gap" between the extensions of 'Φ' and 'Φ^*.' Second, the incompatibilist's 'not-Φ' is not the weak negation I mentioned earlier: 'x is not-Φ' is true just in case 'x is Φ' is false. The incompatibilist's 'not-Φ' is a classical negation, and a classical semantics does not distinguish between strong and weak negations. Also, as far as the definition of borderline cases is concerned, any distinction between so-called internal and external negations collapses: 'x is not-Φ' and 'It is not the case that x is Φ' mean the same.

Third, unlike some authors, I do not define borderline cases as items that permit variable classification.[10] As noted above, Shapiro defines borderline cases for 'Φ' as items that "can go either way," that is, as items that can competently be classified either as Φ or as not-Φ. In a similar vein, Wright says that "for an item to be a borderline case on the red-orange border is for it to have a status consistent both with being red and with being orange (so not red)" (1994, 139).[11] In contrast, the incompatibilist's borderline cases are not-Φ and not-Φ^*. What is true is that any item that can competently be classified as $\Phi[\Phi^*]$ borderline can also competently be classified as Φ and as Φ^*. But that is not what being borderline *consists* in. For convenience I use the term 'variable' to refer to items that are competently classifiable as Φ and as Φ^* and as $\Phi[\Phi^*]$ borderline. (One might also call these items 'transitional,' since they are found in the transitions between categories.) My present point then is that any item that can competently be classified as $\Phi[\Phi^*]$ borderline is variable with respect to 'Φ' and 'Φ^*,' and conversely (though see section 2.4, point 3, for a warning).

I said above that patch #15 (for example) could competently be classified as blue, as not-blue, as green, as not-green, and as border-line—whatever 'borderline' means. Working with the incompatibilist analysis, we can now say that #15 can be classified as blue, as not-blue, as green, as not-green, and as (belonging to a blue/green ordering but) neither blue nor green. We may permissibly vary in our judgments of patch #15 among these alternatives. Whereas I am (on this occasion) classifying #15 as borderline, which entails that '#15 is blue' is false, you might classify it as blue and say that the sentence '#15 is blue' is true; and neither of us would or should think the other mistaken.

Fourth and last, I have not claimed that on the incompatibilist analysis, the predicates 'not-rich' and 'not-blue' lack borderline cases. I have claimed only that borderline cases for 'rich' and for 'blue' are not borderline cases for 'not-rich' and for 'not-blue,' contrary to all versions of the standard analysis.[12] That said, what *does* the incompatibilist say about borderline cases for 'not-rich' and 'not-blue?' Like all vague terms, these predicates have borderline cases if and only if they have proximate incompatibles. Consider for example the converse of our rich-ordering from $200,000 to $50,000, namely a not-rich-ordering extending from a not-rich salary to a not-not-rich one. Does 'not-rich' have borderline cases in this ordering? What about 'not-not-rich?'

Proponents of the standard analysis would presumably say that 'not-rich' and 'not-not-rich' share borderline cases that are neither-definitely-not-rich-nor-definitely-not-not-rich, which is equivalent to being neither-definitely-rich-nor-definitely-not-rich. The incompatibilist, on the other hand, will reply that these predicates do not share borderline cases, since they are contradictories, but that 'not-not-rich' shares borderline cases with its proximate incompatible 'middle income.' The latter borderline cases belong to a not-not-rich/middle income ordering but are neither not-not-rich

42

nor middle income, that is, neither rich nor middle income. In general, borderline cases for 'not-not-rich' are neither not-not-rich nor not-not-rich*—which is, of course, the same as being neither rich nor rich*. Unsurprisingly, the borderline cases for 'not-not-rich' are just the borderline cases for 'rich.' The sentence 'x is not-not-rich' is false of these borderline cases, as is the equivalent sentence 'x is rich'; and the sentence 'x is not-not-not-rich' is true, as is the sentence 'x is not-rich.'

If 'not-rich' doesn't share borderline cases with either 'rich' or 'not-not-rich,' does this mean that it has no borderline cases at all? I think so. You might have thought that the salaries in the ordering from $200,000 to $50,000 could be sorted into categories other than *rich* (or *not-not-rich*), *middle income*, and *rich[middle income] borderline*. For instance, you might have thought that the category *not-rich* could have as a proximate incompatible the category *super-rich*, with the intervening neither-not-rich-nor-super-rich (i.e., rich but not super-rich) salaries as their shared borderline cases. However, 'not-rich' and 'super-rich' probably are not proximate incompatibles, since it is hard to see how there could be a salary in a not-rich/ super-rich ordering that can competently be called 'not-rich' and competently be called 'super-rich' (relative to a single context). And if 'not-rich' and 'super-rich' are not proximate incompatibles, they do not share borderline cases.[13]

In the next section we take up some potential objections to the incompatibilist analysis. Before turning to those, I want to emphasize that while I have chosen to develop the incompatibilist analysis as a revision of the standard analysis, this way of developing it is not essential. I think it is the most illuminating way, but only the most illuminating. Even if the incompatibilist analysis is not properly conceived as a descendant of the standard analysis, it will stand as an alternative semantic definition of borderline cases that can be considered on independent grounds.

2.4. OBJECTIONS AND REPLIES

1. Perhaps defenders of the standard analysis will contend that their strong 'not-Φ' is just equivalent to the incompatible predicate 'Φ^*' in a Φ/Φ^* ordering and so the incompatibilist analysis simply collapses into the standard view. For instance, they may contend that within the span of a blue/green ordering, all not-blue items are green; hence, since all green items are not-blue, 'not-blue' and 'green' are equivalent. (One prominent theorist of vagueness has put it to me that each particular incompatible 'Φ^*' simply "stands in" for 'not-Φ' in a particular Φ/Φ^* ordering. Perhaps this view explains why defenders of the standard analysis have felt free to slide between talk of contradictories and talk of incompatibles when characterizing borderline cases.)

However, as long as we are speaking English, 'not-blue' and 'green' cannot be equivalent, even within a blue/green ordering. 'Green' is a contrary of 'blue,' whereas 'not-green' is the contradictory— even within the range from blue to green; hues in that range can fail both to be blue and to be green, but not both to be blue and to be not-blue.

this is sort of beg-ging the Q [handwritten margin note]

To put the point another way, classical principles require that every value in the range from blue to green be either blue or not-blue—not that every such value be either blue or green. Dummett says the following about a borderline case between red and orange:

> The statement 'That is red' will…be neither definitely true nor definitely false: but, since the object is on the borderline between being orange and being red—there is no other colour which is a candidate for being the colour of the object—the disjunctive

statement, 'That is either orange or red,' will be definitely true, even though neither of its disjuncts is. (1997, 106)

What, is it supposed to have no color?

This is a non sequitur. From the fact that 'there is no other colour which is a candidate for being the colour of the object,' how does it follow that the object is either orange or red? There are borderline cases: neither orange nor red, but somewhere in between.[14] Keefe and, evidently, Edgington make the same mistake:

Suppose that a is on the borderline between being F and being G....It would then be appropriate to say 'a is either F or G.'...Edgington cites some particularly strong candidates for disjunctions that are penumbral truths. With non-instantaneous sex changes, x can, at some time, be a borderline case of a brother and a borderline case of a sister, but a clear case of a sibling, where 'x is a brother or a sister' is true. (2000, 163)

On the contrary, if x is a brother or a sister, then x either is a brother or is a sister, and either or both of those kinds turns out to be different from what we had thought; whereas if x is a borderline case, then some siblings are neither brothers nor sisters. *that isn't entailed*

Perhaps our opponent will claim instead that 'not-Φ' in the standard analysis is equivalent to the disjunction of all (possible?) incompatibles of 'Φ.' For example, maybe he thinks that 'not-blue' is equivalent to the disjunction 'green or blue green or blue blue green...or green green yellow or green yellow or yellow or...or red or...etc.'[15] (Assume that every incompatible has a name.) But then to say that an item is neither-definitely-blue-nor-definitely-not-blue is to say that it has no hue at all: Any hue is a "definite" case of some hue category or other—for example, a blue[green] borderline case may be definitely cyan or definitely turquoise—hence no colored object will count as borderline blue (worse, Godel's Theorem and the plays of Shakespeare *will*). For the same reason, claiming that 'not-blue' is equivalent to the disjunction of all incompatibles of 'blue' in a blue/green ordering is a non-starter, since any item in a blue/green ordering satisfies either 'blue' or one of its incompatibles in that ordering. As far as I can see, other attempts to show that the incompatibilist account collapses into the standard analysis will face the same sorts of difficulties.

When I ask proponents of the standard analysis what they take to be the relationship between, for example, being neither-definitely-a-dog-nor-definitely-not-a-dog, on the one hand, and being neither definitely a dog nor definitely a wolf, on the other, they typically reply with some version of an objection we considered in section 2.3, namely, that a formulation in terms of contradictories is required in order to refer to borderline dogs in general. In other words, they claim that we need the standard analysis in order to say that an animal is a borderline case of a dog, full stop, without having to specify that it is borderline between dog and wolf, or between dog and coyote, or between dog and fox, and so on. (Similarly, a borderline case of blue, full stop, not just between blue and green, or blue and cyan, or blue and red, etc.) But this explanation cannot be right: The standard analysis is not required in order to express borderline status in general, for the incompatibilist analysis does that as well.

2. Remembering Russell's admonition about higher-order borderline cases, friends of the standard analysis might suppose that the incompatibilist has merely postponed the inevitable. If there can be items that are borderline between 'Φ' and 'Φ^*' in a Φ/Φ^* ordering, then surely there can be items that are borderline between 'Φ' and '$\Phi[\Phi^*]$ borderline.' And since $\Phi[\Phi^*]$ borderlines are not-Φ, won't the latter items be borderline between 'Φ' and 'not-Φ?' For example, if there can be

salaries that are borderline between 'rich' and 'middle income' in our ordering from $200,000 to $50,000, then there can be salaries that are borderline between 'rich' and 'rich[middle income] borderline,' that is, between 'rich' and 'rich[middle income] not-rich-and-not-middle-income.' Won't the incompatibilist have to say that these second-order borderline cases are neither-definitely-rich-nor-definitely-not-rich? Won't the incompatibilist analysis now collapse into the standard analysis at one remove, as it were?

I will answer this question (negatively) in a moment. First let me supply some background. Many advocates of the standard analysis suppose that a Φ-ordering that defines borderline cases for 'Φ' also contains indefinitely many higher-order borderline cases. If first-order borderline cases are neither-definitely-Φ-nor-definitely-not-Φ, second-order borderlines are neither-definitely-definitely-Φ-nor-definitely-not-definitely-Φ, third-order borderlines are neither-definitely-definitely-definitely-Φ-nor-definitely-not-definitely-definitely-Φ, and so on ad indefinitum. (To keep things simple, I mention only one set of borderline cases of each order.) Such a hierarchy is said to be essential to the vagueness of 'Φ,' ensuring the absence of any sharp boundaries in the predicate's application (e.g., Burns 1995, 29). Possession of first-order borderlines is not by itself supposed to be sufficient for blurred boundaries. Keefe and Smith write,

> Imagine a hypothetical predicate G that has a sharply-bounded set of clear positive cases, a sharply-bounded set of clear negative cases, and a sharply-bounded set of cases falling in between. Although G is stipulated to have borderline cases in the sense of instances which are neither clearly G nor clearly not-G, it is not vague.... Merely having borderline cases is not sufficient for

vagueness; rather, with a genuinely vague predicate, the sets of clearly positive, clearly negative and borderline cases will each be fuzzily bounded. (1999, 15)

In effect, then, these defenders of the standard analysis will present the incompatibilist with a dilemma: Either higher-order borderline cases can be defined between 'Φ' and 'not-Φ,' and the incompatibilist analysis collapses into the standard analysis, or else 'Φ' has sharp boundaries of application.

The incompatibilist will reject the dilemma as false. As regards the first horn, there are no higher-order borderline cases, because borderline cases, 'higher-order' or otherwise, are not defined between contradictories. The indefinitely many higher-order borderline cases posited on the standard analysis are just the indefinitely many $\Phi[\Phi^*]$ borderline cases in a replete Φ/Φ^* ordering. (If a replete ordering turns out not to contain indefinitely many values, then it does not contain indefinitely many $\Phi[\Phi^*]$ borderline cases—but of course it does not contain indefinitely many higher-order borderline cases either.) In our example, putative higher-order borderline cases for 'rich' are just some of the indefinitely many rich[middle income] ("first-order") borderline salaries in a replete rich/middle income ordering. Generally speaking, on the incompatibilist analysis, any Φ-ordering that defines borderline cases for 'Φ' is exhausted by three categories of items: Φ items, Φ^* items for relevant 'Φ*,' and $\Phi[\Phi^*]$ borderline cases. (In chapter 4 we will see that this result does not entail the presence of sharp boundaries, because the distinction between blurred and sharp boundaries is not properly understood in terms of borderline cases.)

From the vantage of the standard analysis, the possibility of higher-order borderline cases may seem inevitable. The following passage from Keefe and Smith is indicative:

Big worry

The lack of sharp boundaries between the Fs and the not-Fs shows that there are values of x for which it is indeterminate whether x is F and equally indeterminate whether it is not-F. So similarly, the lack of a sharp boundary between the clear Fs and the borderline Fs must imply that there are borderline borderline cases—values of x for which it is indeterminate whether Fx is borderline [and so on ad indefinitum]. (1999, 15–16)

A moral of the incompatibilist story, however, is that higher-order borderline cases seem inevitable only if borderline cases are defined in terms of contradictories. On the incompatibilist analysis, borderline cases cannot be defined between the clear Fs and the borderline Fs, because the borderline Fs are not-F.

One might have thought that in a rich[middle income] ordering, 'rich[middle income] borderline' is a proximate incompatible of 'rich,' since a salary could fail to be either rich or borderline by dint of being middle income. But recall the definition of 'incompatible': Incompatible predicates 'Φ' and 'Φ*' are contraries such that some linear ordering of values on a dimension decisive of the application of both 'Φ' and 'Φ*,' is both a Φ-ordering and conversely a Φ*-ordering. That is, 'Φ' and 'Φ*' must be contraries *in a Φ/Φ* ordering*. In order to be incompatibles, then, 'rich' and 'rich[middle income] borderline' would need to be contraries in that segment of the rich/middle income ordering that extends from 'rich' at \$200,000 to 'rich[middle income] borderline' at, say, \$125,000. And they are not: In the latter, shorter segment they are contradictories. (Borderline rich salaries are not-rich; in particular, rich[middle income] borderline salaries are rich[middle income] not-rich.) Intuitively, 'rich' and 'rich[middle income] borderline' are contraries in the full ordering from 'rich' to 'middle income' only trivially, by dint of the presence of the middle income salaries; whereas in the segment from 'rich' to 'rich[middle income] borderline,' the middle income salaries have dropped out.

49

Alternatively, one might imagine that second-order borderline cases could be defined in an ordering from 'rich' to 'rich[middle income] borderline' that extends from $200,000 to $125,000 but is not simply a segment of the rich/middle income ordering from $200,000 to $50,000. The idea would be that in this distinct shorter (still replete) ordering, the extension of 'rich' shrinks to make room for new second-order borderlines, and so the predicate 'rich[middle income] borderline' now becomes an incompatible of 'rich.' (Since there would be no middle income salaries in this shorter ordering, we can characterize the rich[middle income] borderline cases therein as, simply, *rich[middle income] not-rich.*) In other words, some salaries that are rich in the rich/middle income ordering (say, $150,000) will be second-order borderline cases for 'rich' in the new shorter ordering: They will belong to a rich/rich[middle income] not-rich ordering but be *neither rich nor rich[middle income] not-rich.* Third-order borderline cases will be defined in a still shorter rich-ordering from 'rich' at $200,000 to 'second-order borderline' or 'rich[rich[middle income] not-rich] not-rich' at, say, $165,000, and so on ad indefinitum. Thus the indefinite hierarchy of higher-order borderline cases posited by the standard analysis would be replaced by an indefinite hierarchy of higher-order Φ-orderings associated with any given Φ/Φ* ordering, each defining a class of higher-order borderline cases. (Figure 2.1, if ungrammatical, may convey the idea. 'B1,' 'B2,' and 'B3' stand for first-, second-, and third-order borderline cases.)

I think such a view is untenable for various reasons, but we needn't worry about those here, since even if higher-order borderline cases could be generated in the way just outlined, they would pose no threat to the incompatibilist analysis. For Russell's worry to get hold, the borderline cases of a given order (i.e., in a given rich-ordering) would need to lie between the rich salaries and the not-rich salaries *in that ordering*—in other words, in the ordering that defines them as borderline cases. We might express the point generally by saying

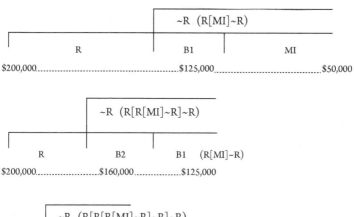

Figure 2.1. A hierarchy of higher-order borderlines?

that in order for Russell's worry to get hold, the *nth*-order borderline cases for 'Φ' would need to lie between the Φ items and the not-Φ items *in the nth-order ordering*; more simply, the *nth*-order borderline cases would need to lie between the *nth*-order Φ items and the *nth*-order not-Φ items. So, for example, the second-order borderline rich salaries would need to lie between the second-order rich salaries and the second-order not-rich salaries. But they don't. As can be seen in Figure 2.1, the second-order borderline cases lie between the second-order rich salaries and the *first-order* not-rich (namely, B1) salaries. In the second-order ordering, the second-order borderline cases are, like all borderline cases for 'rich,' not-rich. They are second-order not-rich, or rich [rich [middle income] not-rich] not-rich; analogously at higher orders. In any Φ-ordering that defines borderline cases for 'Φ,' the borderlines are not-Φ.

All that said, the incompatibilist analysis does provide for something rather like higher-order borderline cases. In addition to our

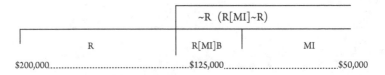

	~R (R[MI]~R)	
R	R[MI]B	MI
$200,000...$125,000...$50,000		

	~R (R[UMI]~R)	
R	R[UMI]B	UMI
$200,000......................$160,000...............$125,000		

	~R (R[UUMI]~R)	
R	R[UUMI]B	UUMI
$200,000.......$180,000.....$160,000		

Figure 2.2. Two fractals of a rich/middle income ordering.

rich/middle income ordering from $200,000 to $50,000, there is inter alia a distinct, rich/upper middle income ordering extending from $200,000 to, say, $125,000, containing rich[upper middle income] borderline cases, and maybe also a rich/upper upper middle income ordering extending from $200,000 to $160,000, containing rich[upper upper middle income] borderline cases, and so on, in theory, ad indefinitum.[16] (See Figure 2.2.) This progression of increasingly shorter rich-orderings, employing new and increasingly finer-grained incompatible predicates, may capture much of what advocates of higher-order borderline cases have had in mind— absent anything higher order.[17] Using the term loosely, I call these new shorter orderings *fractals* of the original rich/middle income ordering, and their borderline cases *fractal borderlines*.

Unlike the situation depicted in Figure 2.1, the fractals of a Φ[Φ*] ordering probably cross-classify one another. The introduction of a new incompatible predicate in each ordering—'upper middle income,' 'upper upper middle income,' and so on—forces a new classification. I have not done an experiment to confirm this prediction, but support comes from related observations. For instance, Sainsbury notes that "subjects asked to classify a range of test objects using just 'young' and 'old' make different assignments to these words from those they make to them when asked to classify using, in addition, 'middle-aged' " (1997, 259). C. L. Hardin makes the same point about hue predicates:

> The boundary of red in the broadest sense extends to the immediate neighborhood of unique yellow, and the breadth of that spread we acknowledge by our use of the modifier 'reddish.' But, in a somewhat narrower sense, the boundary between red and yellow falls at the point at which the perceptual "pull" of yellow is equal to that of red. This point is, of course, orange. But once we introduce orange as a distinct hue category, its boundary with red is at issue, and the extension of 'red' must be contracted to make room for the oranges. The natural red-orange boundary would seem to fall at the 75 per cent red, 25 per cent yellow region which was well within the scope we took 'red' to have when we were concerned to compare red with yellow. (1988, 184)

We can plausibly view the introduction of each new fractal ordering as raising the standards for satisfying the predicate in question. For example, things that are blue in a blue/blue green (or blue/turquoise) ordering are bluer, on average, than things that are blue in a blue/green ordering, and people who are rich in a rich/upper middle income ordering are richer than people who are rich in a rich/middle income ordering.

The fact that 'borderline' cannot have borderline cases underscores the difference between being a borderline case and being a variable item. I noted in section 2.3 that any item (value) that can competently be classified as $\Phi[\Phi^*]$ borderline is variable with respect to 'Φ' and 'Φ^*' and conversely. It is important to see that this biconditional relationship holds only for incompatible predicates, not for contradictories: Some values are variable between vague 'Φ' and 'not-Φ,' but it doesn't follow that they can competently be classified as Φ[not-Φ] borderline, for there is no such thing as being Φ[not-Φ] borderline. For example, in a rich/rich[middle income] borderline ordering of salaries, some salaries can be classified both as rich and as rich[middle income] borderline, and the shifting point from 'rich' to 'borderline' will vary from one occasion to the next. However, it doesn't follow that those salaries are borderline cases between *rich* and *rich[middle income] borderline*, which are contradictories. The upshot is that whereas any borderline case is variable, only those variable items whose competent classifications vary between incompatible categories, not merely contradictory ones, are also borderline cases.

So much for the first horn of the dilemma. What about the second? If the incompatibilist analysis does not allow for higher-order borderline cases, doesn't it follow that 'Φ' has sharp boundaries of application? Specifically, won't there be a sharp boundary between the Φ items and the $\Phi[\Phi^*]$ borderline cases, and another between the $\Phi[\Phi^*]$ borderline cases and the Φ^* items?

The answer is 'no,' though the reasons why will not emerge fully until chapter 4 when we discover simpler and more plausible ways to understand the blurred boundaries of a vague predicate.[18] For the moment it suffices to observe that defenders of the standard analysis with higher-order borderline cases are not entitled to raise this objection against the incompatibilist, for their view equally yields a tripartite classification: Any Φ-ordering that defines borderline cases for 'Φ' is exhausted by three categories of items: Φ items, not-Φ items, and borderline cases of one order or another. Sainsbury explains:

> Suppose we have a finished account of a [vague] predicate, associating it with some possibly infinite number of boundaries, and

some possibly infinite number of sets. Given the aims of the description, we must be able to organize the sets in the following threefold way: one of them is the set supposedly corresponding to the things of which the predicate is absolutely definitely and unimpugnably true, the things to which the predicate's application is untainted by the shadow of vagueness; one of them is the set supposedly corresponding to the things of which the predicate is absolutely definitely and unimpugnably false, the things to which the predicate's non-application is untainted by the shadow of vagueness; the union of the remaining sets would supposedly correspond to one or another kind of borderline case. So the old problem re-emerges: no sharp cut-off to the shadow of vagueness is marked in our linguistic practice, so to attribute it to the predicate is to misdescribe it. (1997, 255)[19]

Thus, even if the incompatibilist analysis did entail the existence of sharp boundaries, the standard analysis would enjoy no advantage. On both accounts the supposed sharp boundaries would flank the region of borderline cases: If there are no sharp boundaries among the various orders of borderline cases on the standard analysis, there are equally no sharp boundaries within the class of $\Phi[\Phi^*]$ borderline cases on the incompatibilist analysis. So the latter view seems no more likely to install sharp boundaries than the former.

> 3. The incompatibilist analysis does not acknowledge even "first-order" borderline cases between 'Φ' and 'not-Φ' in a Φ/Φ^* ordering. Doesn't it follow from this alone that 'Φ' has sharp boundaries of application?

Again the answer is 'no,' and again most of the explanation must wait for chapter 4. For now it will be enough to point out that the claim that an absence of borderline cases between 'Φ' and 'not-Φ'

This is really irksome. Of course there must be a sharp cutoff between rich and not rich then!

entails that 'Φ' is sharply bounded presupposes that borderline cases are defined in terms of a predicate and its contradictory. According to the incompatibilist, however, borderline cases are not defined in terms of contradictories. Claiming that the predicate 'rich' has sharp boundaries because there are no borderline cases between 'rich' and 'not-rich' is rather like claiming that 'rich' has sharp boundaries because there are no borderline cases between 'rich' and 'blue': 'rich' and 'not-rich' are not the sort of predicates that can share borderline cases. Also, again, even if a sharp boundary did obtain between the Φ items and the not-Φ (borderline) items on the incompatibilist analysis, an equally sharp boundary would obtain between the Φ items and the variously ordered borderline cases on the standard analysis.

4. Doesn't the incompatibilist fail to capture the indeterminacy (indefiniteness, uncertainty) associated with borderline cases? On the incompatibilist analysis, borderline cases for 'Φ' are not-Φ and not-Φ*. Where is the indeterminacy in that?

Of course, if 'indeterminacy' just means something expressible only in terms of an opposition between contradictories or only in terms of a definiteness operator, then the incompatibilist analysis does not capture it. The incompatibilist denies that borderline cases have such a feature. Nevertheless, she does allow that being a borderline case can be regarded as an indeterminate status, where 'indeterminate' is understood in either of two different, logically innocuous ways. First, the claim that a borderline case belongs to a Φ/Φ* ordering but is neither Φ nor Φ* just is a way of saying that the category membership of the item is indeterminate. For example, to say that patch #15 belongs to a blue/green ordering but is neither blue nor green is to say that its hue is no more determinate than that: Its hue lies in the range from blue to green, but no further hue classification can be made—given that 'blue' and 'green' are the only categories available. One might say that where *blue* and *green* are the only options, patch #15 has no particular, that is, no determinate, hue. (It "falls into the gap" between blue and green.) Of course #15 is, among other things, blue green (cyan, aqua, turquoise, etc.), but insofar as #15 is a borderline case for 'blue' and 'green,' the category *blue green* is not available. Similarly, to classify $125,000 as a rich[middle income] borderline case is to say that it lies between *rich* and *middle income* but belongs to no particular, no determinate, income category. The second innocuous understanding of indeterminacy rests on the fact that items that can competently be classified as borderline are variable: They can also competently be classified as Φ and as Φ*, and this variability can be understood as a form of indeterminacy. There is no single correct way to classify these items. (In this chapter we have learned that borderline cases do not require a nonclassical logic or semantics for their analysis; in chapter 4 we'll see that the same is true of variable items.)

The uncertainty associated with borderline cases is merely an accompanying feeling, not a constitutive feature; 'discomfort' would be a better name. Such a feeling may have several sources. First, some of the discomfort may be general in nature, deriving from the fact that when we classify an item as borderline, we know that we could equally have classified it as Φ or as Φ*; any classification in such a case is largely arbitrary. By the same token, however, in some cases when we classify an item as Φ, we know that we could equally have classified it as Φ[Φ*] borderline, hence not-Φ. Thus the uncertainty or discomfort is not limited to judgments of 'borderline': We may feel equally uncomfortable on those occasions when we arbitrarily judge #15 blue, or green, or when we judge $125,000 rich, or middle income. Hence we should not build this feeling into the analysis of 'borderline.'

[handwritten margin note:] this I would question. That means the last borderline case in the direction of blue is the last that could still be competently called green

Second, some of the discomfort must owe to the fact that on those occasions when we do classify an item as borderline, we are saying that it belongs to no hue or income category currently in play. (The item is, in this sense, indeterminate.) This makes it a classificatory loose end, and loose ends make us uncomfortable. Our discomfort must be especially acute when the predicates at issue are socially or ethically or legally significant, like 'person' and 'fetus,' or 'adult' and 'juvenile.' In such cases we may be forced to classify an item as Φ or as Φ*; borderline cases may be prohibited. Third, the restriction to two predicates that makes borderline cases possible may carry with it the pragmatic implication that one of the two ought to apply, especially since we know that either predicate *could* competently be applied. Thus we may feel a certain pressure to apply one predicate or the other. (Perhaps this is what misleads Dummett into supposing that the disjunctive statement, 'That is either orange or red,' will be definitely true". [1997, 106]) This pressure may contribute to our discomfort on those occasions when we judge something borderline.[20]

Defenders of the standard analysis like to point out that ordinary English often expresses an absence of borderline cases by asserting excluded middle: 'Either he *is* your father or he *isn't*'; 'Either you're pregnant or you're *not*.' But it uses incompatibles too: 'You're either with us or against us,' 'Take it or leave it,' 'You'll either love it or hate it,' 'He'll either sink or swim.' (See how the latter statements are trivialized if the incompatibles are replaced by contradictories: 'You'll either love it or not love it,' 'He'll either sink or not sink,' etc.) Friends of the standard view want to say that in borderline cases we feel uncertain as to whether an item is Φ *or not*: '*Is* he your father or *isn't* he?' 'Are you pregnant or not?' But such examples are not decisive, for we may feel the same way when asked whether an item is Φ or Φ*: 'Are you with us or against us?' 'Is Tarmin a dog or a wolf?' 'Is he friend or foe?' Maybe, where no lexical incompatible is readily available, we resort to the contradictory 'not-Φ' because that is easier than introducing a new predicate, and ordinary language has no variable like 'Φ*.' (Strictly speaking this is to ascribe an error to ordinary speech—but only if ordinary speakers do in fact sometimes characterize borderline cases in terms of contradictories. That's a big 'if,' in my view. See the next two paragraphs.)

5. If no definiteness operator occurs in the analysis of borderline cases, and the indeterminacy of, and uncertainty associated with, borderline cases are to be understood in the manner I have suggested, <u>what do ordinary speakers mean when they use the term 'definitely' in connection with borderline cases?</u> What do ordinary speakers mean by saying that an item is, or is not, definitely Φ?

More could be said on this topic than I will say here, not least because some work will be required to discover just how, if at all, the word 'definitely' is used in connection with borderline cases in ordinary speech. For now let me offer two speculations. First, maybe 'x is definitely Φ' means something like 'x mandates application of "Φ",' that is, 'x must be classified as Φ on pain of incompetence or at least error.' If that is right, then 'definitely' serves to distinguish the item in question from a variable item: x cannot also be competently classified as Φ[Φ*] borderline or as Φ*, that is, cannot also be classified as not-Φ. Second, perhaps 'definitely' is used to indicate or express a feeling of being comfortable with a certain classification. Maybe it even functions in something like the manner of a "sentence adverb" like 'hopefully.' When we say 'Hopefully it won't rain,' we mean that we hope it won't rain. If we say 'Definitely x is blue,' maybe we mean that we feel comfortable—we feel certain or definite, if you like—in saying that x is blue.

No doubt other interpretations of 'definitely' are possible, and the term may be polysemous in any event; but I will leave it there for now.

2.5. REPLIES TO THE FOUR ARGUMENTS, AND SOME ADVANTAGES OF THE INCOMPATIBILIST ANALYSIS

Recall that the arguments from symmetry, indeterminacy, higher-order borderline cases, and accessibility have been offered by defenders of the standard analysis against the idea that borderline cases for 'Φ' are not-Φ. How does the incompatibilist reply?

(1) In response to the argument from symmetry, the incompatibilist grants that there is a symmetry but locates it between 'Φ' and a proximate incompatible predicate 'Φ*,' rather than between 'Φ' and 'not-Φ.' (2) The incompatibilist also grants that borderline cases occupy an indeterminate status, but she conceives of the indeterminacy differently: First, a borderline case as such 'falls within the gap' between proximate incompatible categories and hence belongs to no category currently in play; and second, variable items admit of no single correct classification. (3) The worry about higher-order borderline cases is allayed by the fact that there can be no such cases. Borderline cases are defined between incompatibles, not contradictories. Finally, (4) in reply to the argument from accessibility, the incompatibilist agrees that when 'x is Φ' is true we can tell that it is true, and when 'x is Φ' is false we can tell that it is false; but she contends that 'x is Φ' is false in a borderline case.[21]

The incompatibilist analysis appears to enjoy several advantages over the standard view in addition to the ones already noted. First, the incompatibilist dispenses with the definiteness operator in the analysis of borderline cases and so is freed from the severe complications that come with that device.[22] Any potential draw-backs of eliminating the operator are mitigated by the fact that the word 'definitely,' as used (multifariously) by advocates of the standard analysis, is a term of art with no clear basis in ordinary speech. Indeed Keefe, herself a patron of the definiteness operator, warns against

> constructing an account of D via one's theory and assuming that it corresponds exactly to a pre-theoretic notion.... The ordinary use and apprehension of 'definitely' may well not straightfor-wardly conform to the kind of formal theory of the D operator that theorists seek. Intuitions about the operator may be incon-sistent... [and] anyway, the consequences of the theory of D will outstrip the consequences we would expect given only our intuitions about 'definitely'... It is thus reasonable, and perhaps necessary, to give 'definitely' a technical sense that depends on and is dictated by the theory of vagueness offered for the D-free part of language. (2000, 30)

Second, since it rules out the possibility of higher-order borderline cases, the incompatibilist analysis is freed of the complications that come with that notion as well. As with the definiteness operator, any potential drawbacks of eliminating higher-order borderlines are mitigated by the fact that the notion has no obvious basis in com-monsense. I have not heard an ordinary speaker call something a borderline case of a borderline case, much less a borderline border-line borderline etc. case. In fact I doubt that ordinary speakers would make much sense of the idea. The supposed need to accommodate higher-order borderline cases is often used as a club by one or another side in disputes among theorists of vagueness (e.g., Williamson 1994,

*But ordinary speakers refuse
to make sharp cut-offs to borderline cases.*

156-161, Keefe 2000, 112ff), but such cases are probably an artifact of the standard analysis.

Third, by defining borderline cases in terms of incompatible predicates rather than contradictories, the incompatibilist analysis avoids the following, counterintuitive consequence of the standard analysis. Consider again our blue/green ordering of patches #1 to #30. As we saw earlier, the strong 'not-Φ' of the standard analysis is not equivalent to any incompatible or disjunction of incompatibles of 'Φ'—in a given Φ/Φ^* ordering or otherwise; so 'not-blue' is not equivalent to any incompatible 'blue*' or disjunction of such incompatibles. What then is the extension of 'definitely not-blue' in the blue/green ordering, according to the standard view? Presumably the extension of 'definitely not-blue' in that ordering is larger, contains more patches (hues), than the extension of 'definitely green.' (It certainly cannot contain fewer.) By the same token, since 'not-green' and 'blue' cannot just be equivalent, the extension of 'definitely not-green' in the blue/ green ordering must be larger than the extension of 'definitely blue.' But then the class of patches that are neither-definitely-blue-nor-definitely-not-blue is not coextensive with the class of patches that are neither-definitely-green-nor-definitely-not-green. Does the blue/green ordering contain two kinds of borderline cases? Such a result seems implausible at best. (Figure 2.3 illustrates one possible way in which the values in question might be

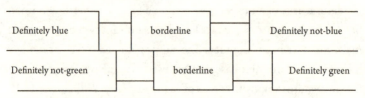

Definitely blue	borderline	Definitely not-blue
Definitely not-green	borderline	Definitely green

Figure 2.3. Two kinds of borderline cases?

distributed. The smaller sections flanking the borderline cases include any higher-order borderlines.) More perplexing still, proponents of the standard analysis do sometimes characterize borderline cases in terms of incompatible predicates, as we saw earlier. Is there then a third class of borderline cases, namely the $\Phi[\Phi^*]$ borderline cases, in a Φ/Φ^* ordering? Where exactly are these items supposed to be located? For example, where exactly are the blue[green] borderline cases supposed to be located in Figure 2.3, according to the standard analysis?

The incompatibilist analysis doesn't generate these conundrums. In keeping with commonsense, only one class of borderline cases exists in a Φ/Φ^* ordering that defines borderline cases for 'Φ'; and the items (values) contained therein are borderline for both of the opposed predicates. All borderline cases defined in a given Φ/Φ^* ordering are $\Phi[\Phi^*]$ borderline and, equivalently, $\Phi^*[\Phi]$ borderline. The borderline cases for 'blue' in a blue/green ordering just are the borderline cases for 'green' in that ordering; blue[green] borderlines just are green[blue] borderlines; and rich[middle income] borderlines just are middle income[rich] borderlines.

In retrospect, the idea of a symmetry between contradictories in the definition of a borderline case should have given us pause, for the extensions of a predicate and its contradictory are not in general symmetrical. At least as far as lexical predicates like 'blue,' 'rich,' 'tall,' and 'bald' are concerned, the extension of 'not-Φ' is significantly larger (and more heterogeneous) than the extension of 'Φ.' There are many more not-blue things in the universe than blue ones, many more not-rich things than rich ones. Is there any nontendentious reason to think that the situation is otherwise within a blue-ordering or a rich-ordering? Granted, such an ordering provides a restricted domain, but a compelling argument would be needed nonetheless.

2.6. INDEPENDENTLY FISHY FEATURES OF HIGHER-ORDER BORDERLINES

I will close this chapter by articulating some independent, mostly intuitive worries about higher-order borderline cases. I'll do this by setting out a series of informal questions and criticisms—I call them 'ruminations'—that help to reveal just how problematic the notion is, even if we assume that the standard analysis is correct.

Rumination 1. Consider the set containing all possible borderline cases of any order for vague predicate 'Φ,' as in Sainsbury's "finished account." Why aren't all of these items just first-order borderline cases? Don't they all fall within a gap between the extensions of 'Φ' and 'not-Φ?' Alternatively, why aren't these items just more (first-order) borderlines, definitely Φ items, and definitely not-Φ items? In fact I think we have no grasp at all on the idea of an item that doesn't fit into any of the latter three categories.

Rumination 2. Even supposing that borderline cases can be defined in terms of contradictories, the standard analysis overlooks a crucial possibility, namely, that there can be borderline cases between 'Φ' and 'not-Φ' only insofar as $\underline{\Phi}$ and $\underline{\text{not-}\Phi}$ are not themselves borderline categories. Maybe only *non*-borderline categories can have borderline cases. Notice that borderline cases are defined negatively in terms of an absence or lack—specifically, a lack of definite category membership: They are neither-definitely-Φ-nor-definitely-not-Φ. On the standard analysis, borderlines are possible only insofar as the extensions of 'Φ' and 'not-Φ' are not together exhaustive over the range of values in a Φ-ordering. This is why borderline cases are said to "fall into the gap" between the extensions of 'Φ' and 'not-Φ.' To put the point another way, there is nothing more to being borderline than failing to (definitely) belong either in the category $\underline{\Phi}$ or in the category $\underline{\text{not-}\Phi}$. Consider how items are classified as borderline: Presumably we assess their distance from the definite cases of Φ

and the definite cases of not-Φ. But if there were definite borderline cases, surely we would classify items as borderline by judging their distance from *those*.

The idea then is that <u>borderline Φ</u> may not be the right kind of category to have borderline cases of application; it is not sufficiently centered or anchored, one might say. Thus, talk of definite borderline cases no longer treats the items in question (namely, the "first-order" borderlines) as defined negatively, as falling within a gap. Such talk in effect transforms the borderline cases into a new, non-borderline category with its own center of gravity, a full-fledged competitor—an incompatible—of Φ and <u>not-Φ</u>.

To illustrate, consider a series of heights progressing by, say, sixteenths of an inch, from one that is definitely tall (e.g., 6 feet 5 inches) to one that is definitely average (e.g., 5 feet 9 inches) for, say, Canadian men.[23] And suppose that 5 feet 10½ inches can competently be classified as a first-order borderline case for 'tall' (see Figure 2.4). The putative second-order borderlines (B2) are then supposed to be located as in Figure 2.5. However, I predict that if a competent speaker were asked to proceed along this series from the definitely tall 6 feet 5 inches to the definitely borderline 5 feet 10½ inches and to classify each height as definitely definitely tall, definitely first-order borderline, or second-order borderline (B2), she would locate any second-order borderline cases not as in Figure 2.5, but roughly as in Figure 2.6. In particular, she would now classify as borderline borderline some heights that she previously classified as definitely tall. The definite first-order borderlines would spread out, pushing everything to the left, as it were.

Figure 2.6 still isn't right though. For in classifying the heights in this new, shorter tall-ordering, the speaker would not in fact be classifying them as definitely definitely tall, definitely first-order borderline, and second-order borderline. Instead, she would be classifying them as tall (or definitely tall, if you like), first-order

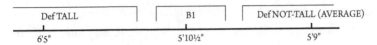

Figure 2.4. Is 5'10 ½" *definitely* borderline tall?

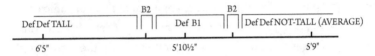

Figure 2.5.

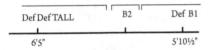

Figure 2.6.

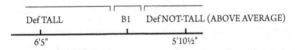

Figure 2.7.

borderline, and, say, above average, as in Figure 2.7. She would be defining a new, shorter tall-ordering (in effect a fractal of the original tall/average ordering—a tall/above average ordering) and thereby replacing what had been first-order borderline cases with a new height category <u>above average</u>. This new category would have its own "first-order" borderline cases that are neither-definitely-tall-nor-definitely-not-tall. (Again, we are assuming for the sake of argument that the standard analysis, which defines borderlines in terms of contradictories, is correct). Some heights that are definitely tall when 'tall' is opposed to 'average' would be borderline when 'tall' is opposed to 'above average.' We could repeat this process of subdividing the original series, never encountering a higher-order borderline case.

Rumination 3. The impossibility of higher-order borderline cases seems to follow from two intuitively plausible claims. For any vague predicates 'Φ' and 'Ψ':

(i) If an item is definitely Φ, then failure to classify it as Φ (when queried, etc.) is mistaken or in some way improper or at least legitimately questionable.

(ii) Failure to classify an item as borderline Ψ cannot be mistaken or in any way improper or even legitimately questionable. Intuitively, one is never required to classify something as borderline; a judgment of 'borderline' is always optional.

If (i) and (ii) are true, then (iii) is true:

(iii) Therefore no item can be definitely borderline Ψ.

Finally, (iv) follows from (iii):

(iv) Therefore no item can be borderline borderline Ψ.

This argument is so simple that it may seem to involve some sleight of hand, so let me spell out the justification for each step.

Premise (i) makes an extremely weak claim about the character of definitely Φ items. Even if 'definitely' is defined stipulatively as a term of art, if definitely Φ items can also permissibly be classified as not-Φ and as borderline Φ, then it is hard to see what the distinction between being definitely Φ and being borderline Φ comes to. I have urged that items that can competently be classified as borderline Φ can also competently be classified as Φ and as not-Φ; in other words, items that can be classified as borderline are variable. But the analogous claim does not hold for 'Φ' and 'not-Φ': It is not the case that any item that can competently be classified as Φ (not-Φ) can also competently be classified as borderline Φ and as not-Φ (Φ). 'Definitely' must carry some sort of legislative force, making failure to apply 'Φ' to a definitely Φ item at least legitimately questionable.

Premise (ii) follows from the claim (or is just another way of saying) that any item that can competently be classified as borderline Ψ can also competently be classified as Ψ and as not-Ψ. But I think (ii) is also intuitively plausible and, as I will show in chapter 5, it enjoys empirical support. Premise (iii) then follows. Premise (iv) is secured from (iii) not merely because 'definitely Ψ' and 'borderline Ψ' are interdefinable but because 'borderline Ψ' is defined by 'definitely Ψ' *in a wholly negative fashion.* As I observed above, there is nothing more to being borderline Ψ than (lying between Ψ and not-Ψ but) failing to be either definitely Ψ or definitely not-Ψ. Hence if definite borderline cases are impossible, so are borderline borderline cases. There is no way to define them.

Stewart Shapiro and Elia Zardini have objected (in conversation) that if definite borderline cases are impossible, then it seems to follow, absurdly, that all first-order borderlines are second-order borderlines. For if nothing can be definitely borderline, then, trivially, first-order borderlines are not definitely borderline (~DefBx). But first-order borderlines are also not-definitely-not-borderline (~Def~Bx). Therefore first-order borderline cases are neither-definitely-borderline-nor-definitely-not-borderline (~Def Bx & ~Def~Bx), which is just the definition of a second-order borderline case.

The trouble with this clever objection is that if there can be no definitely borderline items, if there are only plain old regular "first-order" borderlines, then any second-order borderlines must lie between the definitely-not-borderline (definitely-definitely-Φ) items and those first-order borderlines; there is nothing else for them to lie between. In other words, any second-order borderlines are neither-definitely-not-borderline-*nor-borderline* (see

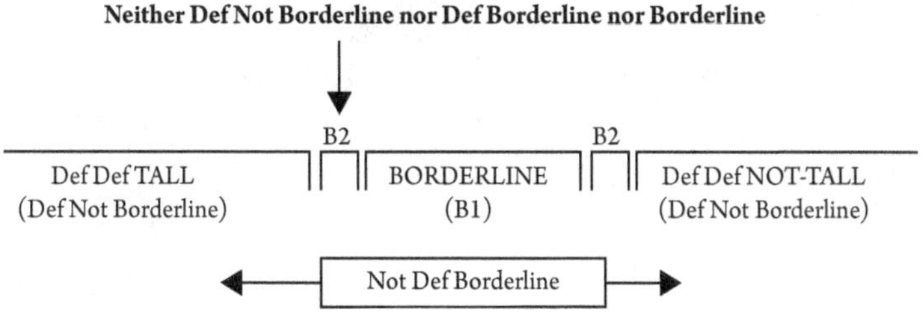

Neither Def Not Borderline nor Def Borderline nor Borderline

Figure 2.8. If there can be no definite borderline cases, there can be no second-order borderline cases.

Figure 2.8). (Specified fully, they are neither-definitely-borderline-nor-definitely-not-borderline-*nor-borderline*.) And anything that is not-borderline ($\sim[\sim\text{Def}\Phi x \ \& \ \sim\text{Def}\sim\Phi x]$) is definitely Φ or definitely not-Φ ($\text{Def}\Phi x \ V \ \text{Def}\sim\Phi x$), which is incompatible with being a borderline case of any order. Therefore, contrary to the objection, first-order borderlines are not second-order borderlines. Nothing can be second-order borderline. Perhaps we have thought that higher-order borderline cases were possible because we allowed technique to lead intuition: We were bewitched by the formal permissibility of generating certain expressions with the definiteness operator. What is possible, even coherent, in natural language is a different matter.

Rumination 4. Borderline cases are supposed to be of indefinite or indeterminate or uncertain status with respect to being Φ. Φ items don't have this status, so borderline cases have a status other than being Φ, where being other than Φ is supposed to be distinct from (weaker than) being not-Φ. Therefore, definite borderline cases definitely have a status other than being Φ. But then, however we interpret 'other than Φ,' how could it be indefinite whether an item that is *definitely other than Φ* is Φ? How could it be indefinite rather than just false? And if it is false, then an item that is definitely other than Φ is, after all, not-Φ. So such an item cannot be a borderline case.

Even if these ruminations are not decisive, I think they reveal some of the difficulties facing the notion of higher-order borderlines and, thereby, underscore an advantage of the incompatibilist approach.

2.7. SELECTIVE REVIEW

(1) Borderline cases for a vague word 'Φ' are not-Φ, and the negation is classical.

(2) Not all vague words can have borderline cases. For example, insofar as 'not-rich' and 'borderline rich' cannot have proximate incompatibles, they cannot have borderline cases. Hence the common definition of vagueness as possession of (possible) borderline cases is incorrect: There is no essential connection between blurred boundaries and borderline cases. Let me repeat that: Some vague words don't (can't) have borderline cases, so vagueness cannot be defined by possession of borderlines. It is easy to forget this and slide back into the usual way of thinking.

(3) If 'borderline' cannot have borderlines, there can be no higher-order borderline cases, that is, no borderline borderline cases or borderline borderline borderline etc. cases.

(4) The standard analysis of borderline cases is plagued by difficulties for which there is no obvious remedy. In particular, insofar as its adherents wish to acknowledge the existence (or possibility) of things that are borderline between blue and green, or between dogs and wolves, or between hills and mountains, they appear committed to the existence of two types of borderline cases: some that violate excluded middle and some that do not. (The mistaken assumption that every item in a Φ/Φ* ordering is either Φ or Φ* is at

least partly to blame.) For reasons given above, being borderline between proximate incompatibles Φ and Φ* cannot be identified with being borderline between Φ and not-Φ.

(5) While higher-order borderline cases are impossible, there can be what I have called *fractal* borderline cases, which are to some extent structurally similar. The crucial difference is that fractal borderline cases are just "first-order" borderline cases of new, more fine-grained predicates.[24]

2.8. LOOKING AHEAD

The impossibility of higher-order borderline cases does not rule out the possibility of higher-order vagueness altogether. In fact, it will turn out that any vague word sustains a certain form of higher-order vagueness. I will discuss some instances of higher-order vagueness in chapter 4, once we have a clearer idea of what vagueness is.

We now have in place some machinery needed to begin work on a semantics of vagueness. That will be the project of the next two chapters.

OK, but we can still define some other kind of borderline: Just those things that can competently be called Φ, Φ* (or neither)

→ We don't have to call them borderline, but these still exist.

And with those you can re-generate the problems.

Chapter 3

Framework for a Semantics of Vagueness

"Vagueness and context dependence are separate phenomena.... Vagueness remains even when the context is fixed. In principle, a vague word might exhibit no context dependence whatsoever.
In practice, the lack of natural boundaries for vague words makes
context dependence hard to avoid, but that is an empirical correlation, not an *a priori* law."

Timothy Williamson (1994, 215)

Over the course of the next two chapters, I will begin to develop a
semantics for vague predicates within the familiar framework of a distinction between sense and reference. Chapter 3 will outline a theory
of sense, and chapter 4 will lay out the main elements of a theory
of reference. As will become clear, the sense of a vague word can be
viewed as the source of its vagueness, but the vagueness itself is an
aspect of the word's reference, not its sense. Working out the theory
of sense helps us to isolate the referential nature of vagueness and
also to understand the relationship between vagueness and context-
sensitivity. As I noted at the start, most if not all vague words are
context-sensitive, so it is important to see how these two features of
language are related. On the view I will propose, the context-sensitivity of vague words is an aspect of their sense and is only contingently

related to their vagueness. In principle a vague word could be insensitive to contextual factors, and nothing essential to the theory of vagueness depends on the details of the account of sense provided here. Again, I am not advancing a contextualist theory of vagueness.

In general I am going to pitch my semantics for vague words at a relatively high level of abstraction. I make a point of this for two reasons. First, I will not lay out a full-fledged formal semantics; that will be an interesting and important exercise but can be saved for later. Here my principal aim will be to characterize the large-scale architecture of the theory; what I mean by this will become clear. Second, the phenomenon of vagueness has received a good deal of attention lately from linguists and linguistically minded philosophers (e.g., Kennedy 1999, 2002, 2007, Barker 2002, van Deemter 2010), and I will leave many technical details to those experts.

3.1. VAGUENESS AND INDEXICALITY

Vague words that are context-sensitive are in some respects like indexical expressions. Suppose I say to you, pointing, 'That's a tall one,' but you cannot see, and don't otherwise know, what I am pointing at. It seems to me that in your present epistemic state, you would be as ignorant, or nearly as ignorant, of the object's height as you would be of its identity, and for analogous reasons. Just as you would need to see the object in order to know what my demonstration picks out, you would need to know the operative comparison class in order to know what I have said about its height. Is it tall compared to buildings? mountains? tomato plants? The point is that with regard to both the demonstrative 'that' and the predicate 'tall,' you would need to know the operative context.

While most or even all vague words are contextually sensitive, they are not plausibly viewed as indexicals, for reasons that will soon come to light; but the epistemic parallel just described suggests a semantic parallel between the two types of expressions. In fact, my semantics for vague words is modeled partly on David Kaplan's semantics for indexicals (e.g., 1977, 1978).[1] Let me start by reviewing the relevant aspects of Kaplan's account. Readers of this book are likely to be familiar with his view, so I will be brief.[2]

Kaplan contends that in order to accommodate the special context-sensitivity of indexical expressions, a semantics must distinguish between two species of sense—what he calls *character* and *content*—both of which are, broadly speaking, contextually sensitive. On his view, the meaning of an indexical expression is made of three elements: character, content, and referent or extension. Intuitively, a word's character is that element of meaning that comes closest to the dictionary definition and is what a speaker knows when we say that he knows what the word means. Character is "set by linguistic conventions" and remains the same across contexts of use (Kaplan 1977, 505). For instance, the character of the first-person indexical 'I' is given by something like the rule '*I' refers to the speaker or writer* (Kaplan 1977, 505).[3] Thus if both Elizabeth and Mary say, 'I will be queen,' their utterances have the same character. What they say, however—the propositions they express—are different: Elizabeth says that Elizabeth will be queen, whereas Mary says that Mary will. The contents of the two utterances differ because they are made in different contexts, where a context consists of things like an agent (speaker or writer), a time, and a position (spatial location) in a possible world.[4] Elizabeth's 'I' is uttered in a context whose speaker is Elizabeth, whereas Mary's 'I' is uttered in a context whose speaker is Mary.

Assuming with Kaplan that indexicals are directly referential, their contents just are their referents. Thus to say that the character of an indexical comes closest to the dictionary definition is not to say that its character enters into what is said or expressed by an utterance of the word; rather, the character of an indexical serves only to fix the referent of the word in a given context. For example, when Elizabeth says, 'I will be queen,' it is no part of what she says, no part of the content of her utterance, that her 'I' refers to the speaker or writer of the context. The character of 'I' serves merely to fix Elizabeth as the referent (content) of her use of the term in the given context; and the proposition she expresses, namely, that Elizabeth will be queen, can then be assessed as true or false at different worlds or circumstances of evaluation. In Kaplan's framework, character is represented as a function from contexts to contents, and contents in turn as functions from circumstances of evaluation to extensions in those circumstances.[5]

By introducing the distinction between character and content, Kaplan is able to explain how it can be that in one respect, occurrences of 'I' or 'now' or 'here' in different contexts mean the same, while in another respect they don't: They have the same character but different contents. His theory also makes sense of the fact that the sentence 'I am here now' is "universally" contingently true (i.e., contingently true—the speaker might always have been elsewhere) in any context in which it is uttered or occurs. At the world of a (proper) context, the speaker of the context is located at the position and time of the context; therefore, since the character of 'I' is given by the rule *refers to the speaker of the context* and similarly *mutatis mutandis* for 'here' and 'now', 'I am here now' is always true at the world of a context in which it is uttered. It is valid in the logic of indexicals, as Kaplan puts it.

I am going to propose a semantics for vague words that shares certain structural features with Kaplan's analysis of indexicals. Kaplan himself claims that the character of a nonindexical term like 'blue' or 'rich' is insensitive to the contexts in which the term is used:

> Nonindexicals have a fixed character. The same content is invoked in all contexts. This content will typically be sensitive

to circumstances, that is, the nonindexicals are typically not rigid designators but will vary in extension from circumstance to circumstance. Eternal sentences are generally good examples of expressions with a fixed character. 'All persons alive in 1977 will have died by 2077' expresses the same proposition no matter when said, by whom, or under what circumstances. The truth-value of that proposition may, of course, vary with possible circumstances, but the character is fixed. (1977, 506)

The distinction between character and content was unlikely to be noticed before demonstratives came under consideration, because demonstrative-free expressions have a constant character, i.e., they express the same content in every context. Thus character becomes an uninteresting complication in the theory. (1978, 404)

I think Kaplan is mistaken about the semantics of demonstrative-free expressions—in particular about the semantics of vague words. Character, or anyway something quite like it, is not an 'uninteresting complication' in the theory of sense for vague words. Let's see why.

3.2.   TWO INGREDIENTS OF SENSE FOR VAGUE WORDS

Consider again the example in which I point and say to you, 'That's a tall one,' but you cannot see what I am pointing at. Assuming you are a competent speaker of English, you understand at least part of what I have said—roughly, *that that* [to which I am pointing] *is large in spatial height*, or, perhaps better, *relatively large in spatial height*. What you understand is something like a character of the predicate 'tall.' Since this element of sense will prove somewhat different from a character, let's call it, for now, a 'quasi-character.' Like the character of an indexical, the quasi-character of 'tall' is set by linguistic conventions and remains the same across contexts of use: In any context, the tall things are large in spatial height. Quasi-character is the ingredient of the word's meaning that corresponds most closely to the dictionary definition and is what a speaker knows when we say that he knows what the word 'tall' means in English.

However, while you understand the quasi-character of 'tall,' you need additional contextual information before you can fully understand, and so determine the truth-value of, what I have said. One might say: You need additional contextual information in order to grasp the proposition expressed by my utterance. Again: tall compared to what? buildings? mountains? tomato plants? And tall in contrast to what? average? short? above average? (Something could be tall in contrast to average but not in contrast to above average.) Only after learning the answers to these questions do you fully understand what I have said. For example, I have said that the object to which I am pointing is large in height, in contrast to average, compared to buildings, or that it is large in height, in contrast to above average, compared to tomato plants. Similarly, suppose I ask you whether Brazil is rich. As a competent speaker of English you know the quasi-character of 'rich'—something like *well off*—but in order to fully understand the question, you need to be told what respect is at issue: richness in respect of financial assets, or natural resources, or cultural history, or what? Also, rich compared to what? other South American countries? Saudi Arabia? Canada? Perhaps you are being asked whether Brazil is rich in financial assets compared to other South American countries; or whether Brazil is rich in natural resources compared to Saudi Arabia; and so on.

In specifying the quasi-characters of 'tall' and 'rich,' we have used the words 'large' and 'well-off,' which are probably themselves vague predicates whose contents vary with context. Is there a risk of pernicious circularity or regress here? I don't think so, for we specify the quasi-characters of 'tall' and 'rich' in terms of the quasi-characters, not in terms of any contextually determined contents, of 'large' and 'well-off.' We could find the quasi-characters of 'large' and 'well-off' in a dictionary; in general the dictionary specifies context-invariant elements of meaning. Hence if there is any circularity in our account of the quasi-character of a vague word, it is no worse than the kind of circularity we find in the dictionary. The relationship between a term and its quasi-character(s) is not meant to be reductive or simplifying. Rather, quasi-character is the context-invariant meaning of a vague word rendered in a way that is more informative than saying simply 'tall' means tall or 'rich' means rich.

Despite the obvious parallels, quasi-characters differ importantly from characters. Unlike a character, the quasi-character of a vague predicate is an element of each of the word's contents and so is expressed by any utterance of the word. When I say 'Brazil is rich' relative to a given context, I am saying that Brazil is *well-off* relative to that context, and when I say 'Shaquille is tall' relative to a given context, I am saying that Shaquille is *large in height* relative to that context. I think we can say that the quasi-character of a vague predicate is a context-invariant element of the word's content: It is that element of content that is common to all contents of the predicate. In any context, being tall consists in being large in height, and being rich consists in being well-off. From now on I will call this element of meaning the *stable content* of a predicate.[6]

If 'tall' has a stable content that is common to all of its contents, then a context can be viewed as an operator on contents that takes that stable content to a richer, contextually relativized content of the sort that a speaker would typically mean to express by uttering the word. For example, the stable content *large in height* might be taken to the context-relative content *large in height compared to basketball players in North America in 2001,* or *large in height compared to basketball players in North America in September of 2001,* or *large in height, in contrast to above average, compared to basketball players in North America in September of 2001,* and so forth, depending on what the speaker means to say. Thus the stable contents of context-sensitive vague words are like the characters of indexicals in their context-invariance and their determination by linguistic conventions, but their status as contents sets them apart.[7]

It is worth noting that context-sensitive vague words appear to differ from indexicals in at least two other significant ways. First, recall Kaplan's claim that the characters of indexical words generate certain universal contingent truths—truths of the logic of indexicals. For example, the sentence 'I am here now' is contingently true in any context in which it is uttered. The stable contents of vague predicates also spawn trivial truths, such as 'Tall people are large in height' and 'Rich people are well-off,' which are true relative to any context of use. However, because stable contents are *contents,* not mere characters, the latter sentences are necessarily true, true at every world, whether they are uttered or not. (Maybe we could say that they are analytic. In chapter 4 I'll say more about necessary truths containing vague words.)

Second, it appears that the content of a vague predicate, but not the content of an indexical, can vary under verb phrase (VP) ellipsis or deletion. Peter Ludlow explains:

> Under VP ellipsis, the content of deictic expressions is understood as fixed. Thus in [1], for example,
>   [1] John likes him and Bill does too.
> [the] instance of him in the ellipsed VP must be understood as designating the same individual picked out by the overt instance of him in the first conjunct...
>   [2] That elephant is large and that flea is too.

In [2] it seems possible to read the adjectives as relativized to different [comparison] classes. That is, it is possible to understand this sentence as asserting largeness of an elephant with respect to elephants, and largeness of a flea with respect to fleas. (1989, 519–520)

'Large' is a vague predicate. By the same token we might say 'Shaquille is tall, and so is the Empire State Building,' or 'Federer is uniquely gifted, and Clinton is too.' In the former sentence the vague predicate 'tall' is relativized to different comparison classes in the two clauses (e.g., people and buildings), despite the ellipsis. In the latter, 'gifted' is relativized to different respects or dimensions or activities (e.g., tennis and politics).

Thus, despite some commonalities, context-sensitive vague words are importantly different from indexicals.[8] Klein observes that "there are certain kinds of context-dependent phenomena in semantics which cannot be forced into the pattern of indexical reference by pronouns" (1980, 16). The context-sensitivity of vague predicates is probably among them.

Just what factors constitute a linguistic context is often a delicate question, whether it be in connection with indexicals, observational predicates, epistemic predicates, or moral predicates, to name just a few.[9] David Lewis, citing Max Cresswell (1972), characterizes the situation this way:

The dependence of truth on context [is] surprisingly multifarious. It would be no easy matter to devise a list of all the features of context that are sometimes relevant to truth-in-English. In [1970] I gave a list that was long for its day, but not nearly long enough. Cresswell rightly complained: "Writers who, like David Lewis…try to give a bit more body to these notions talk about times, places, speakers, hearers…etc. and then go through agonies of conscience in trying to decide whether they have taken account of enough. It seems to me impossible to lay down in advance what sort of thing is going to count [as a relevant feature of context] ... The moral here seems to be that there is no way of specifying a finite list of contextual coordinates". (1980, 87)

If Cresswell means that in general we cannot specify exhaustively, or in advance, the contextual factors that will be relevant to a given application of a term, then his point is surely true of vague words. The relevance of a given factor is typically decided by competent speakers on a case-by-case basis. Speakers may choose among a variety of contextual factors and be as general or specific as their communicative goals require. Contexts, and therewith the contents expressed, are determined largely by speakers' intentions. I will come back to this point.

For the sake of argument, let us suppose that a typical context for a vague predicate specifies a respect (dimension, activity) r, an opposed or contrastive category c, and a comparison class cc that is usually defined in part by a time, place, and world. For the time being we can call such a context a *V-context* and represent it as having three coordinates: $\{r; \underline{c}; cc\}$. For example, a V-context relative to which the predicate 'rich' could be applied is $\{$salary; poor; factory workers in the United States, 1940, $w_@\}$. This context operates on the stable content of 'rich,' namely *well-off*, to yield the contextually determined content *well-off with respect to salary, in contrast to poor, compared to factory workers in the United States in 1940 at the actual world*. Another V-context for 'rich' would be $\{$financial assets; average; European countries, 2001, $w_\gamma\}$, where w_γ is a world at which Germany won World War II. This context yields the content *well-off in financial assets, in contrast to average, compared to European countries in 2001 at a world where Germany won World War II*. A very different V-context for 'rich,' $\{$nutrients; average; farmland in Maine, 1800,

$w_@$ }, yields the content *well-off in nutrients, in contrast to average, compared to farmland in Maine in 1800 at the actual world.*[10]

A question arises about the coordinate for a comparison class: Must the item to which a vague predicate is applied be a member of the operative comparison class? The examples just given for 'rich' suggest not. For instance, Canada might be well-off in financial assets, in contrast to average, compared to European countries in 2001, and so on. But Ewan Klein is dubious:[11]

> Suppose
>   [1] Bill is tall
> is uttered in the context [c] of watching jockeys weigh in before a horse race. The appropriate comparison class for tall will be the set of jockeys... The question is then what value should be assigned in c to [2], where Sam is no jockey, but a rather tall basketball player:
>   [2] Sam is tall.
> The first option is to take [2] as true in c. But this will nullify the introduction of comparison classes, for though it may make good sense to say that Bill is tall relative to the set of jockeys in c, it would not be consistent with our usual understanding of tall to say that both Bill and Sam are tall. As soon as we take Sam into consideration, [1] will be judged false.... On the other hand, it also seems odd to say that [2] is false in c. For Sam is much taller than Bill. (1980, 13–14)

But why should [1] be judged false when we take Sam into consideration? Aren't Sam and Bill both tall compared to jockeys? Aren't Warren Buffett and Hillary Clinton both rich compared to welfare recipients, though one is much richer than the other? The difference in their richness is evident in the fact that Buffett is rich compared to more classes of people than Clinton. I don't deny that the item or person to which a vague predicate is applied does often belong to the operative comparison class, and we can mark such cases by using the construction 'x is Φ for an A': Gerry is tall for a jockey, and Buffett is rich (even) for a businessman. We can also use the predicate attributively and say that Gerry is a tall jockey. But the latter cases are presumably a subset of the cases in which something is Φ compared to A's. Surely Shaquille O'Neal is tall compared to jockeys. And though it might be pragmatically bizarre to say that Big Ben is tall compared to jockeys, I think that if pressed we would say it is true. (On the other hand, perhaps in these cases we are saying, roughly, that a jockey whose height was the same as O'Neal's, or *per impossibile* the same as Big Ben's, would be tall for a jockey.)

However the latter issue is resolved, in ordinary language we usually don't need to specify explicitly the V-contextual coordinates that are operative on a given occasion, since these are obvious from the preceding text or conversation or implicit in the shared background beliefs and expectations of the speakers involved. For instance, we have already been talking about financial assets in connection with factory workers, or European countries, and have already been employing the contrastive word 'poor.' Also, the V-contexts we employ in ordinary speech are vastly less fine-grained than such a context can be in principle. In principle a V-context could specify a comparison class of, say, American women aged from 40 years and 3 hours to 40 years and 10 hours, employed in jobs having two or more coffee breaks but no lunch break, in US cities that have populations over 500,017 but are not state capitals, and so on, ad indefinitum. While we could employ such a detailed comparison class if the need arose, we are usually interested in more coarse-grained classes like, say, Scottish farmers in the late 19th century, or communists during the Cold War, or African Americans in executive positions during the 1990s. For that matter, in the absence of some indication otherwise, we often (rightly) assume that the world and time of an operative comparison class are the world and time at which we are currently speaking. In general we assign V-contextual coordinates in an ad hoc, task-relevant fashion; and, finite beings that we are, we take account of only a small number of factors at any given time. When we use hue predicates, for example, the question of a comparison class may be irrelevant; we may want to say simply that something is red in contrast to orange, or red in contrast to pink, where the question 'compared to what?' does not arise. Our theory can represent an empty coordinate with a zero, as in $\{$hue; <u>orange</u>; $0\}$, which specifies no comparison class.

No doubt the contexts relative to which vague words can be applied contain coordinates additional to the three I have suggested. For instance, maybe the meaning of the operator 'for an A,' discussed above, should be captured in the form of a coordinate for a domain—say, jockeys or mountains. Maybe we should add a coordinate for a purpose: Eve may be tall for the purpose of reaching the cookie jar but not for the purpose of dusting the ceiling fan. But nothing of significance hinges on these details. The important, fundamental idea is that a sentence containing a V-context-sensitive vague word can express different contents and hence take different truth-values relative to different V-contexts.

3.3. REFINEMENT: INTENDED CONTEXTS, NOT CONTEXTS OF UTTERANCE

Before turning to the theory of reference and the account of vagueness itself, I want to call attention to a distinction between two roles that can be played by linguistic contexts and to clarify which of them is likely to be played by a V-context. While nothing essential to our understanding of vagueness depends on this, it will give us a clearer picture of the context-sensitivity of vague words.

Suppose that Roger is an outstanding tennis player but a mediocre golfer. And suppose we are watching him play in a golf tournament. He shoots a triple bogey on the 18th hole, and you remark, "Roger is terrible." If I have been thinking about his latest triumph at Wimbledon, as is likely given the quality of his golf game, I might reply by saying, "I think he's outstanding," meaning that he's outstanding at tennis. It seems to me that I can make my utterance express the content *that Roger is outstanding at tennis* even in response to your remark at the golf tournament. I can do this simply by intending to. If you fail to grasp that content, or anyway fail to acquiesce in or "accommodate" my contextual relativization, and insist that Roger is terrible, still *my* utterance expresses the content *that Roger is outstanding at tennis*. What I've said may be pragmatically anomalous—may violate maxims of relevance in particular—and its content may be opaque to you as a result.[12] (To make my meaning clear, I may need to make my contextual relativization explicit; I may need to say, for instance, 'I agree about the golf, but he's outstanding on the tennis court.' See note 13 of this chapter.) But the semantics is straightforward. As far as content fixation is concerned, the context in which the utterance is produced is irrelevant.

The distinction I want to employ is elaborated by, for example, Stefano Predelli (1998) and Claudia Bianchi (2001) in work on the difference between "pure" and "intentional" or "discretionary" indexicals. On a usual view, the words 'I,' 'now,' and 'here' are said to be *pure* or *automatic* indexicals whose content in a given utterance is determined entirely by their characters together with their contexts of utterance, independently of the speaker's referential intentions (e.g., Kaplan 1977, Perry 1997, 1998; King 2012). The latter terms are supposed to differ in this respect from demonstratives or *intentional* indexicals like 'that' and 'he,' whose contents are fixed only by the addition of a speaker's intention to refer to a particular thing or person. Against this standard view, Predelli (1998) and

Bianchi (2001) assemble an array of examples to show that at least some utterances of 'I' and 'now' and 'here' also have their contents fixed partly by speaker intentions.[13] For example, suppose you are stuck in traffic and you're going to arrive late for your office hours. You might call the department secretary and ask him to put a note on your office door saying 'I'll be about 15 minutes late.' Although the occurrence of 'I' in the note would be uttered (inscribed) in a context whose speaker (inscriber) is the secretary, it would refer not to him but to you. This appears to be a case in which the referent (content) of the first-person indexical is fixed not by the situation in which it is uttered or produced but rather, at least in part, by the secretary's intention that it refer to *you*. To accommodate such "impurities," Bianchi writes, we must

> distinguish between the context of utterance (or inscription)—which I will call the *context of* (material) *production*—and a context the speaker considers semantically relevant, the *context of interpretation*... which I will call *intended context*. The character... [of 'I', in 'I'll be about 15 minutes late']... appl[ies] to the intended context and not to the context of utterance/inscription. (2001, 79)[14]

Making the same point about 'now,' Predelli illustrates with this passage from a book about World War II, written in 1996:

> It is May 1940. Germany outflanks the Maginot line. Now, nothing stands between Hitler's troops and Paris. (1998, 72)

My present concern is not with the apparent impurity of certain utterances of 'I' and 'now' but rather with the nature of the contexts relative to which vague words are applied.[15] I suggest that the content of a given utterance (use, occurrence) of a vague word is determined not by its context of utterance—that is, not by the situation in which the utterance is produced—but by the speaker's intended context. The individual speaker's intention to relativize to a certain set of factors is (along with the word's stable content) the sole determinant of the context-relative content of his utterance of a vague word, and the latter factors may diverge from the factors to which his interlocutors are relativizing or which would otherwise constitute the situation of his utterance.[16] Thus the content of my utterance of 'I think he's outstanding' is determined not by the context of the conversation at the golf tournament but by my intended context, namely, tennis playing.

One might think that the individual speaker's intention just is a feature of the context of utterance—for example, that my intention to relativize to tennis just is a feature, among various others, of the context of our conversation at the golf tournament.[17] And indeed my intention may be a feature of the latter context, but the question is whether it can be a content-fixing feature. (Contexts may have indefinitely many features that are not content-fixing.) That is what seems implausible, because my intent to relativize to tennis is an intent to relativize to a context distinct from the situational context of our conversation at the golf tournament. How could one context determine that another, distinct context is currently operative? How could the context of the conversation at the golf tournament determine that the context of tennis playing is in effect *in the context of the conversation at the golf tournament*? Rather, V-contexts are intended contexts: They are determined by speaker intentions independently of contexts of material production. As far as vague predicates are concerned, I think Fodor and Lepore have it right:

> Nothing about the context of an utterance is a metaphysical determinant of its content. The only metaphysical determinants of utterance content are (i) the linguistic structure of the utterance (the syntax and lexical inventory of the expression type

that it's a token of), and (ii) the communicative intentions of the speaker. Nothing else. Ever. (2005, 8)[18]

Certainly there is a sense in which the context of utterance of a vague predicate may determine the word's content in that utterance. If I say "Eve is short" during a conversation about the players at a basketball game, that context will probably determine that my utterance expresses the content *that Eve is short compared to basketball players*; but this is not determination in the strong metaphysical sense. The topic of conversation determines the content of my utterance in the merely pragmatic sense that it influences my choice of intended context and, as a result, helps my hearers figure out which context I am relativizing to.[19] If I am a competent and sincere speaker wanting to contribute to an ongoing conversation, I am likely to choose the context that is already operative so that my hearers will easily recognize it and I can say something relevant. But I am not obliged to do this; *semantically* speaking, I can choose any context I like. If I refuse or otherwise fail to relativize to the context already in play, I may say something that seems false or inappropriate or even incomprehensible to my fellow conversationalists or something misleading or simply irrelevant, but that will be a merely pragmatic blunder. (Situational context of utterance may not determine content, but it does determine relevance.)

To help us remember that the individual speaker has discretion over the intended contexts of his utterances and that the latter may be wholly distinct from the situational contexts in which his utterances are produced, I suggest that we think of V-contexts not as situations but as formal indices—as sets of coordinates for whatever factors (contrastive category, comparison class, etc.) are needed for the semantics. I am going to replace reference to V-contexts with reference to V-indices in our semantics and say that a vague predicate 'Φ' has a content relative to a *V-index* $\{r;$

$\underline{c}$; cc }, abbreviated as { i }. The content of the predicate relative to a given V-index is determined, in the strong metaphysical sense of 'fixed', by that V-index. On the view I am advancing, then, a V-index operates upon the stable content of a V-index-sensitive (f. V-context-sensitive) vague word, yielding a richer, more fine-grained content of the word relative to that V-index. And many vague predicates will have indefinitely many V-index-relative contents.

From now on, for ease of discussion, I will often specify only one or two coordinates of a V-index, usually a comparison class and sometimes a time. I will say for example that Hillary Clinton is rich { average Americans, 2001 } or that Shaquille O'Neal is tall { basketball players }. This may be about as much detail as speakers usually have in mind anyway. Also I will take for granted that the world of an index, specifically of the comparison class, is the actual world.

[handwritten margin notes: OK, so the comparison class is part of the meaning for vague terms]

3.4. SELECTIVE REVIEW

(1) The apparent context-sensitivity of many vague words may be best conceived as sensitivity to the coordinates of formal indices determined by speakers' intentions. For discussion, we are supposing that a V-index specifies a respect (dimension, activity) r, contrastive category $\underline{c}$, and comparison class cc.

(2) An (unambiguous) V-index-sensitive word can plausibly be viewed as having a stable content and different V-index-relative contents determined by different V-indices. A stable content shares some features with, but differs importantly from, a character. In general, contrary to what some authors have supposed, the context-sensitivity

of context-sensitive vague words differs importantly from indexicality.

(3) The V-index-sensitivity of vague words bears no essential relationship to their vagueness. In principle, a vague term could be insensitive to contextual (V-indexical) factors.

3.5. LOOKING AHEAD

In this chapter I have set out some elements of a theory of sense for vague words. While the latter account could be regarded as a form of semantic contextualism, even if correct it doesn't touch the vagueness of a vague word. We are about to see why.

Chapter 4

The Multiple Range
Theory of Vagueness

Vague.
1. Que l'esprit a du mal à saisir, à cause de son caractère mouvant...
[tr. *Hard for the mind to grasp, because of its fluid character....*]

Le Grand Robert (1970)

So far the basic architecture of our semantics for vague words has fol-
lowed that of Kaplan's semantics for indexicals fairly closely. Kaplan
holds that indexical words have a stable or context-insensitive character that, together with a context, determines a content relative to
that context. We hold that V-index-sensitive vague predicates have a
stable or V-index-insensitive content that, when operated upon by a
V-index, yields a richer content relative to that V-index. Kaplan com-
pletes his semantics by representing content in turn as combining
with a circumstance of evaluation to yield an extension in that circumstance. Our semantics of vagueness cannot proceed so directly,
however. At this point the structure of our theory must diverge from
that of Kaplan's in order to account for an additional element in the
meaning of a vague word.

4.1. VAGUENESS AND REFERENCE

The crucial point is that even after a V-index, and hence a V-index-relative content, have been fixed, competent speakers will vary both inter- and intrasubjectively in their applications of a vague word.[1] Even having settled on, say, the V-index $\{$ height; above average; five-year-olds in public schools of fewer than 250 students in Ukrainian cities whose names begin with 'M,' September 1954, $w_@ \}$—make it as specific, as fine-grained as you like—still you and I will vary arbitrarily in some of our judgments as to whether a given height makes a person tall. Because 'tall' is vague, its application will vary even if all variation with V-index is eliminated. To frame the point in terms of a sorites series: Even given a V-index, hence a V-index-relative content, multiple stopping places are equally competent or permissible. This means that the choice of any particular stopping place is, from the viewpoint of semantics, arbitrary, and hence not legislative; when I stop at a particular place in a sorites series, I do so without reason or justification (recall section 1.2). It also means that when we diverge in our classifications, we merely diverge: We do not disagree, where by 'disagreement' I mean a divergence in which argument is appropriate and mistakes are possible. We are using the predicate in question with the same content—one of us applying the predicate, the other applying its negation—and so we contradict each other, but we do not disagree in the relevant sense of that term, and neither of us need be mistaken.[2] (Similarly, if I like the taste of arugula I may say, 'Arugula tastes delicious,' whereas if you dislike it you may say, 'Arugula does not taste delicious.' We can be using our terms with the same contents, and so we contradict each other. But we do not disagree in the sense here at issue.) In such a case, the absence of genuine disagreement between us results not from a difference in the contents of our utterances, as semantic contextualists typically claim, but rather from the arbitrariness of

92

our divergent stopping places. I will say more about divergence and disagreement shortly.

To keep things simple, let's work again with the predicate 'rich' relative to the V-index {salary; middle income; Americans aged forty to sixty, 2001, $w_@$}. (Call this V-index 'Vinny.') Our sorites series contains salaries extending from rich at $200,000 to middle income at $50,000, so ordered that each salary is one dollar lower than its predecessor. Suppose also that $125,000 can competently be classified as rich[middle income] borderline. (Therefore it can also competently be classified as rich and as middle income.) Perhaps, on a given occasion, I stop applying 'rich' and shift to 'borderline' at $150,000, while you don't stop until $140,000. Another time I may stop at $140,000 while you stop at $137,000. *There are multiple equally competent ways of applying the vague predicate 'rich' relative to Vinny*: $150,000, $140,000, and $137,000 are different, equally competent stopping places, among many others. Assuming that all of the salaries higher than the stopping place in each case would make a person rich, we can say that on one competent way of applying 'rich' relative to Vinny, salaries from $200,000 to $150,000 are rich, while on another competent way of applying the predicate, salaries from $200,000 to $140,000 are rich, and so forth. That is, on one competent way of applying 'rich' relative to Vinny, *all and only* the salaries from $200,000 to $150,000 are rich, while on another competent way of applying the predicate, *all and only* salaries from $200,000 to $140,000 are rich, and so forth.

When I say that applying 'rich' to the salaries from $200,000 to $150,000 is a competent way of applying the predicate, I don't mean, or don't mean only, that applying 'rich' to those salaries *seriatim* is a competent way of applying it. Naturally if we are talking about a sorites series, then to say that the range $200,000 to $150,000 is a competent way of applying 'rich' is to say that $150,000 is a competent stopping place. But generally when I say that application of 'rich' to the salaries $200,000 to $150,000 is competent or permissible, I mean just that 'rich' can competently be applied to any of those salaries.

When I say that I stop applying 'rich' at a particular location (e.g., $125,000) without reason or justification, I mean *without independent or nontrivial reason or justification in the nature of the case.* Of course someone could hold a gun to my head, or bribe me, thereby giving me reason to classify $125,000 as rich, but this would not be a reason *in the nature of the case.* Similarly, we set the US voting age at eighteen years rather than at eighteen years plus one day for reasons of convenience and easy remembering, not for any reason in the nature of the case, that is, not because a difference of one day is relevantly significant with regard to the maturity required for voting (see, e.g., Marmor 2012, 4–5.) I don't mean to say that my arbitrary stopping place is a shot in the dark: I classify $125,000 as rich *because it seems rich* (to me on this occasion); it strikes me as being rich, impresses me as being a salary that would make a person rich relative to Vinny. Rather, the point is that my classification is made without independent or nontrivial—here, non-question-begging—justification.[3] I classify $125,000 as rich because it strikes me as rich, but I can provide nothing further in the way of justification for classifying it that way rather than as, for example, middle income or rich[middle income] borderline. Similarly, I classify patch #15 as blue *because it looks blue,* as opposed to looking green or looking blue[green] borderline, but I can provide no further grounds for my judgment. Of course I may mistakenly believe that I have grounds, that I have nontrivial reason to classify the patch as I do, but in fact no such grounds can exist. This is why argument (genuine disagreement) over the classification of variable, transitional items is impossible. In contrast, when I classify $200,000 as rich or patch #1 as blue—central cases—I can cite linguistic rules for 'rich' and 'blue' that require their application, or point to the uncomprehending

That is really a weak justification [handwritten marginal note]

or disapproving reactions from competent speakers if I fail to apply them.

It's worth noting that epistemicist Williamson tries unsuccessfully to knock down the idea that vague words are multiply applicable in the way I have described. He writes,

> On the view that nothing is hidden, it should be harmless to imagine omniscient speakers, ignorant of nothing relevant to the borderline case...Accompanied by an omniscient speaker of English, you remove grain after grain from a heap. After each removal you ask 'Is there still a heap?'...For some number n, she says 'Yes' after each of the first n removals, but not after n + 1. ...You repeat the experiment with other omniscient speakers.... If they all stop at the same point, it evidently does mark some sort of previously hidden boundary.... [A non-epistemic view] must therefore hold that different omniscient speakers would stop at different points. They are conceived as having some sort of discretion....
>
> You can instruct the omniscient speakers...to use their discretion...conservatively, so that they answer 'Yes' to as few questions as is permissible.... Now if two omniscient speakers stop answering 'Yes' at different points, both having been instructed to be conservative, the one who stops later has disobeyed your instructions, for the actions of the other show that the former could have used her discretion to answer 'Yes' to fewer questions than she actually did. But the omniscient speakers are cooperative. They will...obey your instructions.... It is not as though, however many times they said 'yes', they could have said it fewer times, for the sorites series is finite.... Thus if all [omniscient speakers] are instructed to be conservative, all will stop at the same point. You do not know in advance where it will come. It marks some sort of previously hidden boundary. (1994, 199–200)

The trouble with this argument is that the instruction to "answer 'Yes' to as few questions as is permissible" is equivalent to an instruction to stop applying 'heap' at the earliest (most conservative) permissible place. And those who think that vagueness is semantic deny that there is any such place; the instruction cannot be carried out. Only someone already in the clutches of an epistemic view will imagine that it can. We find these apt remarks in Wittgenstein:

> 'Make me a heap of sand here.'—'Fine, that is certainly something he would call a heap.' I was able to obey the command, so it was in order. But what about this command 'Make me the smallest heap you would still call a heap'? I would say: that is nonsense. (1974, 240)

Assuming then that competent application of a vague term is variable and divergent in the ways described above, so what? What does this show about the term's semantics, specifically its reference? I made it my goal early on to develop a theory of vagueness that is grounded "as deeply as possible in commonsense intuition and our actual competent use of vague words" (p. 12). All else being equal, a semantics should square with competent use. Hence at this juncture I propose to take the character of competent use as evidence of the semantic structure of vague words. Specifically, I propose that the multiple competent ways of applying a vague predicate relative to a given V-index reflect multiple *ranges of application* in the semantics of the term. By 'range of application' I mean simply a set of values (types, properties, categories) to whose instantiations or tokens the predicate can competently be applied. (Here and in what follows I use the term 'set' in its ordinary, nontechnical sense, as when we talk of a set of dishes or golf clubs.) For example, a range of application of 'tall' is a set of tall heights, and a range of application of 'blue' is a set of blue hues (shades of blue). One range of application of 'rich,' relative to Vinny, is the set of salaries $200,000 to $150,000; another is the set $200,000 to $127,240, and so on; a competent speaker could apply 'rich' to all and only the salaries $200,000 to $150,000, or to all and only the salaries $200,000 to $127,240, and so on.[4] Relative to a different V-index—say, $\{$ salary; <u>upper middle income</u>; Americans aged forty to sixty, 2001, $w_{@}$ $\}$—'rich' will have a different content that determines a different multiplicity of ranges of application. My proposal is that *each V-index-relative content of a vague predicate determines multiple ranges of application*—as many as there are competent ways of applying the predicate relative to that V-index. If some vague words are not V-index-sensitive (we are leaving open this possibility), their single contents determine multiple ranges of application.

Three points need emphasis. First, ranges of application correspond to *competent* ways of applying a predicate; for example, a set containing the salaries $200,000 to $150,025 and $150,000 to $130,000 is not a range of application of 'rich,' nor is a set containing the salaries $200,000 to $10. We might represent some ranges of application of 'rich' as in Figure 4.1. We could of course extend the series of dollar amounts upward ad indefinitum and say that one range consists of salaries greater than or equal to $130,000, another of salaries greater than or equal to $150,000, and so forth. For convenience I will often speak of a predicate as having its ranges of application relative to a V-index rather than determined by a (V-index-relative) content, but these ways of talking are equivalent.

Second, a range of application is not a set of *objects*, such as a set of tall buildings, or blue objects, or rich people. Rather it is a set of values or properties, namely, a set of heights, or hues, or numbers of dollars of salary. In other words, a range is a set of values or types whose instantiations are the tall buildings, the blue objects, the rich people. I will use the term *V-extensions of* 'Φ' to refer to the sets of objects (tall buildings, rich people) that instantiate the ranges of application of

$200,000..................................$150,000

$200,000..................................$149,999

$200,000..................................$145,050

$200,000...$135,000

$200,000...$133,000

$200,000..$130,100

$200,000..$127,240

$200,000...$125,000

$200,000...$120,000

$200,000...$111,003

Figure 4.1. Some ranges of application of 'rich' relative to the V-index $\{$salary; <u>middle income</u>; Americans aged 40–60, 2001, $w_@\}$.

a vague predicate. In any given circumstance of evaluation (for simplicity I'll assume that circumstances are just worlds), a vague predicate will have multiple V-extensions relative to each V-index—one V-extension picked out by each of its ranges. I would have preferred to use the term 'extensions' for these sets of objects and to say that a vague predicate has multiple extensions relative to each V-index at a given world (circumstance). Since it is commonplace to say that a predicate has different extensions at different worlds and different extensions relative to different contexts at each world, it seems to me natural to say, on the present view, that a vague predicate has different extensions relative to each range of application for each context (V-index). However, the term 'extension' is so theoretically loaded—some philosophers insist that it comes with a uniqueness condition, others that an extension must have sharp boundaries in a sense antithetical to vagueness—that using it in this way causes more trouble than it's worth. So I am going to compromise and use the term 'V-extension'. The upshot is that a vague predicate does not have a (single) extension in the usual sense.[5]

Third, although I have defined 'V-extension' in a way that employs some formal machinery, the term is really just a fancy name for the innocuous notion of a set of objects that instantiate the values or properties in a given range, and 'range of application' is just a fancy name for those values—namely, a set of values that a competent speaker could classify as satisfying a certain vague word. For example, a competent speaker could apply 'rich' to the salaries $200,000 to $130,000, and relative to that way of applying the predicate, the rich people at each world are the people earning those salaries; another competent speaker can apply 'rich' to the salaries $200,000 to $127,240, and relative to that way of applying the predicate, the rich people at each world are the people earning *those* salaries, and so forth. As it seems to me, the notion of a range of application is so innocuous that it should be acceptable to anyone (even the epistemicist) who thinks that competent speakers are permitted to stop applying a vague predicate 'Φ' at different places in a sorites series. (What's distinctive of the present view is not the concept of a range of application but the role played by that concept in the semantics of vague terms.) In particular: *the fact that a range of application has a last member does not indicate the presence of a sharp boundary; it signifies only that the item or value in question is a permissible stopping place.* As I observed in chapter 1, virtually all theorists of vagueness seem to agree on at least these two points: (i) that competent speakers must stop applying the predicate before the end of a sorites series and (ii) that the existence of permissible stopping places does not reflect the presence of sharp boundaries in the application of the term.

Just how a (V-index-relative) content of a vague predicate determines multiple ranges of application may seem obscure. But determination of multiple ranges should be no more mysterious than determination of a single range. Commonly we think of a predicate, vague or otherwise, as picking out its extension by way of determining a set of decisive properties or values. For instance, 'old' picks out its extension at a world (perhaps relative to a context) by way of determining a set of ages whose instantiations at that world (relative to that context) are the things that are old at that world (relative to that context). In other words, 'old' picks out the ages that are old, and then the things that instantiate those ages are the old things. That set of old ages just is a range of application of 'old.' And if 'old' can determine a single such set of ages as the old ones, why should it not determine multiple such sets—specifically, multiple sets corresponding to the multiple permissible ways of applying the predicate? Our idea, recall, was that the competent use of a vague word reflects—is evidence of—its semantic structure.

Rather than building the multiplicity of ranges of application of a vague word into its semantics, as I am proposing, why not think that we are simply making mistakes, simply being inconsistent in some faulty way, when we vary in our classifications of the values in a sorites series? I have been asked this question more than once,[6] but I confess I am baffled by it. Surely it is a fundamental tenet of good theory construction that, all else being equal, a theory that does not have us chronically, irremediably (and hitherto unbeknownst to us) mistaken in the application of our own ordinary words is preferable to one that does. As long as a viable "non-error" theory is available, the burden of argument lies with the error theorist. The right question is: Why think we are mistaken?[7]

In rejecting an error theory, I do not suppose that competent speakers are infallible in any substantive sense. With respect to what I have called 'variable' items, competent speakers are vacuously infallible, one might say. They are infallible only in the sense that their divergent classifications of variable items do not occur within a normative framework in which error as such could exist. Hence talk of mistaken applications, eo ipso of correct applications, of a vague word to a variable item is misplaced. Granted if you classify a blue/green variable patch as *red*, you are mistaken, but not if you classify it as blue or as green or as blue[green] borderline. In this connection it is also worth noting that because our judgments of variable items are made arbitrarily, without independent reason or justification, a judgment that such an item is Φ (Φ^*, $\Phi[\Phi^*]$ borderline) probably should not be regarded as knowledge. I do not mean to suggest, like the epistemicist, that there is something, some fact, of which we are ignorant in a variable case. Rather, a crucial possibility of justification or warrant is missing; hence the question of correct and incorrect applications, and therewith the question of knowledge, does not arise.

Lest there be any confusion: I am not claiming that vague predicates are *response-dependent*.[8] The responses or judgments of competent speakers do not determine whether a vague word applies to a given item; in other words, the responses or judgments of competent speakers do not determine which items belong to the V-extensions of vague words. Whether an item satisfies a given vague predicate is determined by the predicate's semantics. (In still other words: Only the use of a vague word, not its semantics, is *variable*; the semantics is *multiple*, not variable.) For example, whether an item satisfies 'blue' relative to a certain V-index is determined by the semantics of 'blue,' in particular by its ranges of application (which are themselves determined by the predicate's content relative to that V-index) and of course by the item's hue—not by speakers' responses or dispositions to respond. An item may belong to the extension of 'blue' relative to every one of the predicate's ranges for a given V-index, or relative to none of its ranges, or relative to some but not every one—independently of anything to do with judging subjects or speakers. The most that competent speakers determine is which range(s) of application they will "use" or "employ" on a given occasion. (In the next chapter I will say more about what is involved in using ranges of application; cf. section 5.4.)

Of course, we need also to allow for the more familiar kind of variability of application across possible circumstances or worlds—the idea that the set of rich people or tall buildings or bald heads will vary in its membership from world to world. Our semantics for vague words makes an adjustment from singular to plural: The *sets* of rich people and the *sets* of tall buildings vary in their memberships from world to world. We can speak of a single set of such items if we relativize to a particular V-index, range of application, and circumstance or world. For instance, the set of people at the actual world who are rich relative to Vinny and the range $200,000 to $150,000 may differ from the set of people who are rich, relative to Vinny and that same range, at some other world.[9]

4.2. WHY RANGES OF APPLICATION ARE NOT PRECISIFICATIONS

On the surface, ranges of application may seem rather like the supervaluationist's precisifications. But the two notions differ crucially in several ways. (1) Most important, a complete admissible precisification of 'Φ' contains Φ items and not-Φ items with a sharp boundary between, whereas a range of application of 'Φ' contains (all and) only Φ items and no boundary. In terms of a sorites series, a range of 'Φ' contains a last member, but the latter signifies only a permissible stopping point, not a boundary: A competent speaker could stop applying 'Φ' *here*. Again, a range of application is simply an abstract representation of a permissible way of applying a word; in no sense does it precisify the word. (2) An admissible precisification can contain "gappy" items, that is, items with respect to which 'x is Φ' receives no truth-value, whereas there can be no gappy items in a range of application (or anywhere else, on the present view).[10] (3) The predicate *but it has a longest and a shortest range!*

'borderline Φ' has multiple ranges and V-extensions like any other vague predicate; in other words, some ranges of application, namely those for the predicate 'borderline Φ,' contain all and only borderline items. No precisification contains only borderline (gappy) cases; any admissible precisification must classify some items as Φ and some items as not-Φ. Lastly, (4) whereas the supervaluationist identifies ordinary everyday truth with truth on all admissible precisifications or "super-truth," the present view identifies ordinary everyday truth with truth relative to a single range of application. The present view has no need to generalize over ranges of application, no need to locate truth at one remove, as it were, from the ranges of a vague word. Fine writes that "Truth is super-truth, truth from above" (1975, 127). We say: Truth is plain old regular truth, truth from straight ahead.

4.3. PROGRESS REPORT AND A CRITERION OF VAGUENESS

Let us review the elements of our semantics that are now in place.

V-index-sensitive vague expressions have a stable content that remains the same across V-indices. For argument's sake we have supposed that a V-index specifies inter alia a respect, a contrastive category, and a comparison class. A V-index can be thought of as a content operator: it takes the stable content of a vague term to a richer, V-index-relative content. Each V-index-relative content determines multiple ranges of application of the predicate relative to that V-index. And, unless the word is rigid, each range of application in turn picks out different V-extensions in different circumstances or worlds. (If a vague expression is not V-index-sensitive—we are allowing this possibility—its single content determines multiple ranges.)

this is precise!

Structurally speaking, our account extends Kaplan's semantics for indexicals so as to capture the distinctive multiplicity in the meaning of a vague word. It does this by means of the intervening determination of multiple ranges of application by each V-index-relative content. In effect, a vague word has two kinds of referents: sets of values or properties, and sets of things that instantiate those properties. Figures 4.2 to 4.4 may help to bring out the differences between our semantics and Kaplan's. Kaplan's scheme can be represented as in Figure 4.2; our semantics for vague words can then be represented as in Figure 4.3.

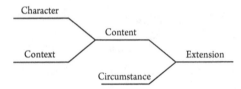

Figure 4.2. Kaplan's semantics for indexicals (adapting Lewis 1980).

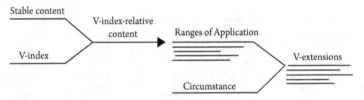

Figure 4.3. Our semantics for V-index-sensitive vague predicates.

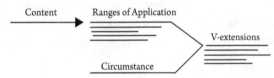

Figure 4.4. Our semantics for V-index-insensitive vague predicates.

As these diagrams show, the front and back ends of our semantics are structurally analogous to Kaplan's. We extend Kaplan's scheme in the middle, where the V-index-relative content of a vague predicate generates multiple ranges of application. The semantic structure of a vague word that is V-index-*in*sensitive, sustaining no distinction between stable and V-index-relative contents, could be pictured as in Figure 4.4. Thus, whereas Kaplan's semantics for indexicals isolates three ingredients in the meaning of an indexical word—character, content, and extension—our semantics isolates four ingredients in the meaning of a (V-index-sensitive) vague predicate: stable content, V-index-relative content, ranges of application, and V-extensions. Where Kaplan distinguishes two elements of sense, our theory distinguishes in addition two elements of reference.

Possession of multiple arbitrarily different ranges of application is probably not by itself sufficient for vagueness. In particular, it may be that in order for 'Φ' to be vague, the higher-order predicate 'range of application of "Φ"' also must have multiple arbitrarily different ranges of application. In other words, maybe if 'Φ' is vague, competent speakers must be permitted to vary and diverge arbitrarily not only in their applications of 'Φ' but also in their applications of 'range of application of "Φ"': They must be permitted to vary and diverge as to what counts as a competent way of applying 'Φ' relative to a given V-index.[11] To see why, consider a predicate 'srich' that competent speakers apply by stopping arbitrarily at one of three places in our series of salaries \$200,000 to \$50,000: They can stop at \$120,000, or at \$119,999, or at \$119,998, varying arbitrarily among these from occasion to occasion.[12] If possession of multiple arbitrarily different ranges were sufficient for vagueness, 'srich' would be vague. But intuitively that doesn't seem right: Given its fixed set of ranges, 'srich' comes too close to having sharp boundaries to count as vague. There is a first salary that can competently be classified as not-srich (viz.,

$119,999) and a last salary that can competently be classified as srich (viz., $119,998). If 'srich' were vague, there could be no such salaries.

A moment's reflection then suggests that, for analogous reasons, the still higher higher-order predicate 'range of application of "range of application of 'Φ'"' should also have multiple arbitrarily different ranges of application, and then the predicate 'range of application of "range of application of 'range of application of "Φ"'"' and so forth, in theory, ad indefinitum. If I am right about 'srich,' then, a predicate 'Φ' is vague only if 'Φ,' and also 'range of application of "Φ"' and its indefinitely many iterations, have multiple arbitrarily different ranges of application. The vagueness of these iterative predicates is an instance of higher-order vagueness, about which I will say more later.

I don't mean to suggest that all ineliminable or unresolvable linguistic divergences among competent speakers are symptomatic of vagueness, or, more generally, that unresolvable divergence always reflects the semantic structure of the terms involved. For instance, you and I may diverge chronically as to whether arugula tastes delicious, and arguing about it would be pointless. Opinions on such matters are not the sort of attitude with respect to which justifications can be provided or mistakes can be made; they are mere opinions. However, it doesn't follow that 'delicious' is vague; it may be vague, but not because *this* divergence is unresolvable. The principal reason is that, presumably, neither of us has formed her opinion arbitrarily. When you say that arugula is delicious, you don't think that you could as well—right now, on the basis of the same taste experience—have said it was, say, ordinary, or a fortiori mediocre. And presumably your opinion won't vary arbitrarily from one occasion to the next.

Sometimes even a genuine disagreement may be unresolvable, as in so-called essentially contested cases (e.g., Gallie 1956, Waldron 2002). For example, debates over the moral permissibility of aborting a conceptus, or what counts as a reasonable person or a violation of privacy, may be unresolvable even though they are genuine dis-agreements, namely, divergences with respect to which argument is appropriate, and, presumably, mistakes are possible. Each side in such a debate thinks that opposing views are defective. Indeed, opposing sides in the abortion debate diverge over cases they both take to be *clear*: For instance, the pro-life side holds that a conceptus clearly is, while the pro-choice side holds that a conceptus clearly is not, a person. In contrast, divergences resulting from the vague-ness of 'person' are restricted to transitional values (e.g., gestational stages) in the progression from a non-person to a person. This is what makes the latter divergence arbitrary, and the giving of rea-sons inappropriate, and mistakes impossible. It is *mere* divergence. Moreover, application of a vague word is intrasubjectively, not just intersubjectively, variable: Each speaker varies arbitrarily in her own applications of a vague term and will not (or at least should not) sup-pose, on any particular occasion, that she is correcting her past use.[13]

Our discussion suggests that a predicate 'Φ' is vague only if 'Φ' and also 'range of application of "Φ"' and its indefinitely many iter-ations have multiple arbitrarily different ranges of application. This iterated multiplicity is, at least in part, what "blurs" the boundaries of a vague word. Although I have not even tentatively proposed necessary and sufficient conditions for an expression to be vague, I am going to take the liberty of referring to my account as the *mul-tiple range theory* of vagueness, or *multi-range theory* for short. The multi-range theory has the nice consequence that vagueness and ambiguity are two sides of a coin. Both are, or at least essentially involve, multiplicities of meaning: ambiguity a multiplicity of sta-ble contents and vagueness a multiplicity of referents. Precision then consists in possession of a single range of application (per-haps relative to a context); there is one and only one competent way—the correct way—to apply a precise expression (relative to a given context). A sharp boundary between the extension and anti-extension of a term is a unique, legislative division; hence failure to observe such a boundary in one's application of a term constitutes a mistake. On the multi-range view, the distinction between blurred and sharp boundaries is thus understood in terms of the notion of ranges of application, not in terms of bivalence, borderline cases, soriticality, or the other phenomena that have been proposed (cf. section 1.2).

In the broadest terms, vagueness is a form of arbitrariness—ineliminable arbitrariness. No rule dictates a particular stopping place in a sorites series. Thus the application of a vague word is, in this sense, unruly. If there is a rule in the vicinity, it dictates that speakers must stop *at no particular place*. At first blush the idea of a rule requiring us to stop at no particular place—a rule requiring that we follow no rule?—may seem oxymoronic, but it is of the essence of vagueness.[14] Vagueness is standardly characterized as a form of unclarity. Maybe, to pretheoretic eyes, arbitrary variation and divergence look like unclarity.

Our ability to communicate using vague words may seem mysterious, given the inter- and intrasubjective divergence and variation in their use. Keep in mind, however, that the variability is confined to values located in what I have called the 'transitional' region between categories. Communication would be threatened if our classifications of *clear* cases were similarly variable, but I don't think they are. Also, communication would be threatened if we failed to recognize that our classifications of transitional values are arbitrary. Because they are arbitrary, they are, from the viewpoint of semantics, just so much noise—so much blur, if you like. (Since vague predicates are meant to be applicable on the basis of casual consideration, as Wright observes, the noise is essential.) When speaking to one another, we can simply ignore these noisy variations in application, and communication proceeds unimpeded.

In chapter 2 (section 2.2), I promised to say more about the distinction between soritical borderline cases and the multidimensional kind. Multidimensional vagueness, recall, is an unclarity as to which dimensions are decisive of the application of a term. 'Nice' was the example we discussed: We supposed that altruism and thoughtfulness are decisive, but what about being a good listener? Can you be nice even though you repeatedly monopolize conversations? The answer seemed unclear, and intuitions will diverge. Equipped now with a better understanding of the nature of vagueness, we can elaborate the distinction this way: Soritical vagueness is an unclarity (here, multiplicity) in the reference of a term, whereas multidimensional vagueness is an unclarity in the stable content. Thus understood, multidimensional vagueness is a closer relative to ambiguity than to vagueness.

4.4. EVALUATION

If the reference of a vague word is multiple in the way I have suggested, how are sentences and arguments containing vague words to be evaluated for truth and validity?

According to the multiple range theory, the truth or falsity of a sentence containing a vague word is relative to a V-index and a range of application. By 'truth' and 'falsity' I mean plain old regular truth and falsity: Again, unlike supervaluationism, the multi-range theory does not identify ordinary truth with any generalized or higher-order property defined over ranges of application. Certainly a sentence 'x is Φ' may be true relative to every range of application of 'Φ' for a given V-index, or false relative to every one, or true relative to some and false relative to others. For instance, presumably Shaquille O'Neal is tall (at the actual world) relative to every range of application of 'tall' for the V-index $\{$height; <u>above average</u>; jockeys$\}$; and Warren Buffett is rich relative to every range of 'rich' for the V-index { portfolio size; <u>above average</u>; philosophy professors }. Maybe this indicates that O'Neal is *very* tall relative to that V-index and Buffett *very* rich. But such generalizations do not figure in the definition of ordinary truth for 'tall.' (They do figure in the definition of validity for sentences and arguments containing 'tall,' however; see below.)

Relativization of truth to a range of application may seem implausible in extreme cases, such as O'Neal's tallness or Buffett's richness. O'Neal and Buffett may seem unequivocally or unqualifiedly or absolutely tall or rich, independently of any such relativization. But consider that O'Neal isn't tall compared to buildings, and Buffett is not rich compared to nations; and neither is tall or rich at all worlds. They are tall or rich only relative to certain comparison classes and at certain worlds. Inasmuch as their tallness and richness are already "qualified" or relativized in these ways, a relativization to ranges of application can be seen merely as a further refinement—a refinement characteristic of vagueness. Relativizing to possible worlds enables us to (among other things) distinguish necessary propositions from contingent ones; relativizing to comparison classes enables us to distinguish context-sensitive (V-index-sensitive) terms from context-insensitive ones, and relativizing to ranges of application enables us to distinguish vague terms from non-vague ones.[15]

We need to see the multi-range semantics in action in some specific examples. What follows is a first, modest stab at spelling things out, and I will work mostly with familiar lexical predicates. (Some additional, more complex examples are discussed in the appendix on pp. 181–7.) The remainder of this section will be a slog, but once we get through it, the sailing will be smoother.

Consider again 'rich' relative to Vinny. This meaning of the predicate might be represented by the tree diagram in Figure 4.5. I have pictured only four ranges of application, that is, four different

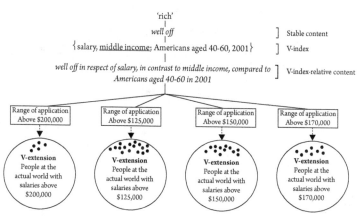

Figure 4.5. Part of a semantic tree for 'rich' with the V-index {salary; <u>middle income</u>; Americans aged 40–60, 2001 }.

competent ways of applying the predicate, and only one V-extension (assume it is the V-extension at the actual world) picked out by each of the four. Here each branch of the tree comprises the predicate, its stable content, Vinny, a richer content relative to Vinny, a range of application, and the V-extension picked out by that range at the actual world (Figure 4.6). So there are four branches in the figure, each picking out one set of all and only those people at the actual world who are well-off with respect to salary, in contrast to middle income, compared to Americans aged forty to sixty in 2001 at the actual world.

Each semantic tree for a given predicate is individuated by a stable content together with a V-index, and within a tree, each branch is individuated by a range of application. Assuming that we are working with unambiguous terms, we can say that a semantic tree for a vague term is individuated by the term together with a V-index. (Sometimes I will use the expression 'predicate/V-index combination.') Since branches are individuated by ranges of application, we can say—roughly, for now—that a vague word applies (or fails to apply) to an item relative to a certain branch in a semantic tree. (A

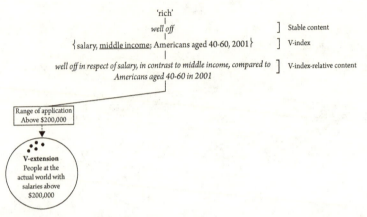

Figure 4.6. Leftmost branch of the semantic tree in Figure 4.5.

semantic tree for a V-index-*in*sensitive predicate, if such there be, is represented in Figure 4.7.)

In general, the evaluation procedure for a sentence containing vague words depends on (a) the number of distinct semantic trees (or sets of trees—see below) it implicates and (b) where more than one tree (or set of trees) is implicated, whether the V-indices in those trees differ in more than their contrastive categories. (V-indices differing at most in their contrastive categories will be called *siblings*.) Whether a sentence is evaluated relative to single trees or sets of trees depends on the amount of V-indexical information that is specified or otherwise available for the utterance in question; I will say more about this in a moment. For practical purposes, the evaluation of a sentence containing vague predicates depends on the number of predicate/V-index combinations that speakers are interested in on a given occasion.

As a simple first example, consider the sentence

(S1) Jeff is rich

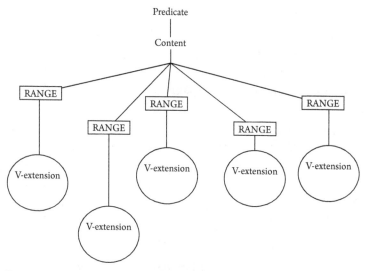

Figure 4.7. Part of a semantic tree for a V-index-insensitive vague word.

relative to Vinny. S1 implicates only one semantic tree, defined by 'rich' together with Vinny, and so is evaluated relative to singleton branches. S1 is true (at the actual world) relative to a given branch in the tree only if Jeff is in the V-extension picked out by that branch. Equivalently: S1 is true relative to a given branch only if Jeff's salary is an instance of a salary (type) contained in the range of application of 'rich' on that branch. Depending on Jeff's salary at the actual world, S1 may be true relative to every (i.e., each) branch in the tree, or false relative to every branch, or true relative to some branches and false relative to others. So, for example, if Jeff's annual salary at the actual world is $500,000, he will probably be rich relative to every branch in this tree; if Jeff earns $150,000, he will probably be rich relative to some branches and not-rich relative to others. Again, this is ordinary, everyday truth or falsity: As far as vague predicates are concerned, ordinary truth *is* truth relative to a branch in a semantic tree, or, what comes to the same: Ordinary truth is truth relative to a competent way of applying a predicate.[16]

Consider next the sentence

(S2) Jeff is rich and tall

relative to Vinny and the V-index $\{$ height; <u>above average</u>; American men, 2001, $w_@ \}$. (See Figure 4.8.) Since S2 implicates two predicate/V-index combinations, it has two semantic trees and will be evaluated relative to pairs of branches. These pairs come from the Cartesian product of the set of branches in the 'rich' tree and the set of branches in the 'tall' tree.[17] In this simplified example I have pictured twelve such pairs of branches. No pair contains sibling branches, since the two V-indices differ in their comparison classes among other things;[18] hence S2 is evaluated relative to each of the twelve pairs. As far as 'rich' and 'tall' are concerned, S2 is true relative to every pair of branches whose V-extensions both contain Jeff and false otherwise.

Sometimes we make V-indexical coordinates explicit, as in S3:

(S3) Nancy is rich in contrast to middle income but not in contrast to upper middle income.

Suppose that the operative V-indices for the two occurrences of 'rich' are, respectively, Vinny and $\{$ salary; <u>upper middle income</u>; Americans aged forty to sixty, 2001, $w_@ \}$. (Presumably, to evaluate S3 we need to use V-indices that differ only in their contrastive categories.) S3 implicates two predicate/V-index combinations and so has two trees: Both are trees for 'rich,' but one contrasts <u>rich</u> with <u>middle income</u> while the other contrasts <u>rich</u> with <u>upper middle income</u>. Therefore the sentence will be evaluated relative to pairs of branches from the Cartesian product of the two sets of branches from the two trees. In this instance, however, the V-indices in those trees are siblings: They differ only in their contrastive categories. This raises the possibility that some pairings of branches are impermissible and so

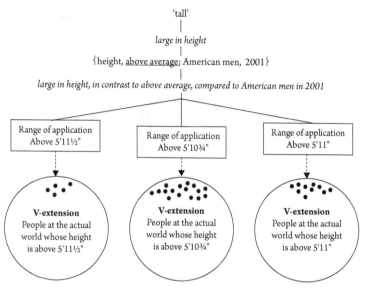

Figure 4.8. Part of a semantic tree for 'tall' with the V-index {height; <u>above average</u>; American men, 2001 }.

must be excluded from the evaluation of S3. Specifically, we must prune out any pairs whose ranges of application together violate certain intuitive semantic principles. For example, no permissible pair of branches can contain co-extensive ranges of application of 'rich' or ranges of application such that some middle income salary on the one branch is higher than any upper middle income salary on the other branch.[19] The ranges of application on the two branches in a permissible pair must be mutually compatible, semantically speaking. Thus the pair of branches whose ranges of application effect the classifications shown in Figure 4.9 would be permissible, whereas the pair in Figure 4.10 would not.

As far as 'rich' is concerned, S3 is true relative to permissible pairs of branches in which the branch that contrasts *rich* with *middle income* contains Nancy in its V-extension, but the branch that contrasts *rich*

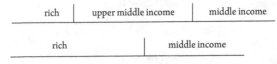

Figure 4.9. Permissible pair of branches for evaluating S3.

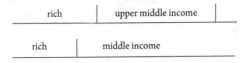

Figure 4.10. Impermissible pair of branches for S3.

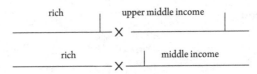

Figure 4.11. Pair of branches that makes S3 true.

with *upper middle income* does not. For example, the pair of branches whose ranges of application are pictured in Figure 4.11 will make S3 true if Nancy's salary is located at the 'x'.

We evaluated S3 indirectly, one might say, by evaluating the application of 'rich' relative to the two V-indices specified. I think we are free to handle S3 that way, but suppose we want to evaluate S3 as it stands; in other words, suppose we want to evaluate its application of the predicates 'rich in contrast to middle income' and 'rich in contrast to upper middle income.' The latter predicates themselves are vague and V-index-sensitive. Presumably a speaker uttering S3 would intend both predicates to be relativized to the same V-index—for example, the V-index ⟨ salary; 0; Americans aged forty to sixty, 2001 ⟩. (See Figure 4.12. Since the operative contrast categories are built into the two predicates, we don't specify those in the V-index.) Therefore we need to watch out for siblings: S3 will be evaluated relative to each *permissible* pair of branches from the Cartesian product of the set of branches from the 'rich in contrast

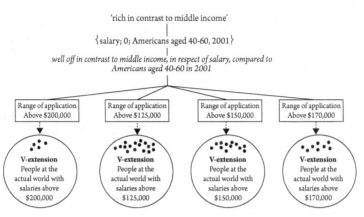

Figure 4.12. Part of a semantic tree for the vague predicate 'rich in contrast to middle income' with the V-index {salary; 0; Americans aged 40–60, 2001}.

to middle income' tree and the set of branches from the 'rich in contrast to upper middle income' tree.[20]

What about a case like S4?

> (S4) The Prince of Wales is rich with respect to salary, in contrast to middle income, compared to philosophy professors in 2001.

It seems to me that even if no substantive V-indexical coordinates are specified (implicitly or explicitly) for the predicate in S4, in other words, even if we treat 'rich in salary, in contrast to middle income...2001' as relativized to the V-index {0; 0; 0}, that predicate has multiple arbitrarily different ranges of application. Not as many as 'rich' alone, perhaps, but still it is vague by our lights: There would be multiple equally competent places to stop applying the predicate in a sorites series of salaries. In that case, (part of) its semantic tree could be pictured as in Figure 4.13. Presumably, at the actual world, S4 is true relative to every one of its branches. (Of course, at some other worlds, the prince is not rich in salary, in contrast to middle income, compared to philosophy professors etc.)

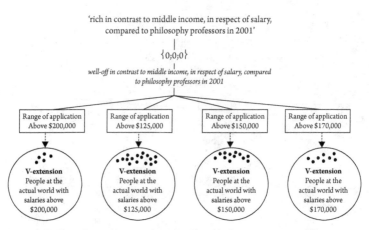

'rich in contrast to middle income, in respect of salary, compared to philosophy professors in 2001'

$\{0;0;0\}$

well-off in contrast to middle income, in respect of salary, compared to philosophy professors in 2001

Range of application Above \$200,000	Range of application Above \$125,000	Range of application Above \$150,000	Range of application Above \$170,000
V-extension People at the actual world with salaries above \$200,000	**V-extension** People at the actual world with salaries above \$125,000	**V-extension** People at the actual world with salaries above \$150,000	**V-extension** People at the actual world with salaries above \$170,000

Figure 4.13. Part of a semantic tree for the predicate 'rich in contrast to middle income, in respect of salary, compared to philosophy professors in 2001,' with the V-index $\{0; 0; 0\}$.

Consider next the vagueness of 'big' in S5:

(S5) Tony Soprano is a big guy.

As we saw earlier, 'big' is multidimensionally vague; there is unclarity not only with respect to the extension of 'big' on certain decisive dimension(s) but also with respect to which dimensions are the decisive ones.[21] Suppose that in S5 the two dimensions of height and girth are at issue. In that case we can suppose that 'big' is applied relative to two V-indices: say, $\{$height; <u>average</u>; Sicilian men, 2001, $w_@\}$ and $\{$girth; <u>average</u>; Sicilian men, 2001, $w_@\}$. If the relevant stable content of 'big' is something like *of considerable size*, then S5 expresses the V-index-relative content that *Tony Soprano is of considerable size in both height and girth, as opposed to average, compared to Sicilian men in 2001 at the actual world*. S5 implicates two semantic trees and so will be evaluated relative to pairs of branches. No pairs will be siblings, so all will be permissible. As far as 'big' is concerned, S5 will be true relative to those pairs in which Tony belongs to the V-extensions of both branches.

I have said that in ordinary speech we usually don't need to make V-indices explicit. But sometimes we mean to use a V-index-sensitive vague predicate apart from any particular V-index; we mean to speak in a universal, V-index-invariant way. For example, we may be speaking this way if we say

(S6) Nothing is both tall and short.

We can suppose that, spelled out more fully, S6 says:

Relative to any V-index $\{i\}$, at any world, nothing is both tall $\{i\}$ and short $\{i\}$.[22]

Here the evaluation procedure is slightly more complicated. Because no V-indexical coordinates are specified for S6, we have to consider all possible V-indices for the predicates at issue. So the initial question is not how many semantic trees are implicated in the sentence but rather how many sets of semantic trees. In the first instance, S6 implicates two sets of trees: the set of all trees (hence all V-indices) for 'tall' and the set of all trees (hence all V-indices) for 'short.' Then from the Cartesian product of the set of all branches from all of the 'tall' trees and the set of all branches from all of the 'short' trees, we select those pairs in which both branches contain the same V-index. (A pair whose branches share the V-index $\{$height; <u>average</u>; jockeys$\}$ would be an example.) This means that all of the selected pairs will contain sibling branches; so S6 will be evaluated relative to the permissible selected pairs. (Of course, the necessary truth of S6 partly dictates which pairs are permissible; S6 itself states an 'intuitive semantic principle' that constrains the parings of the branches. Hence its evaluation is, as you might expect, rather trivial; see again this chapter, note 19.) S6 will be true relative to every permissible selected pair of branches for 'tall' and 'short' at every world.

The elliptical sentence S7 employs V-indices that differ in their respect or dimension coordinates:

(S7) Yul Brynner is bald and so is Ben Nevis.

Suppose for the sake of argument that the stable content of 'bald' is *lacking some usual surface covering*. And suppose the first instance of 'bald' in S7 is relativized to the V-index ⟨ number of hairs on the head; <u>hairy</u>; adult men ⟩, while the second (tacit) occurrence is relativized to the V-index ⟨ number of trees at the summit; <u>forested</u>; the Berkshires ⟩. The permissible pairs of branches for evaluation of S7 will then come from, indeed will just *be*, the Cartesian product of the set of all branches for 'bald' containing the first V-index and the set of all branches for 'bald' containing the second. There will be no siblings. As far as 'bald' is concerned, S7 is true relative to each pair that contains Yul Brynner in the one V-extension and Ben Nevis in the other, and false otherwise.

With these examples in mind, we can state a necessary condition on validity of sentences and arguments containing vague words:

1. A sentence containing vague predicates is valid only if, at every world, it is true relative to every permissible selected n-tuple of branches, where n is the number of (sets of) semantic trees implicated in the sentence.

2. An argument containing vague predicates is valid only if, at every world, every permissible selected n-tuple of branches that makes its premises true also makes its conclusion true, where n is the number of (sets of) semantic trees implicated in the argument.

Consider for instance the simple argument

(1) Rita is either rich or middle income.

(2) Rita is not middle income.

(3) Therefore Rita is rich.

The argument implicates two sets of semantic trees: the set of all trees for 'rich' and the set of all trees for 'middle income.' Presumably the two predicates are to be evaluated relative to the same V-index. Hence, from the Cartesian product of the set of all 'rich' branches and the set of all 'middle income' branches, we select those pairs in which both branches contain the same V-index. Then we evaluate the argument relative to the permissible selected pairs. Here all of the branches will be siblings because all contain the same V-index, so some pruning will be necessary in order to isolate the permissible pairs. The argument is valid since, at every world, Rita is in the V-extension picked out by the 'rich' branch in every permissible pair in which she is in the V-extension picked out by the 'rich' branch and not in the V-extension picked out by the 'middle income' branch.

Taxing though this section has been, these examples merely scratch the surface of an evaluation procedure for sentences containing vague words. I hope they have been instructive nonetheless, if only in suggesting that a multi-range evaluation procedure could be worked out. More complex examples are provided in the appendix.

4.5. SOLVING THE SORITES

The multi-range theory of vagueness delivers a straightforward solution to the sorites paradox. Consider a series of thirty colored patches proceeding from a central blue to a central green, so ordered that each patch is incrementally different in hue, that is, either indiscriminable or just noticeably different, from the next.[23] We have an apparent paradox:

This implies that each permissible use makes a sharp cut-off!

UNRULY WORDS

#2 is blue

(1) Patch #1 is blue.

(2) For any n, if patch #n is blue, then patch #$(n + 1)$ is blue.

(3) Therefore patch #30 is blue. *# 29 is blue*

The argument implicates one set of semantic trees, namely, the set of all trees for 'blue,' so it can be evaluated relative to each singleton branch from those trees. The argument is valid: At every world, the conclusion is true relative to any branch that makes the premises true. The trouble with the argument is that the major premise (2) is never true: It is false relative to every branch from every semantic tree for 'blue' at every world. On any branch for 'blue,' specifically in any range of application of 'blue,' there is a last value—where, again, this final shade marks not a boundary but simply a permissible stopping place. Therefore the major premise is necessarily false, and the argument is valid but unsound. (Evidently the vagueness of a vague predicate—its permanent multiplicity of ranges of application—is the cure for the paradox, not the cause of it.) On reflection, we should not be surprised that the major premise of the paradox is necessarily false, for it is not a contingent fact about 'blue,' or any other vague predicate, that its application stops before the end of a sorites series. No particular stopping place is mandatory, but stopping *someplace* is.

but where?

An adequate response to the sorites paradox must answer at least two critical questions: (1) How, intuitively, can the major premise be false? and (2) Given that it is false, why does it seem true? Our incipient semantic theory addresses the first question by showing how the major premise can be false in the absence of sharp boundaries: The premise is false because each range of application of a vague word 'Φ', each permissible way of applying it, contains a last Φ item, marking a permissible stopping place. Our semantics also points toward a partial answer to the second question. The major premise may seem true at least in part because we have confused two claims:

122

(a)   The increments between adjacent items in a sorites series
      are sufficiently small as to leave the application of the predi-
      cate unaffected; in other words, if an item in the series satis-
      fies the predicate, so do its immediate neighbors.

(b)   The increments between adjacent items in a sorites series
      are sufficiently small as to make any differential application
      of the predicate as between them, that is, any application of
      'Φ' to one but not to the other, *arbitrary*.[24]

No! It wouldn't be arbitrary
to call $30 blue if we call $29
green

Once (b) is on the table, we can see that (a) could be expressed in the
following way, making the contrast clear:

(a)   The increments between adjacent items in a sorites series
      are sufficiently small as to make any differential application
      of the predicate as between them, that is, any application of
      'Φ' to one but not to the other, *impermissible*.

Claim (a) is required to generate a paradox, but only the weaker claim
(b) is true. The major premise seems true because we mistake (b) for
(a).[25] Interestingly, Fine hypothesizes that

> [the] temptation to say that the second premise is true may have
> two causes. The first is that the value of a falsifying n appears to
> be arbitrary. This arbitrariness has nothing to do with vagueness
> as such. (1975, 139)

On the contrary, this arbitrariness has everything to do with vagueness as such.

I think these responses to the two critical questions about the
major premise are correct as far as they go, but they tell only part of
the story. They do not yet fully (i.e., intuitively) dissolve the puzzle.
To do that, we will need to look more closely at certain pragmatic
features of vague words. That will be the project of the next chapter.

4.6. VERDICTS ON SOME SPECIFIC PREDICATES

I want to spell out our theory's verdicts on some specific predicates whose vagueness, or lack thereof, has been of particular interest to philosophers. These include natural kind terms, the predicate 'vague' itself, the predicate 'true,' and certain linguistically normative expressions such as 'mandates application of "Φ",' 'permissible stopping place in a sorites series for "Φ",' and 'is competently classified as Φ'.

(1) **'Strawberry,' 'dog,' and other natural kind terms.** These predicates are often thought to be vague. As we have seen, Sainsbury supposes that there could be a series of incrementally different plants extending from a strawberry to a raspberry, in which the transition from the one category to the other is seamless or boundaryless. Similarly, given a series of animals with incrementally different genetic profiles progressing from a dog to a wolf, just where *dog* ends and *wolf* begins may seem vague. Nevertheless, natural kind terms probably are not vague. In particular, these words are not plausibly viewed as having multiple arbitrarily different ranges of application. For example, if two biologists diverged in their classification of an animal located midway in the progression from dog to wolf, or a plant midway between strawberry and raspberry, presumably each would think the other's judgment, if not mistaken, at least open to legitimate question. Arguments would be demanded, and could be given, on both sides. Hence neither judgment would be arbitrary in the requisite sense; such a divergence would be a genuine disagreement, and at most one of them could be correct. By the same token, the biologists would not vary arbitrarily in their own judgments. They might vary, but not arbitrarily; they would have reasons for changing their classifications and would take themselves to be correcting their previous judgments.[26]

Perhaps natural kind terms have what Frederich Waismann calls *open texture*.[27] This would be to say that

> we cannot foresee completely all possible conditions in which [natural kind terms] are to be used; there will always remain a possibility, however faint, that we have not taken into account something or other that may be relevant to their usage; and that means that we cannot foresee completely all the possible circumstances in which the statement is true or in which it is false. (1945, 123)

Open texture may give the impression of vagueness inasmuch as open-textured terms lack sharp boundaries—and chronically so, if Waismann is right. But the relevant classifications of new ("unforeseen") items will not, or anyway need not, be arbitrary. Presumably the biologists cannot foresee all possible plants between strawberries and raspberries, or all possible animals between dogs and wolves. Nevertheless, when they do encounter an intermediate case, their classification of it will not be arbitrary (or so I am supposing), and a word has blurred boundaries only insofar as there can be cases with respect to which any classification must be arbitrary. Evidently vagueness—possession of blurred boundaries— requires more than a lack, even a chronic or permanent lack, of sharp boundaries.[28]

(2) **'Vague.'** 'Vague' itself is often said to be vague (e.g., Tye 1994, Sorensen 2006). Achille Varzi explains why the issue has been thought important:

> Is 'vague' vague?...[A] lot depends on how we settle the question. For example, Frege (1903, §56) famously remarked that logic must be restricted to non-vague predicates. But if 'vague' is vague, then so is 'non-vague', hence the restriction

is itself vague and, therefore, helpless. For another example, incoherence theorists such as Unger (1979) have claimed that vague terms have no clear instances, blocking the sorites paradox at the base step. If 'vague' is vague, however, then either it is a clear instance of itself, in which case the incoherentist claim is plainly false, or it has an empty extension, in which case the claim is vacuously true (there are no vague predicates) and the paradox strikes back. Finally, if 'vague' is vague, then—as Hyde (1994) has argued—vague predicates must suffer from the phenomenon of higher-order vagueness.... [T]his is no small issue and we need to look at it closely. (2005, 695)

On the multi-range view, the question of whether 'vague' is vague comes down to the question of whether it has multiple arbitrarily different ranges of application, that is, whether competent speakers may vary and diverge arbitrarily in their judgments as to whether a given word is vague. More fully, that is the question of whether competent speakers may vary and diverge arbitrarily in their judgments as to whether competent speakers may vary and diverge arbitrarily in their applications of a given word.

Certainly competent speakers may vary and diverge in their judgments as to whether a word permits arbitrary variation and divergence, but it is hard to see how the former variation and divergence could be arbitrary. If you and I, competent speakers, diverge in our judgments as to the vagueness of some predicate, surely we *disagree*: We make (or at least can make) our respective judgments for certain reasons and are prepared to offer arguments and willing to charge each other with error. Similarly, if I vary in my own judgment, it will not be arbitrarily; if I am competent, I will (or at least should) take each such variation to be *correcting* my previous view. If that's right, then 'vague' is not vague. (If it's wrong, then 'vague' may be vague after all; see again the last paragraph of section 1.7.)

(3) **'True.'** Is it vague? Many philosophers have thought so (e.g., Sorensen 1985, McGee 1990). Consider for instance the series of sentences of the form

The sentence '$n is rich' is true

ascribed to the salaries in our sorites series for 'rich.' (Suppose we are relativizing to Vinny.) You might reasonably suppose that 'true' has multiple ranges of application that ride piggyback on the multiple ranges of application of 'rich' relative to Vinny. Intuitively, you might think that our competent application of the two expressions varies in tandem. Fine writes:

> The vagueness of 'true' waxes and wanes, as it were, with the vagueness of the given sentence; so that if a denotes a borderline case of F then Fa is a borderline case of 'true'. (1975, 149)[29]

But doesn't it seem far-fetched that the vagueness of 'true' (or any other expression) should wax and wane? A fortiori that it should wax and wane with the vagueness of a distinct predicate?[30] Compare:

The sentence '$n is a prime number of dollars' is true.

Here 'true' seems precise—and not because we have arbitrarily precisified any of the terms involved. In the terms of the multi-range theory, 'true' does not impress us here as having multiple ranges of application, as permitting arbitrary variation and divergence in its application. It seems to have only a single permissible way of being applied, corresponding to the single, sharply bounded set of prime numbers.

The upshot is that 'true' seems to behave like a vague predicate (or operator) when applied to a sentence containing a vague predicate such as 'rich' but like a precise predicate (or operator) when applied to a sentence containing a precise predicate such as 'prime number.' This suggests that the apparent vagueness and precision of 'true' are just the vagueness of 'rich' and the precision of 'prime number.' Thus the right thing to say, I think, is that 'true' itself is neither vague nor precise; it has neither blurred boundaries nor sharp ones. It merely *behaves as if* it were vague or precise depending on the vagueness or precision of the predicates to which it is applied. I will call 'true' a *reflector*, signifying that it merely reflects the vagueness or precision of other terms. The distinction between vagueness and precision is often seen as exhaustive, but I know of no good reason why. As a matter of fact, Russell says that 'vague' and 'precise' are contraries, in the sense of opposites: 'We are able to conceive precision; indeed, if we could not do so, we could not conceive vagueness, which is merely the contrary of precision' (1999, 65). (We have already seen that lacking sharp boundaries is no guarantee of having blurred ones; for instance, natural kind terms may have neither blurred nor sharp boundaries.)

It may be worth pointing out that, on our view, 'true' is also not gradable: *pace* degree theorists, it is not the case that one sentence can be more or less true than another—closer to or farther from being true, maybe, or more or less similar to a true sentence, but not more or less true. (Saying that one sentence is truer than another may be rather like saying that one action is more permissible or more mandatory than another.) Nor can a sentence be so true, very true, or insufficiently true, except in some epistemic or else merely figurative or elliptical sense. If we say that a sentence 'Fa' is so true or very true or insufficiently true, we probably mean that a is so F or very F or insufficiently F. Moreover, since our semantics of vagueness is bivalent, 'true' has no incompatibles; its contradictory 'false' is its only competitor, so neither 'true' nor 'false' has borderline cases. For reasons discussed earlier, these observations about gradability and borderline cases are not decisive, but they fit well with the idea that 'true' is not vague.

Normative metalinguistic predicates like 'mandates application of "Φ",' 'satisfies "Φ",' and 'range of application of "Φ"' appear to be reflectors as well. For example, 'mandates application of "rich"' seems vague but 'mandates application of "prime number"' seems precise; 'satisfies "rich"' seems vague but 'satisfies "prime number"' seems precise; 'range of application of "rich"' seems vague but 'range of application of "prime number"' seems precise; and so forth. I think this shows that the predicates 'mandates application of "Φ"' and 'satisfies "Φ"' and 'range of application of "Φ"' are *per se* neither vague nor precise. 'Mandates application of "rich"' and 'range of application of "rich"' are vague and 'satisfies "prime number"' is precise, but the vagueness and precision of the latter predicates just are the vagueness of 'rich' and the precision of 'prime number.'

The vagueness of normative metalinguistic expressions like 'mandates application of "rich"' and 'range of application of "rich"' can be regarded as a form of higher-order vagueness. It doesn't come to much, however: In such cases, higher-order vagueness is a merely "reflected" property of the object-linguistic terms in question.[31] In section 4.3 I proposed that a predicate 'Φ' is vague only if 'range of application of "Φ"' and its indefinitely many iterations also have multiple arbitrarily different ranges of application. That amounts to saying that 'Φ' is vague only if 'range of application of

that generates higher-order borderline cases.

"Φ"' is vague, and that is to say that 'Φ' is vague only if it is, in this sense, higher-order vague.

4.7. VAGUENESS, V-INDEX-SENSITIVITY, SORITICALITY, GRADABILITY, BORDERLINES, AND INDETERMINACY: RELATIVES OR JUST FRIENDS?

I predicted at the outset that these phenomena would prove to be less tightly linked than is commonly supposed. Let's sum up what the multi-range theory has to say about their interrelations.

(1) Although rooted in the sense of a term, vagueness itself is a referential phenomenon. V-index-sensitivity, in contrast, is first and foremost a feature of the sense or content of an expression and only consequently of its reference. While it may be that all vague words are in fact V-index-sensitive, nothing in the nature of vagueness indicates that V-index-sensitivity is necessary for it. Also, as we noted in chapter 1, expressions like 'the winning score' and 'the fastest speed' are context-sensitive but intuitively don't seem vague. The multi-range theory concurs: It is hard to see how a divergence as to which score won a game or which speed was the fastest in a race could be arbitrary. Presumably each of us would be prepared to argue that the other is mistaken.

(2) If our treatment of the sorites has been effective, there are no soritical predicates. There is a last Φ value in any range of application of 'Φ,' reflecting in the semantics the fact that there are permissible stopping places in every Φ-ordering or

sorites series for 'Φ.' Vague words appear to generate a para-dox partly because differential application of 'Φ' to neighbor-ing items in a sorites series must be arbitrary, and we confuse that fact with the claim expressed by the major premise of the paradox. (For ease of discussion I will continue to use the term 'soritical vagueness' to refer to the species of vagueness here at issue, but strictly speaking we should replace it with something like 'boundary vagueness' or 'blurred boundary vagueness,' or at least put it in scare quotes.)

(3) Gradability is not necessary for vagueness. For example, 'medium' is vague but not gradable. Whether gradability is sufficient for vagueness, I am not certain. Kennedy says 'no'; he claims that although the adjectives 'dry,' 'closed,' and 'straight' (what he calls *maximum standard absolute adjectives*) are not vague, they are "perfectly acceptable in comparatives and with other degree morphology [as for example in] 'The floor is dryer than the table' and 'This rod is too straight...for this purpose'" (2007, 22). Of course one's verdicts in these cases will depend on one's concep-tion of vagueness, but it may be true that we cannot per-missibly diverge over what is absolutely dry or closed or straight (relative to a given V-index). On the other hand, one might wonder whether the 'dry' ('closed,' 'straight') that is non-vague means the same as the 'dry' that admits of comparatives. For instance, perhaps when I use the word 'dry' in ordinary speech, as when I announce that the recently washed floor is dry, I mean that the floor is close enough to being absolutely dry to justify calling it 'dry' in the present circumstances. And to say that the floor is dryer than the table may be to say that the floor is closer to being absolutely dry than the table is—not that the floor is *more*

absolutely dry than the table. If that's right, the absolute adjective 'dry' may not be gradable after all and so may not be gradable but non-vague as Kennedy contends. Similarly, the expression '6 feet' is not shown to be gradable by the fact that 5 feet is closer to it than 4 feet is; 5 feet is not *more 6 feet* than 4 feet is. These considerations are not decisive; I leave the question open.

(4) Possession of borderline cases is neither necessary nor sufficient for vagueness; the widespread view that vagueness consists in possession of borderline cases is incorrect. We saw in chapter 2 that 'not-rich' probably has no borderlines because it probably has no incompatibles. But that is no bar to its being vague: There are multiple equally competent stopping places between 'rich' and 'not-rich' in a rich-ordering, and the choice of any particular one is arbitrary. Having borderline cases does not appear to be sufficient for vagueness either. Granted, for a predicate 'Φ' to have borderline cases, it must have a proximate incompatible 'Φ^*,' where incompatibles 'Φ' and 'Φ^*' are proximate just in case there are items in a Φ/Φ^* ordering that can competently be classified as Φ and competently be classified as Φ^*, relative to a given V-index. And if 'Φ' and 'Φ^*' are proximate incompatibles, then there are multiple equally competent ways of applying them to the items in a Φ/Φ^* ordering; in other words, they have multiple arbitrarily different ranges of application. However, as we have realized, having multiple ranges is not by itself sufficient for vagueness; in addition, the predicates 'range of application of 'Φ'' and 'range of application of 'Φ^*,'' along with their indefinitely many iterations, must have multiple arbitrarily different ranges of application too. (Recall section 4.3.)

(5) If vagueness is a kind of indeterminacy, it is an innocuous one that involves no violation of excluded middle.[32] If there is "no fact of the matter" as to where the transition from Φ to not-Φ occurs in a sorites series, that is because there is no *single* place where it occurs. If you like: there is no *single* fact of the matter.

I have not yet said anything about tolerance. There are reasons for that, which will come to light in the next chapter.

4.8. SELECTIVE REVIEW

(1) The term 'range of application' is just a fancy name for the anodyne notion of a set of values to which a term can competently be applied. (Again, I use the term 'set' informally.) One could say that ranges of application are just a way of representing, in the semantics, the multiple permissible ways of applying a vague word. Vague words have multiple ranges (relative to each index) whereas precise words have only one. We arrived at this view by taking the variable use of vague words as evidence of their semantic structure.

(2) Ranges of application are importantly different from precisifications (cf. section 4.2). Also, crucially, the multi-range theory does not define truth in terms of a generalization over ranges of application. Rather, a sentence containing a vague predicate is true relative to each range of application that contains the value instantiated by the item to which the predicate is being applied. In the multi-range theory there is no notion of truth analogous to the supervaluationist's super-truth.

(3) Neither 'vague' nor 'true' is vague, though for different reasons. 'Vague' isn't vague because it makes no sense to suppose that competent speakers could vary and diverge *arbitrarily* in their applications of it. 'True' isn't vague because it behaves like a precise expression at least as often as it behaves like a vague one. 'True' merely *reflects* the vagueness or precision of the predicate to which it is applied.

(4) Multidimensional vagueness is an unclarity in the sense of a vague term, whereas soritical vagueness is an "unclarity"—here, a multiplicity—in the reference.

(5) Expressions that are *open-textured*, in Waismann's sense of the term, lack sharp boundaries of application but may not have blurred boundaries, that is, may not be vague. For example, natural kind terms may be open-textured but not vague.

4.9. LOOKING AHEAD

I have said that a resolution of the sorites paradox must answer two critical questions: (1) How can the major premise be false? and (2) Given that it's false, why does it seem true? The answers provided by our semantic theory may be well and good from a formal or theoretical standpoint, but intuitive mysteries remain. In particular, we have said that the last value in a range of application of a vague predicate signifies a permissible stopping place rather than a boundary; but this does not yet explain how a competent speaker proceeding step by step along a sorites series is able to shift categories without disturbing its apparent continuity or seamlessness. Also, the notion that we confuse claims (a) and (b) (cf. section 4.5) does not yet fully diagnose the intuitive appeal of the major premise. There is more to it.

I believe that satisfactory answers to these questions can be had only by investigating certain aspects of the competent use of vague words as distinct from their semantics. This will be our project in the next, final chapter. We will make use of a secondary version of the paradox—the so-called *forced march* or *dynamic* sorites. One might say that there are two sorites paradoxes: One, the paradox proper, belongs to semantics, while the other, the dynamic sorites, belongs to pragmatics or the theory of use. In resolving the pragmatic puzzle, we will learn how competent speakers are able to shift categories "seamlessly," and we will discover the principal reason why the major premises of both paradoxes seem true. In general, we will begin to see how our semantic theory could be implemented in the competent use of a vague word.

Chapter 5

The Competent Use of Vague Words

Vague.
ORIGIN Latin *vagus* 'wandering'.

The Oxford English Dictionary

5.1. A PRAGMATIC SORITES

Following Terence Horgan (e.g., 1994) and Scott Soames (1998), we can distinguish a secondary version of the sorites paradox, the so-called *forced march* or *dynamic* sorites. The dynamic paradox is an informal version of the argument framed in terms of the hypothetical applications of a vague predicate by a competent speaker who proceeds step by step along a sorites series. Consider a blue/green sorites series of thirty incrementally different patches (hues) and a competent speaker who begins at patch #1 and classifies each successive patch as blue, or as green, or as blue[green] borderline. On pain of incompetence, she must classify patch #1 as blue. Then since #2 is so similar to #1, it seems she must classify #2 as blue; and then #3 as blue, and so on until finally she must classify #30 as blue. The dynamic version of the paradox can be expressed this way:

For any competent speaker S proceeding along the sorites series:
(1D) S must classify patch #1 as blue.
(2D) For any n, if S classifies patch #n as blue, then S must also classify patch #$(n + 1)$ as blue.
(3D) Therefore, S must classify patch #30 as blue.

At the same time, and also because she is competent, our speaker is bound to stop applying 'blue' before she reaches patch #30. Thus she is torn between apparently conflicting rules: She must violate either the rule expressed by the major premise (2D) or the rule that says that objects that look like patch #30 are green. Of course she will stop applying 'blue' before the end, and rightly so, but how, intuitively, does she manage to do this without disturbing the seamlessness of the series? I suggested at the end of the preceding chapter that we might think of the dynamic argument as a pragmatic version of the paradox, that is, a version that arises from the way we *use* vague words; and a solution to the semantic version, which we think we have now got, is not yet a solution to the pragmatic one. Only by resolving the pragmatic sorites we will fully understand how speakers manage to shift categories in an apparently seamless series—and indeed why, if they are false, the major premises of both versions of the puzzle seem true.

We can begin to resolve the dynamic sorites by attending to three facts about the competent use of a vague word. (I will continue to use 'blue,' 'green,' and 'blue[green] borderline' as my examples, but they are just examples.)

(1) First, each of the categories *blue, green,* and *borderline* contains a range of more and less central cases. Again, this is not the distinction between clear and borderline cases; the distinction between more and less central cases is drawn within each category: There are more and less central blues, more and less central greens, and more and less central borderline cases. In particular, as our speaker moves along the series away from the initial, most central blue patch (#1), the blue patches start to look more and more like the borderline patches. The result is that some patches that she competently classifies as blue and some patches that she competently classifies as borderline look

very much alike—even the same. (Remember that any patch that can competently be classified as borderline can also competently be classified as blue and as green.) This fact helps to demystify the speaker's ability to stop applying 'blue' and shift to 'borderline' between hues that are so similar. I suspect that when we think about the difference between being blue and being borderline, we think about the difference between looking like patch #1, a central case of blue, and looking like, say, patch #15, a central borderline case. So naturally it seems incredible that two neighboring patches could be one blue and the other borderline (a fortiori one blue and the other green.)

(2) Appeal to this first fact does not by itself dissolve the mystery of the dynamic sorites, since the possibility remains that all competent speakers stop applying 'blue' at the same place on every run along the series. For example, maybe everyone always shifts from 'blue' to 'borderline' at patch #13. This would suggest the presence of a sharp boundary. Hence we need to take account of a second, now familiar fact about the competent use of a vague word, namely, that it varies arbitrarily both within and across competent speakers, even with respect to a single V-index. In particular, different speakers diverge, and individual speakers vary, in their stopping places in a sorites series. In the terms of our semantic theory, a vague predicate has multiple arbitrarily different ranges of application relative to any of its V-indices. This arbitrariness is what enables variation in our use of a vague word without question of error.

(3) Even the first two facts together do not fully resolve the dynamic paradox, it seems to me. To see why, suppose that on a given run our competent speaker shifts from 'blue'

to 'borderline' at patch #15. Then, instead of having her continue along the series to #30, we immediately query her again about patch #14. If she still classifies #14 as blue, and especially if she persists in classifying #15 as borderline and #14 as blue, she would seem to have drawn a sharp boundary (if an idiosyncratic and temporary one) between #14 and #15. However, I predict that she will not classify #14 as blue after shifting to 'borderline' at #15; rather, she will now classify #14 as borderline too. The thought is that when she shifts from 'blue' to 'borderline' at #15, the speaker will undergo a characteristic change in her verbal dispositions so that she is now disposed to judge patch #14 as borderline also, despite having judged it blue just a moment before.[1] If she now continues backward down the series toward patch #1, she will classify some of the preceding patches as borderline before eventually shifting back to 'blue'; and so on. This is the third fact—well, so far it is only a hypothesis—that goes to dissolving the dynamic sorites. Intuitively, when the speaker categorizes patch #15 as borderline, it's not as if #14 still seems blue; instead, it's as if a string of patches shift their category together, so that consecutive patches never seem category-different at the same time (similarly for the later switch from 'borderline' to 'green'). Again, by the time the speaker shifts to 'borderline,' she is already in the midst of variable patches that can competently be called 'blue' and competently be called 'borderline' and competently be called 'green,' relative to a single fixed V-index. So the idea that her classifications should be fluid in this way is not so surprising.

The pattern of judgments that I have just described in (3) may constitute a *hysteresis* effect. As a first approximation, hysteresis is a

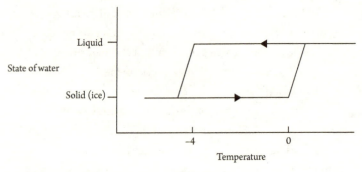

Figure 5.1. Hysteresis loop in the melting and freezing of water.

dynamical effect that occurs when an entity or system shifts discretely from one state to another as the result of an incremental change in the value of some determining parameter, and—here is the crucial bit—the value at the shifting point depends on the direction in which that parameter is changing. Van der Maas, Jansen et al. explain that hysteresis occurs "when the sudden jump [from one state to the other] depends on the direction of change in the normal variable. For instance, ice melts at 0°C but water freezes (in disturbance free conditions) at −4°C" (2004, 137). This pattern is commonly referred to as a 'hysteresis loop,' illustrated in Figure 5.1.

A classic case of hysteresis occurs in the behavior of magnets. The diagram in Figure 5.2 plots a hysteretic change in magnetization of a piece of iron. The x-axis specifies the strength of an externally applied magnetic field source (the 'determining parameter') and the y-axis specifies the degree of magnetization (the effect or 'response') in the iron. From the starting point, the magnetization of the iron increases as the applied magnetic field increases. But notice that when the magnetic field strength decreases from its maximal point, the magnetization of the iron does not simply retrace its steps back down to zero. Rather, as the field decreases, the iron retains its high level of magnetization for a period of time

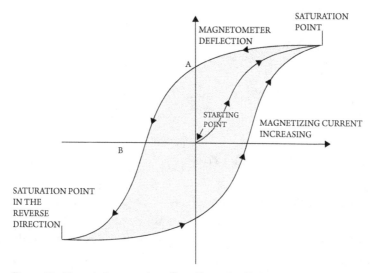

Figure 5.2. Magnetic hysteresis loop (http://www.daviddarling.info/encyclopedia/H/hysteresis_loop.html).

before it begins to drop. The decrease in magnetization lags behind the decrease in the field, and the magnetic field must be reversed and increased past zero in order to bring the iron back to its initial, non-magnetized state. (Hysteresis is sometimes called a 'lag' in, or 'persistence' or 'inertia' of, an effect or response.) Hence the iron's shift from a nonmagnetized state to a magnetized state occurs at a higher value of the applied magnetic field than its shift from magnetized to nonmagnetized.[2]

Hysteresis is also observed in human cognition, perception, and action. Just for example, Raczaszek et al. (1999) report a fascinating hysteresis effect in speakers' interpretations of ambiguous sentences as a function of continuously changing prosodic cues. (Prosodic features of an utterance include its intonation, rhythm, and stress pattern.) When disambiguating contextual information is absent, relative foot duration can disambiguate an utterance of a sentence

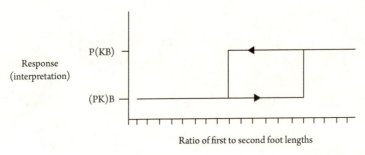

Figure 5.3. Hysteresis loop in interpretations of the sentence 'Pat and Kate or Bob will come.'

if the alternate interpretations of the sentence have different surface syntactic structures or "bracketings." Raczaszek et al. define a
foot to be a 'string of syllables that begins with an accented syllable
and extends to another accented syllable' (1999, 375). (So a foot is
rather like a musical beat.) Consider for example the sentence 'Pat or
Kate and Bob will come,' which has two possible interpretations and
bracketings:

P(KB): [Pat] or [Kate and Bob] will come.

(PK) B: [Pat or Kate] and [Bob] will come.

The sentence has four feet: 1 = 'Pat or', 2 = 'Kate and,' 3 = 'Bob will,'
4 = 'come.' Raczaszek et al. observe that the ratio of the lengths of the
first and second feet determines whether a hearer assigns interpretation P(KB) or interpretation (PK)B. In particular, the ratio of the
first foot to the second is greater in P(KB) than in (PK)B.[3]

For their experiment Raczaszek et al. (1999) synthesized a series
of utterances of the sentence 'Pat or Kate and Bob will come' that
progressed by equal increments of foot duration from one that was
heard as having the PK(B) interpretation to one that was heard as
having P(KB). They found that subjects shifted from one interpretation to the other at different points in the series depending on the

direction in which the stimuli were changing. Specifically, subjects shifted from PK(B) to P(KB) closer to the P(KB) end than where they shifted from P(KB) to PK(B), so that their interpretations in the two directions overlapped (Figure 5.3). This is hysteresis.

Hysteresis is pervasive in the natural world. It is observed in ecological relations among predator and prey (e.g., Côté et al. 2004), in the functioning of labor markets and unemployment rates (e.g., Ball 2008), in decisions to buy or sell stock (Dixit 1992), in dating behavior (e.g., Tesser and Achee 1994), in heart rates (Walker et al. 2003), and in the process of cell differentiation (Kim 2008), to name just a few. Hysteresis is itself a certain pattern of behavior in a system, and instances of it in different systems result from different underlying mechanisms. However, a plausible general explanation for hysteretic behavior is that, all things being equal, many systems like to stay in the state they are currently in. (Among other things, changing from one state to another may expend energy.) I will discuss several forms of psychological hysteresis later. For now, I propose that once our speaker has shifted from 'blue' to 'borderline' in the blue/green dynamic sorites series, her categorizations will exhibit hysteresis: If she then reverses direction, she will categorize some preceding patches as borderline rather than blue as she had done before. The behavior of classifying patches as borderline will *persist* after, or *lag* behind, her category shift and change of direction (Figure 5.4). The idea is that it's *by* changing her dispositions in this hysteretic fashion that the speaker is able to shift categories while preserving the effective continuity, the seamlessness, of the sorites series.

You might think of these category shifts on the model of an automatic transmission in a car. Suppose that as the car accelerates from a stop, the transmission shifts from first gear to second at 20 mph. Once it has shifted to second, it will continue to use that gear as long as it can, even if the car subsequently slows to a speed previously handled by first gear: For example, the transmission will now remain

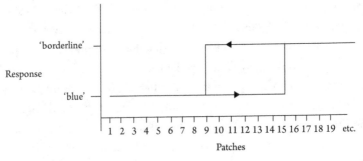

Figure 5.4. Predicted hysteresis in a blue/green dynamic sorites series.

in second gear even if the car slows to 15 mph, a speed previously handled by first gear.[4] The following explanation from a website on kart racing is helpful here:

> What is hysteresis? In racer's terms: (his-ta-'ree-sis) is the difference in engine speeds when the clutch engages and when it disengages. For example, an average clutch on an accelerating engine will engage at 4000 rpm. When slowing down from high speed the same clutch will disengage at 3500 rpm. This clutch has 500 rpm of hysteresis (4000 rpm–3500 rpm).... Hysteresis is a phenomenon in which the response of a physical system to an external influence depends not only on the present magnitude of that influence but also on the previous history of the system. Expressed mathematically, the response to the external influence is a doubled-valued function; one value applies when the influence is increasing, the other applies when the influence is decreasing.[5]

Analogously, once the competent speaker has shifted to 'borderline' and reversed direction, she will persist in using that category even when classifying patches that she formerly called 'blue.'

I don't mean to suggest that changing her verbal dispositions in this manner is under the speaker's conscious or otherwise willful control. For example, it's not as if she arrives at a certain patch and then *decides* to change her dispositions. (Maybe some subpersonal part of her "decides," but that is not something that she does or that she intends.[6]) Rather, when the speaker arrives at patch #15, it just strikes her a certain way—as borderline, for example. And if she reverses direction, some preceding patches will also now strike her as borderline even though they struck her as blue a moment before. The precise location of her category shift, and the associated change of verbal dispositions, must be the work of subpersonal mechanisms. The idea that speakers' applications of a vague predicate owe to the underlying switching machinery in this way accords with the arbitrariness of our stopping places in a sorites series; indeed, it may explain how that arbitrariness is possible. It also sits well with the absence of any normative framework for justification or argument concerning our classifications of variable items. I will say more about the role of mechanism in a theory of vagueness later.

Of course, to do the work I am assigning to it, the hypothesis of hysteresis will need to hold generally: It will need to hold for the competent use of any vague word, not just for predicates, and certainly not just for perceptual predicates like 'blue' and 'green.' For example, a speaker doing a forced march along a sorites series for 'rich' or 'old' or 'rich in contrast to middle income' should likewise (typically) undergo a hysteretic change of verbal dispositions at a category shift. If you proceed along our rich/middle income series of salaries $200,000 to $50,000 until you shift from 'rich' to 'borderline' at, say, $130,000, you should now (typically) be disposed to classify $130,001 and probably some of the preceding salaries as borderline also, in spite of the fact that you previously classified them as rich. Thus when you shift at $130,000, it's not as if you are crossing justification norm

a decisive threshold of richness; on the contrary, it's as if a string of salaries shift their category together, so that $130,000 and $130,001 never seem category-different at the same time. (Again, the 'seeming' needn't be phenomenological; the salaries will strike you, impress you, incline you to judge them, as rich or as borderline.) Remember that salaries in this transitional region of the series can competently be classified as rich and as borderline (hence not-rich) and as middle income, and your classifications of them will vary from occasion to occasion.

N.B. I am not proposing that hysteretic application is either necessary or sufficient for vagueness. Hysteretic application may be necessary for competent *use* of a vague word, but I am not going to argue for even that much here. I mean to propose only that hysteretic application may explain two things: first, how competent speakers are able to shift categories without disturbing the seamless progression of a sorites series, and second, how our multi-range semantics of vagueness could be implemented in competent use.

The idea that hysteresis occurs in a dynamic sorites series in the manner I am suggesting is an empirical hypothesis that needs to be tested. With two psychologists, Delwin Lindsey[7] and Angela Brown[8], I have designed and run an experiment to do that.

5.2. TESTING FOR HYSTERESIS

In designing our study, we faced the challenge of finding stimuli that could ensure that subjects were unaware of the reversal of direction immediately after a category shift. If subjects recognized the reversal, any spontaneous tendency to produce hysteretic judgments might be superseded by the desire not to appear inconsistent. Experimental subjects hate to appear inconsistent. At the reversal of direction, they would likely dig in their heels and think, 'I see what you are doing—you are trying to catch me contradicting myself. But I'm smarter than you think. I'm going to draw a line and stick to it.' For this reason we could not employ sorites series of dollar amounts, or chronological ages, or numbers of sand grains. In fact, the only kind of stimuli we could think of that would serve our purpose were perceptual stimuli varying along a single continuous dimension. It is well known that such stimuli differing only incrementally cannot be reidentified across time. For instance, if I show you a blue patch, you will not be able to recognize it, as distinct from a patch of an incrementally different shade of blue, when you see it again even a few seconds later. In general, we can perceive (discriminate) many more values than we can recognize or even learn to recognize.[9]

With these considerations in mind, Lindsey constructed a set of thirty-seven colored lights progressing from a central blue to a central green, so ordered that each light looked the same in hue as the next.[10] The lights were viewed in a darkened room on a high-resolution hue monitor. Subjects' task throughout the experiment was to classify a single stimulus by clicking on one of three boxes labeled 'B' for blue, 'G' for green, and '?,' respectively. Subjects were instructed to "use the question mark response when, for any reason whatsoever, [they were] not fully satisfied either with 'B' or with 'G.'" The experiment was self-paced, but subjects were told not to spend more than a few seconds on each stimulus. The subjects were nineteen graduate and undergraduate students, postdocs, faculty, and staff from the philosophy and psychology departments at Ohio State University, including four experts in vision research. All testified that, to their knowledge, their hue vision was normal.

The experiment had three parts, each corresponding to a different way of presenting the stimuli. In Part I the lights were presented singly ("one at a time"), as illustrated in Figure 5.5. The colored light changed location in its box randomly from trial to trial, and the three responses 'B,' 'G,' and '?' switched boxes randomly between

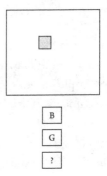

Figure 5.5. Stimulus configuration in Part I of the experiment. See www.oup.com/us/raffman for color illustrations.

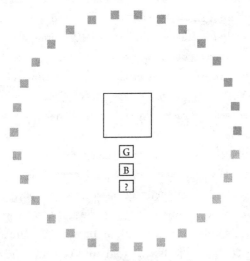

Figure 5.6. Stimulus configuration in Part II of the experiment. See www.oup.com/us/raffman for color illustrations.

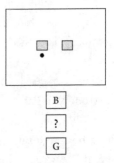

Figure 5.7. Stimulus configuration in Part III of the experiment. See www.oup.com/us/raffman for color illustrations.

conditions. Stimuli were presented in five conditions, each employing a different, randomly selected set of thirty consecutive stimuli from the available thirty-seven:

(1) Straight through the series in order from blue to green (BG)
(2) Straight through the series in order from green to blue (GB)
(3) Random order (Rn)
(4) Reversal ordering starting at the blue end (B[r])
(5) Reversal ordering starting at the green end (G[r]).

Each subject ran the set of five conditions twice. Within each set of five, conditions were presented in random order except that the first condition tested was always one of the two reversal orderings, selected at random. (We began each set with a reversal condition so as to minimize subjects' knowledge or memory of the stimulus set.)

Figures 5.8 and 5.9 (pp.150–151) display data from two individual subjects in Part I. Without defense beyond these few remarks, I have replaced the '?' response with lower-case 'b' for 'borderline.' We chose not to use 'borderline' as a response category in the experiment; since even the philosophers can't agree about what it means, we didn't want our subjects to be confused by it. Strictly speaking, then, the interpretation of the question mark remains open. The columns in each figure display the subject's responses in the five conditions, and each row represents the response on a given trial. The column labeled 'stm' specifies the stimulus being judged in a given trial, and the colored rectangles indicate the initial stimulus in each condition. The starting patch varied at random within a small range.

Notice first that our results provide evidence that competent speakers vary, both inter- and intrasubjectively, in their classifications of the items in a sorites series. For instance, in the first BG condition

stm	BG	GB	Rn	B[r]		G[r]		stm	BG	GB	Rn	B[r]		G[r]	
1	-	-	-	-	-	-	-	1	-	-	-	-	-	-	-
2	-	G	G	-	-	-	-	2	-	G	-	-	-	-	-
3	-	G	G	-	-	-	-	3	-	G	-	-	-	G	-
4	G	G	G	-	-	G	-	4	-	G	G	-	-	G	-
5	G	G	G			G	-	5	-	G	G	-	-	G	-
6	G	G	G	-	-	G	-	6	G	G	G	-	-	G	-
7	G	G	G	-	-	G	-	7	G	G	G	-	-	G	-
8	G	G	G	-	-	G	G	8	G	G	G	-	-	G	G
9	G	G	b	-	-	b	b	9	G	G	G	-	-	G	-
10	G	G	G	-	-	G	b	10	G	G	G	-	-	G	b
11	G	G	G	-	-	G	b	11	G	G	G	-	-	b	-
12	b	b	b	-	-	b	-	12	G	G	G	-	-	-	-
13	b	b	b	-	-	-	-	13	G	G	G	-	-	-	-
14	b	b	b	-	-	-	-	14	b	G	b	-	-	-	-
15	B	b	b	-	-	-	-	15	b	G	b	b	-	-	-
16	B	B	b	G	-	-	-	16	B	G	b	B	b	-	-
17	B	B	B	B	G	-	-	17	B	G	B	B	b	-	-
18	B	B	B	B	G	-	-	18	B	G	B	B	b	-	-
19	B	B	b	B	G	-	-	19	B	B	B	B	b	-	-
20	B	B	B	B	G	-	-	20	B	B	B	B	b	-	-
21	B	B	B	B	G	-	-	21	B	B	B	B	B	-	-
22	B	B	B	B	G	-	-	22	B	B	B	B	-	-	-
23	B	B	B	B	G	-	-	23	B	B	B	B	-	-	-
24	B	B	B	B	G	-	-	24	B	B	B	GB	-	-	-
25	B	B	B	B	G	-	-	25	B	B	B	B	-	-	-
26	B	B	B	B	G	-	-	26	B	B	B	B	-	-	-
27	B	B	B	B	G	-	-	27	B	B	B	B	-	-	-
28	B	B	B	B	G	-	-	28	B	B	B	B	-	-	-
29	B	B	B	B	G	-	-	29	B	B	B	B	-	-	-
30	B	B	B	B	G	-	-	30	B	B	B	B	-	-	-
31	B	B	B	B	G	-	-	31	B	B	B	B	-	-	-
32	B	-	-	B	B	-	-	32	B	-	B	B	-	-	-
33	B	-	-	B	-	-	-	33	B	-	B	B	-	-	-
34	-	-	-	B	-	-	-	34	B	-	-	B	-	-	-
35	-	-	-	-	-	-	-	35	B	-	-	-	-	-	-
36	-	-	-	-	-	-	-	36	-	-	-	-	-	-	-
37	-	-	-	-	-	-	-	37	-	-	-	-	-	-	-

BG = stimuli presented in order (straight through) from blue to green
GB = stimuli presented in order (straight through) from green to blue
Rn = stimuli presented in random order
B[r] = reversal condition starting at blue
G[r] = reversal condition starting at green

Figure 5.8. Data from one subject for Part I of the experiment (single stimulus presentation). Curved arrows indicate reversal of direction and subsequent hysteresis. See www.oup.com/us/ raffman for color illustrations.

in Figure 5.8, the subject shifts from 'blue' to 'borderline' at patch #14 and then from 'borderline' to 'green' at patch #11; whereas in the second BG condition he shifts from 'blue' to 'borderline' at #15 and from 'borderline' to 'green' at #13. In the first GB condition he shifts from 'green' to 'borderline' at #12, while in the second he shifts

stm	BG	GB	Rn	B[r]		G[r]		stm	BG	GB	Rn	B[r]		G[r]	
1	-	-	-	-	-	-	-	1	-	-	-	-	-	-	-
2	-	G	G	-	-	-	-	2	-	G	-	-	-	-	-
3	-	G	G	-	-	-	-	3	-	G	-	-	-	G	-
4	G	G	G	-	-	-	-	4	-	G	G	-	-	G	-
5	G	G	G	-	-	-	-	5	-	G	G	-	-	G	-
6	G	G	G	-	-	G	-	6	G	G	G	-	-	G	-
7	G	G	G	-	-	G	-	7	G	G	G	-	-	G	-
8	G	G	G	-	-	G	-	8	G	G	G	-	-	G	G
9	G	G	G	-	-	G	G	9	G	G	G	-	-	G	b
10	G	b	G	-	-	G	b	10	G	G	G	-	-	G	b
11	G	b	G	-	-	G	b	11	G	G	G	-	-	G	b
12	G	b	G	-	-	G	b	12	G	G	G	-	-	G	b
13	G	b	b	-	-	b	-	13	G	G	G	-	-	b	-
14	G	B	b	G	-	-	-	14	G	b	b	-	-	-	-
15	G	B	b	B	G	-	-	15	G	b	b	-	-	-	-
16	b	B	B	B	G	-	-	16	G	b	b	-	-	-	-
17	b	B	B	B	G	-	-	17	G	B	B	-	-	-	-
18	b	B	B	B	G	-	-	18	b	B	B	b	-	-	-
19	b	B	B	B	G	-	-	19	b	B	B	B	b	-	-
20	B	B	B	B	G	-	-	20	b	B	B	B	b	-	-
21	B	B	B	B	G	-	-	21	b	B	B	B	B	-	-
22	B	B	B	B	G	-	-	22	B	B	B	B	-	-	-
23	B	B	B	B	B	-	-	23	B	B	B	B	-	-	-
24	B	B	B	B	-	-	-	24	B	B	B	B	-	-	-
25	B	B	B	B	-	-	-	25	B	B	B	B	-	-	-
26	B	B	B	B	-	-	-	26	B	B	B	B	-	-	-
27	B	B	B	B	-	-	-	27	B	B	B	B	-	-	-
28	B	B	B	B	-	-	-	28	B	B	B	B	-	-	-
29	B	B	B	B	-	-	-	29	B	B	B	B	-	-	-
30	B	B	B	B	-	-	-	30	B	B	B	B	-	-	-
31	B	B	B	B	-	-	-	31	B	B	B	B	-	-	-
32	B	-	-	B	-	-	-	32	B	-	B	B	-	-	-
33	B	-	-	B	-	-	-	33	B	-	B	B	-	-	-
34	-	-	-	B	-	-	-	34	B	-	-	B	-	-	-
35	-	-	-	-	-	-	-	35	B	-	-	-	-	-	-
36	-	-	-	-	-	-	-	36	-	-	-	-	-	-	-
37	-	-	-	-	-	-	-	37	-	-	-	-	-	-	-

BG = stimuli presented in order (straight through) from blue to green
GB = stimuli presented in order (straight through) from green to blue
Rn = stimuli presented in random order
B[r] = reversal condition starting at blue
G[r] = reversal condition starting at green

Figure 5.9. Data from one subject for Part I of the experiment (single stimulus presentation). See www.oup.com/us/raffman for color illustrations.

directly from 'green' to 'blue' at #19. In Figure 5.9 we see still different classifications by another subject. On the plausible assumption that our subjects were competent speakers, these responses provide support for the claim that there are multiple equally competent stopping places in a sorites series—multiple equally competent ways of applying a vague word.

At present we are most interested in the reversal conditions, which tested for hysteresis. In reversal condition B[r], stimuli were presented starting from the blue end of the series. Immediately after the subject shifted to 'borderline' or to 'green,' the stimuli were then presented in reverse order. Thus if the subject shifted from 'blue' to 'green' at, say, stimulus #16, she was then presented with #17, #18, #19, and so forth until she shifted back to 'blue' (or 'borderline'). The G[r] condition did the same, starting from the green end. Both subjects display hysteresis. (See the curved arrows in the figures.) In the first reversal condition B[r] in Figure 5.8, for example, this subject classified lights #34 through #17 as 'blue' and then shifted to 'green' at #16. The next column then shows that as she was brought back down the series, she continued classifying lights #17 through #31 as 'green' even though she had judged them 'blue' just a moment before. In other words, she persisted in using the green category after her shift. We could say that in this block of trials she underwent a hysteresis of fifteen lights. In the second G[r] condition in Figure 5.9, we see that the subject shifted from 'green' to 'borderline' at light #13; he then displayed hysteresis of four lights until shifting back to 'green' at light #8. (Here is one way in which the idea that vagueness is a form of *wandering* may be embodied in competent use.[11])

Figures 5.8 and 5.9 show two of our most striking cases; often the hysteresis was shorter, around two or three lights. The average length of hysteresis observed in Part I of the experiment was slightly less than three lights. One expert did not exhibit hysteresis in any block of trials. There is nothing in my hypothesis to rule out that possibility—it is simply a limiting case of hysteresis of zero lights—but it should be, and was, exceptional.[12] Another striking aspect of these data is that subjects often did not use the '?' response (see, e.g., the first B[r] and second GB conditions in Figure 5.8). In fact our expert subjects almost never used the question mark. If '?' can indeed be interpreted as meaning 'borderline,' this finding provides support for the idea, floated during our discussion of higher order borderline cases in chapter 2, that a judgment of 'borderline' is always optional; there are no definite borderline cases. Actually it indicates something stronger—namely, that a competent speaker needn't classify *any* items in a sorites series as borderline.

We ran the 'straight through' conditions BG and GB partly in order to see whether our study would replicate the results of a previous, standard test for hysteresis reported in Kalmus (1979). The standard way to test for hysteresis is to run subjects through an entire series of stimuli first in one direction and then in the other, as we did in BG and GB. Subjects' classifications are hysteretic if the shifting point in each direction is displaced toward the opposite endpoint— for example, if the span of patches classified as blue in the blue-to-green direction overlaps with the span of patches classified as green in the green-to-blue direction. Kalmus (1979) performed exactly this test with hue stimuli and found no hysteresis. Instead he found enhanced contrast, which is the opposite of hysteresis: Enhanced contrast consists in a gap, rather than an overlap, between the classifications in the two directions. Our study largely replicates Kalmus's finding. Notice for instance that in Figure 5.9, the last blue patch in the first BG condition is #20, whereas the last green patch in the first GB condition is #9. The last blue patch in the first B[r] condition is #15, whereas the last green patch in the first G[r] condition is #12. Thus, interestingly, we observed hysteresis only after a reversal of direction. A reversal condition has not been investigated previously, so far as we are aware.

In Part II, thirty consecutive stimuli were presented simultaneously, as shown in Figure 5.6 on page 148; all of the patches were in view throughout. On each trial, a small black dot appeared next to the patch that was to be classified. Data from one subject are shown in Figure 5.10 below. These results bear out our expectation that if subjects were aware of the change of direction in the reversal condition, they would tend to select an arbitrary fixed boundary so as to avoid appearing inconsistent, and this would tend to obscure

stm	BG	GB	Rn	B[r]		G[r]		BG	CB	Rn	B[r]		G[r]		stm
1															1
2	G							G							2
3	G	G						G					G		3
4	G	G						G					G		4
5	G	G	G			G		G	G	G			G		5
6	G	G	G			G		G	G	G			G		6
7	G	G	G			G		G	G	G			G		7
8	G	G	G			G		G	G	G			G		8
9	G	G	G			G		G	G	G			G	G	9
10	G	G	G			G	G	G	G	G			b ↓		10
11	G	G	G			b ↓		G	G	G					11
12	b	b	b					G	G	G					12
13	b	b	b	↑				G	G	b					13
14	B	B	b	b				G	b	b					14
15	B	B	G	B	B			G	b	b					15
16	B	B	B	B				b	B	b	↑				16
17	B	B	B	B				B	B	B	G				17
18	B	B	B	B				B	B	B	B	B			18
19	B	B	B	B				B	B	B	B				19
20	B	B	B	B				B	B	B	B				20
21	B	B	B	B				B	B	B	B				21
22	B	B	B	B				B	B	B	B				22
23	B	B	B	B				B	B	B	B				23
24	B	B	B	B				B	B	B	B				24
25	B	B	B	B				B	B	B	B				25
26	B	B	B	B				B	B	B	B				26
27	B	B	B	B				B	B	B	B				27
28	B	B	B	B				B	B	B	B				28
29	B	B	B	B				B	B	B	B				29
30	B	B	B	B				B	B	B	B				30
31	B	B	B	B				B	B	B	B				31
32		B	B	B				B	B	B					32
33		B						B	B	B					33
34			B					B	B						34
35															35
36															36
37															37

BG = stimuli presented in order (straight through) from blue to green
GB = stimuli presented in order (straight through) from green to blue
Rn = stimuli presented in random order
B[r] = reversal condition starting at blue
G[r] = reversal condition starting at green

Figure 5.10. Data from one subject for Part II of the experiment (simultaneous presentation). No hysteresis evident. See www.oup.com/us/raffman for color illustrations.

any hysteresis in their classifications. Nevertheless, some subjects did exhibit a short hysteresis in Part II, as indicated in Figure 5.11, though the average length was only slightly more than one patch. As in Part I, the '?' response was not always used.

Perhaps it will be thought that subjects' judgments exhibited hysteresis in Part I merely because they believed or expected that the stimuli they saw in the reversal conditions B[r] and G[r] were continuing to change in the original direction. For instance, after shifting from 'blue' to 'green,' maybe subjects persisted in saying 'green' not because the stimuli looked green but only because the stimuli had so far been progressing steadily from blue toward green, and so subjects expected them to continue in that direction. After a time, as the stimuli became increasingly blue, subjects realized that the direction had reversed and went back to saying 'blue.'

This is an intelligent objection, and we cannot rule out the possibility it describes. However, we can offer some reasons to favor a hypothesis of perceptual hysteresis. First, in Part II of the experiment, all of the stimuli were presented simultaneously, so subjects presumably did not believe that stimuli were continuing to progress in the same direction. (Call the latter belief the 'continuation belief.') Nevertheless, six subjects displayed a hysteresis of 1 patch, and two displayed a hysteresis two patches long. Hence a continuation belief is unlikely to have been the cause of the hysteresis in either Part I or Part II. Also, in some instances in Part I, the hysteresis was long enough to make it unlikely that the subjects still believed the stimuli were progressing in the original direction, yet they persisted in the new (post-shift) category anyway. Three subjects exhibited hysteresis more than eight patches long, and the subject represented in Figure 5.8 exhibited a hysteresis of fifteen patches. These results suggest that the continuation belief does not explain the hysteretic patterns of judgment we observed.[13]

stm	BG	GB	Rn	B[r]		G[r]		stm	BG	GB	Rn	B[r]		G[r]	
1	-	-	-	-	-	-	-	1	-	-	-	-	-	-	-
2	-	-	G	-	-	-	-	2	G	G	-	-	-	-	-
3	-	-	G	-	-	-	-	3	G	G	-	-	-	-	-
4	G	-	G	-	-	-	-	4	G	G	G	-	-	-	-
5	G	G	G	-	-	-	-	5	G	G	G	-	-	G	-
6	G	G	G	-	-	G	-	6	G	G	G	-	-	G	-
7	G	G	G	-	-	G	-	7	G	G	G	-	-	G	-
8	G	G	G	-	-	G	-	8	G	G	G	-	-	G	-
9	G	G	G	-	-	G	-	9	G	G	G	-	-	G	-
10	G	G	G	-	-	G	-	10	G	G	G	-	-	G	-
11	G	G	G	-	-	G	-	11	G	G	G	-	-	G	-
12	G	G	G	-	-	G	-	12	G	G	G	-	-	G	-
13	G	G	b	-	-	G	-	13	G	G	G	-	-	G	G
14	G	b	b	-	-	G	-	14	G	b	G	-	-	b	↰ -
15	G	b	b	-	-	G	G	15	b	b	G	-	-	-	-
16	b	b	b	-	-	b ↰	-	16	b	b	b	-	-	-	-
17	b	b	b	-	-	-	-	17	b	b	G	-	-	-	-
18	b	b	b	b ↱	-	-	-	18	b	b	G	-	-	-	-
19	b	B	B	B	b	-	-	19	b	B	b	-	-	-	-
20	b	B	B	B	B	-	-	20	B	B	b	b ↱	-	-	-
21	B	B	B	B	-	-	-	21	B	B	b	B	b	-	-
22	B	B	B	B	-	-	-	22	B	B	B	B	b	-	-
23	B	B	B	B	-	-	-	23	B	B	B	B	B	-	-
24	B	B	B	B	-	-	-	24	B	B	B	B	-	-	-
25	B	B	B	B	-	-	-	25	B	B	B	B	-	-	-
26	B	B	B	B	-	-	-	26	B	B	B	B	-	-	-
27	B	B	B	B	-	-	-	27	B	B	B	B	-	-	-
28	B	B	B	B	-	-	-	28	B	B	B	B	-	-	-
29	B	B	B	B	-	-	-	29	B	B	B	B	-	-	-
30	B	B	B	B	-	-	-	30	B	B	B	B	-	-	-
31	B	B	B	B	-	-	-	31	B	B	B	B	-	-	-
32	B	B	-	-	-	-	-	32	-	-	B	B	-	-	-
33	B	B	-	-	-	-	-	33	-	-	B	B	-	-	-
34	-	B	-	-	-	-	-	34	-	-	-	B	-	-	-
35	-	-	-	-	-	-	-	35	-	-	-	-	-	-	-
36	-	-	-	-	-	-	-	36	-	-	-	-	-	-	-
37	-	-	-	-	-	-	-	37	-	-	-	-	-	-	-

BG = stimuli presented in order (straight through) from blue to green
GB = stimuli presented in order (straight through) from green to blue
Rn = stimuli presented in random order
B[r] = reversal condition starting at blue
G[r] = reversal condition starting at green

Figure 5.11. Data from one subject for Part II of the experiment (simultaneous presentation). Small hysteresis in B[r]. See www.oup.com/us/raffman for color illustrations.

5.3. NONPERCEPTUAL HYSTERESIS: DOES OUR HYPOTHESIS GENERALIZE?

Even if applications of hue predicates are hysteretic in the way I predicted, that doesn't yet show that the same holds for nonperceptual vague words like 'rich,' 'old,' and 'person'; maybe our experimental results were elicited by specifically perceptual features of the stimuli. I do not know of any studies of hysteresis effects in nonperceptual categorization in an immediate reversal condition like the one we investigated.[14] However, there is ample evidence of nonperceptual hysteresis effects in other conditions, so I think we can be optimistic that our hypothesis will hold up outside the perceptual domain. Let me provide a few illustrations. (Since it is important to see exactly what these theorists say, I am going to quote several of them at some length.)

With regard to attitudinal change, Van der Maas, Jansen et al. explain:

> Hysteresis in...attitude...means that the informational value at which people change their attitude (the threshold) depends on the person's initial position and the direction of change in information. For instance, people with a positive attitude toward abortion change to a negative attitude only when information is strongly against abortion. People with a negative attitude change to a positive attitude only when information is strongly in favor of abortion. (2003, 131)

Such attitudes toward abortion might be reflected in hysteretic application of vague predicates like 'morally (im)permissible' or 'sinful' or maybe 'person'. Oliva et al. describe hysteresis in the relationship between service delivery and customer satisfaction in marketing:

> Once a sudden shift occurs, a return to the former [behavior] will not occur even if the independent variable values return to the levels they were [at] when the shift was made. There is a lag or hysteresis (inertia) in the process, which tends to keep behavior at its current level. For example, when a brand loyal customer for a high involvement product switches to another brand because of dissatisfaction with the first brand's performance or service,

the customer is not likely to be easily switched back.... The reason is that the [customer's] current behavior...is dependent on
recent past [performance], just as service adjustments provided
to an unhappy customer may not reduce unhappiness, and the
same adjustments made to a happy customer may not reduce
happiness. (1992, 87)

We can perhaps imagine customers applying a vague predicate such
as 'reliable detergent' or 'effective cough suppressant' in a hysteretic
fashion.

Abraham Tesser and John Achee (1994) have developed a model
in which dating behavior in the face of negative social pressure (e.g.,
dating someone of the "wrong" gender, race, or religion) exhibits hysteresis. Here their model is discussed by Jonathan Elster:

As the disposition [to date the "wrong" person] continues to
decrease in the face of strong social pressure, there will come a
point when the person switches from engaging in the behavior to
not engaging in it. In the [opposite] case, as the disposition continues to increase, there will come a point when the person switches
from not engaging in the behavior to engaging in it. Moreover, the
level of disposition at which the first switch occurs is lower than
the level at which the second occurs. A person who has adopted
an unpopular opinion will need to see a lot of the evidence for it
fritter away before he gives it up, whereas an uncommitted person
will need a lot of evidence for it before adopting it. Finally, a given
combination of social pressure and disposition can lead to high as
well as low engagement in the behavior, depending on where the
person initially started up. (1976, 68)

Here the vague terms implicitly at issue might be something like 'datable' or 'mate-worthy.'

Economists also are familiar with hysteresis in human behavior. For instance, Avinash Dixit asks us to

> picture a particular path of the stochastic evolution of net revenues [R] of a company through time.... Suppose the initial R equals 1, and it starts to rise.... Finally it rises above 1.62, and the project is launched. Then the revenue starts to fall, and comes back all the way down to 1. But this does not justify abandonment. The driving force behind the investment decision, namely the currently observed revenue, has been restored to its initial level. But its meandering along the way has left its mark, namely an active project where there was none before.
>
> Similar effects have long been known in physics and other sciences... This phenomenon is called hysteresis, and by analogy the failure of investment decisions to reverse themselves when the underlying causes are fully reversed can be called economic hysteresis.... If our project's current revenue falls even more, it will eventually be abandoned. Then a subsequent rise back to 1 in revenues will not restore the project; there is hysteresis in the reverse direction, too....Very large changes in R in the opposite direction are needed to reverse the effects of a temporary move in either direction. (1992, 121–122)

Here the vague words at issue might be something like 'good (bad) time to invest' or 'adequate revenue to justify launching the new project.'[15]

These examples are not conclusive. As I have said, I do not know how to prove that hysteresis of the sort observed in our experiment, namely, hysteresis in an immediate reversal condition, would occur in applications of nonperceptual vague predicates as well as perceptual ones. Van der Maas et al. don't describe a case in which information about abortion turns negative immediately after an agent has

Test it by playing an economic game

People need to click buttons / choose dialogue options when they give instructions to employes using those terms.

shifted from a negative to a positive attitude toward abortion, and Dixit (1992) doesn't describe a case in which revenue decreases immediately after a project is launched. Plus there remains the difficulty of revealing hysteresis when subjects are aware of the reversal. Thus the best I can offer at present is a plausibility claim: The research cited above suggests that a variety of nonperceptual judgments are hysteretic in "straight-through" conditions, and from there it is not a great leap to the idea that the dynamics of nonperceptual judgments over incremental differences would be relevantly analogous to those observed in our experiment. (Indeed, given that we observed hysteresis only in the reversal conditions, and not in the straight-through conditions, the application of predicates like 'datable,' 'morally impermissible,' and 'reliable detergent,' which are likely to be hysteretic even in straight-through conditions, might exhibit greater hysteresis than the hue words in a reversal condition.) Let us suppose, then, at least for the sake of argument, that our hypothesis holds of vague words across the board.

Wright has raised the worry (in conversation) that competent speakers might exhibit hysteresis in their (perceptually based) applications of some precise predicates also. They might not apply an obviously precise predicate like 'six feet tall' hysteretically; indeed they might decline to apply that predicate at all, just on the basis of looking. But they might apply a less obviously precise predicate hysteretically—say, the predicate 'taller than six feet.' Speakers might apply the latter predicate hysteretically even though arguably it is neither soritical nor vague. If that's right, our finding of hysteresis shows nothing distinctive about vague predicates.

Let me offer two points in reply. First, notice that Wright's worry cannot be allayed by contending that the speakers in his example would implicitly be applying not the predicate 'taller than six feet' but rather 'looks taller than six feet,' for this contention misses the distinction between judging that something looks Φ, on the one hand, and judging, *on the basis of looking*, that something *is* Φ, on the other. We should suppose that the speakers in the example are doing the latter: They are judging, on the basis of looking, whether a given object is taller than six feet. However, Wright's worry *can* be allayed by appeal to the further distinction, often drawn by philosophers of perception, between an object's looking Φ and an object's looking as if it is Φ (or looking to be Φ). For instance, a round object viewed from an angle looks elliptical but does not look as if it is elliptical. It looks as if it is round; round things look elliptical when viewed from an angle. My point then is that if speakers applied the predicate 'taller than six feet' hysteretically, on the basis of looking, they would in fact be judging not that the object in question is taller than six feet, or even that it looks taller than six feet, but rather that it looks *as if it is* taller than six feet, or *looks to be* taller than six feet. (It looks the way things that are taller than six feet look.) Because they would be classifying the object on the basis of looking, they would actually, implicitly, be applying the predicate 'looks as if it is taller than six feet'; when it is applied *on the basis of looking*, the predicate 'taller than six feet' is simply an abbreviation for 'looks as if it is taller than six feet.' And the latter predicate is vague. Hence hysteresis is just what we should expect. Second, as I said above, I am not claiming that hysteresis in the application of a term is either necessary or sufficient for vagueness; at most, hysteresis may be necessary for competent use of a vague term (as opposed to competent use of a precise term). I am claiming only that evidence exists to suggest that competent speakers apply vague words hysteretically and that the hysteresis may explain how they are able to shift categories in a dynamic sorites series without disturbing its apparent continuity.

My hypothesis then is that hysteresis in our applications of a vague predicate to the items in a dynamic sorites series has the effect of smoothing out what would otherwise be sharp or abrupt transitions from one category to another. (There is in fact a mathematical technique called 'hysteresis smoothing' that is used to smooth pixels in digital images and to enable smooth starting in clocks and turntables, for example.) Intuitively, hysteresis in our applications of a vague word allows us to talk about the continuous world around us; it allows our "discrete" language to apply to a seamless environment. Generally speaking, items in the transitional region between vague predicates 'Φ' and 'Φ*' can competently be classified as Φ and as Φ* and as Φ[Φ*] borderline. So we can hardly cast aspersions on our classifications of those items for being hysteretic. If anything, the hysteresis provides a pattern or regularity to our variable judgments. It makes them more intelligible, not less: The permissible variability is hysteretic, not random.

A referee for Oxford University Press asks, "[If the subjects] are trying to be consistent (as, it seems, some are), why not take *that* to be due to semantic features of ['blue' and 'green']? That is, why chalk it up to artificial features of the testing environment?" The thought here, I take it, is either (a) that 'blue' and 'green' have unknowable, or at least unknown, sharp boundaries that our inconsistent use is (unbeknownst to us) aiming at or (b) that the semantics of these predicates is such that although they lack sharp boundaries, our use of them aspires or ought to aspire to such boundaries, that is, we should try to apply them *as if* they had sharp boundaries, and that is why we try to maintain consistency in our applications when the stimuli are presented simultaneously. I cannot see any good reason to endorse either (a) or (b) and many reasons to reject both; and even if such reasons exist, they will be outweighed by considerations favoring the explanation I have offered. Let me mention four of these.

First, my explanation is not ad hoc: Subjects' desire to be consistent in their responses has been observed across a wide range of experimental conditions (see Falk and Zimmermann 2013, for example). Moreover, knowledge of that desire led us to make a correct prediction about the results of Part II of the experiment: We predicted little or no hysteresis in the reversal conditions. Second, fully competent speakers are incapable of applying these predicates consistently. Why would their semantics require that we try to apply them in a humanly impossible way? Third, if the experimental findings are correct, the inconsistency in subjects' applications of vague words is not anomalous: It is hysteretic, and the hysteresis is what enables smooth category shifts. The existence of this pattern, and its apparent purpose, suggest that we apply vague words hysteretically *by design*, as one might put it. Fourth and last, if *per impossibile* we could apply 'blue' and 'rich' and 'bald' consistently, then as Wright points out (cf. p. 3 above), those words would be effectively useless in communication. Why would their semantics dictate that we aspire to apply them in a way that makes them useless?

I said that we could resolve the dynamic version of the paradox by attending to three aspects of vague predicates and their competent use: (1) each category in a sorites series encompasses a range of more and less central cases; (2) there are multiple equally competent ways to apply a vague predicate—in particular, multiple equally competent places to stop applying it in a sorites series; and (3) competent applications of a vague predicate are hysteretic in the manner observed in our experiment (we are supposing). It seems to me that, taken together, these features of competent use demystify our ability to shift categories without introducing an abrupt transition into a seamless sorites series. In so doing they show how the major premise of the dynamic paradox can be false: It is not true that if a speaker has applied the predicate in question to one item in a sorites series, she must also apply it to the next.

If the major premise of the dynamic sorites is false, indeed necessarily false, why does it seem true? I will offer an answer to this pressing question shortly.

5.4. MEANING AND USE: IMPLEMENTING THE MULTIPLE RANGE SEMANTICS

In developing the multiple range theory, I have placed significant weight on the idea that the character of the competent use of vague words provides evidence of their semantic structure. In particular, the hypothesis that vague words have multiple arbitrarily different ranges of application in their semantics is motivated in part by the variability of their competent use. Our experiment has now revealed additional aspects of the competent use of vague words, in particular its hysteretic character, that would not otherwise have been apparent. Can the hysteresis observed in the experiment also be seen as implementing the multi-range semantic theory, and if so, how?

Think of the use of vague words on the model of an imaginary board game. You have a game piece, and the game board contains an array of twelve colored patches progressing from a blue one to a green one, as illustrated in the top panel in Figure 5.12. (I have used twelve patches merely for practical reasons; it helps to imagine a more populated series having, say, thirty hues as in our experiment.) Suppose that the operative V-index for 'blue' is $\{$hue; green; $0\}$, the V-index for 'green' is $\{$hue; blue; $0\}$, and the V-index for 'borderline' is $\{$hue; blue, green; $0\}$. The object of the game is to produce a competent classification of all twelve patches seriatim, that is, to produce a dynamic sorites series, by landing your game piece on various squares in the rows $(i\text{-}x)$ on the board. Rows α and β at the top of the game board illustrate two possible ways of classifying the patches.

As an exercise, let's try producing the classifications in row α (Figure 5.12, bottom panel). You begin at patch #1 and classify one patch on each move by "using" the rows on the game board. For example, you can classify patch #1 as blue ('B') using any of rows i through iii; let's suppose you choose row ii, so your place your game piece on

α	B	B	B	B	B	B	B	b	G	G	G	G	
β	B	B	B	B	B	b	b	G	G	G	G	G	

	1	2	3	4	5	6	7	8	9	10	11	12	
i	B	B	B	B	B								i
ii	B	B	B	B	B	B							ii
iii	B	B	B	B	B	B	B						iii
iv			b	b	b	b							iv
v			b	b	b								v
vi					b	b	b	b					vi
vii			b	b	b	b							vii
viii						G	G	G	G	G	G	G	viii
ix					G	G	G	G	G	G	G	G	ix
x							G	G	G	G	G	G	x

i	B	B	(B)	B	B								i
ii	(B)	(B)	B	B	B	(B)							ii
iii	B	B	B	(B)	(B)	B	(B)						iii
iv			b	b	b	b							iv
v			b	b	b								v
vi					b	b	b	b					vi
vii			b	b	b	(b)							vii
viii						G	G	G	(G)	G	G		viii
ix					G	G	G	(G)	G	G	G		ix
x							G	G	G	(G)	(G)		x

Figure 5.12. Top panel shows the game board. Bottom panel shows the rows that could be used to produce the classifications in row α, with a particular sequence of moves circled. See www.oup.com/us/raffman for color illustrations.

the first square of that row (#1: *ii*). You can also classify patches #2 through #5 as blue by using any of rows *i* through *iii*; let's suppose that you move your piece to the second square of row *ii* (#2: *ii*), then to the third square of row *i* (#3: *i*), then to the fourth square of row *iii* (#4: *iii*), and then to the fifth square of row *iii* (#5: *iii*). You can classify #6 as blue by placing your game piece on either row *ii* or row *iii*, and classify #7 as blue using row *iii*. Patch #8 is classified as borderline ('b') using *vi* or *vii*, and patches #9-#12 can be classified as green ('G') using any of rows *viii* through *x*. On this particular game board, you can classify patch #6 as blue or as borderline or as green, but you can classify patch #8 only as borderline or as green and patch #1 only as blue. A judgment of 'borderline' is always optional; there are no patches having only 'b' rows below them.

Granted *Monopoly* has nothing to fear, but this toy example helps us to see how the multi-range semantic theory might be implemented in our competent use of a vague word. Using a vague word in a dynamic sorites series may be similar in certain respects to playing the game. Think of the rows on the board as different ranges of application of 'blue', 'borderline', and 'green': Rows *i* through *iii* as ranges of 'blue', rows *iv* through *vii* as ranges of 'borderline', and rows *viii* through *x* as ranges of 'green'. Then think of classifying a patch using a given row as analogous to classifying an item relative to a corresponding range of application. Where a player is permitted to classify a patch as, for example, green by using a 'green' row containing the hue of that patch, a speaker is permitted to classify an item as green by "using" a range of application of 'green' that contains the hue of that item. Where the player traverses the board by jumping among overlapping rows of different categories, the speaker traverses a sorites series by "jumping" among different overlapping ranges of the relevant predicates, much as one might bridge a crevasse by jumping from one to another of a series of overlapping planks of different lengths.

We can also understand the hysteresis in speakers' applications of vague words by analogy with possible moves on the game board. Suppose you want to produce the assignments shown in row β. You would classify patches #1 through #5 using any of rows *i–iii*, patches #6 and #7 relative to any of *iv–vii*, and patches #8–#12 relative to any of *viii–x*. Now suppose that, for whatever reason, you decide to reverse direction after classifying #8 as green. The overlaps among the rows would enable a hysteretic pattern in the reversal. You would trace a hysteretic path if you classified some preceding patches as green also; for example, if you classified patch #7 using row *viii*, patch #6 using row *ix*, #5 also using *ix*, and then shifted back to blue at #4. (See the bottom panel of Figure 5.13.) By analogy, a speaker could classify patch #7 as green relative to ("using") range *viii*, patch #6 using range *ix*, and so forth.

The analogy goes only so far, however. In particular, whereas the player in the game selects a single row to use on each move, it does not seem plausible that, in any given application of a vague word, a competent speaker uses or relativizes to a particular unique range of application. What could determine a particular range? When I say that the sky is blue, what facts about me or the language or the world could determine that I am applying 'blue' relative to, for example, range *i* rather than range *ii* or range *iii*? I think we should say instead that for any V-index, a speaker applies a vague predicate (truly) relative to *each* range of application that contains the value in question. For example, when producing the classifications in row β, you would classify patches #1 through #5 relative to each of the ranges *i–iii* (i.e., relative to *i* and relative to *ii* and relative to *iii*), patches #6 and #7 relative to each of *iv–vii*, and patches #8 through #12 relative to each of ranges *viii–x*.

What I have just proposed may sound like saying that the competent speaker has somehow to find out, independently of the classifications she makes or is disposed to make using a given vague word,

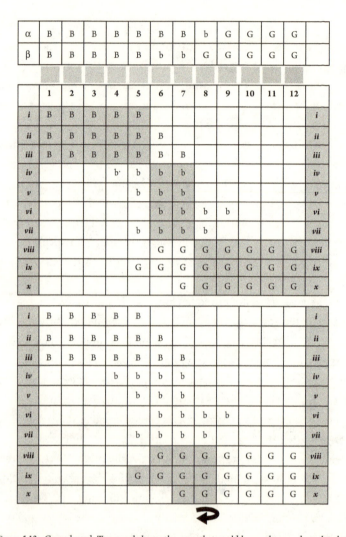

Figure 5.13. Game board. Top panel shows the rows that could be used to produce the classifications in row β. Bottom panel shows a sequence of rows that could be used in a reversal condition with hysteresis after the player has shifted to green at patch #8. On this game board the hysteresis could be up to three patches long. See www.oup.com/us/raffman for color illustrations.

Complaint: This Prediction Unrealistic infallible

whether any ranges of that word include the relevant value. But that is not what I mean. Simply in virtue of her competence with the word, her applications of it are "automatically" relativized to the appropriate ranges of application. Suppose you are looking at patch #6 on the game board; on this occasion it strikes you as blue, and so you classify it as blue. Because you are competent with 'blue,' your very act of classifying #6 automatically relativizes your application of 'blue' to range *ii* and to range *iii*. Or perhaps it would be better to say that you relativize your application of 'blue' to the relevant ranges—you use those ranges—*in the very act* of classifying the patch. You don't need to do anything else in order to relativize your judgment to the proper ranges of application. Similarly, you relativize your application of 'rich' to certain of its ranges in the very act of classifying $165,000 as rich relative to Vinny.

Ok. This is important for the justification bit?

Let me repeat: I am not saying that vague predicates are response-dependent.[16] The responses or judgments of competent speakers do not determine whether an item satisfies a given predicate. Whether an item satisfies 'blue' relative to a given V-index is determined by the semantics of the predicate, in particular by its ranges of application relative to that V-index, and by the item's hue. An item may satisfy 'blue' relative to every range of the predicate for a given V-index, or relative to none, or relative to some but not all ranges— independently of anything to do with judging subjects or speakers. Variable (transitional) items satisfy more than one predicate: For instance, patch #6 on the game board is blue relative to range *ii* and to range *iii*, borderline relative to each of ranges *iv* through *vii*, and green relative to each of ranges *viii* and *ix*. All that competent speakers (or maybe some of their subpersonal parts) are allowed to determine is how they will classify an item, and to that extent which ranges they will use, in a particular utterance.

But now what constitute a misapplication

One might have wondered whether relativity to ranges of application is itself just a fine-grained species of V-index-relativity

(f. context-relativity). We can now see why the answer is 'no.' A V-index is a set of factors that speakers can select, that is, intentionally choose, to take into account in their application of a term. For instance, I can choose to relativize my use of 'tall' to jockeys instead of basketball players, and I can choose to take into account the number of hairs on a head rather than their arrangement, in a given application of 'bald.' Speakers are typically aware of, and can say, which V-index they are relativizing to in a given utterance. (They also typically know which V-indices their interlocutors are relativizing to and so are aware of changes of V-index during a conversation.) More important, a V-index can be, and usually is, chosen *for a reason*—for example, because it is topically relevant to a current conversation, or simply because it is the one currently in use. In contrast, as I have just explained, speakers do not *choose* or *decide* the ranges to which they will relativize their applications of vague words, and do not take those ranges *into account*. Rather, they simply decide how they will classify a given item, and relativization to (each of) the corresponding ranges of application comes along automatically, for free, as it were. Furthermore, in the variable transitional region between categories, speakers' classifications, a fortiori the ranges to which those classifications are relativized, are determined by brute psychological mechanisms. Thus they are not made *for a reason*; as I have explained, our classifications of variable items are made without (nontrivial) justification. For these reasons, among others, range-relativity is not plausibly viewed as a species of index-relativity.[17]

5.5. AN ETYMOLOGICAL SPECULATION

After working out this hysteretic solution to the dynamic sorites, I discovered some evidence of a possible etymological link between the notions of vagueness and hysteresis. The English adjective 'vague' and cognates 'vagrant,' 'vagabond,' 'vagary,' and so on originate in the Latin 'vagus,' meaning 'wandering.'[18] (The French noun 'vague,' whose primary meaning is 'wave,' as in an ocean wave or a sound wave or, less literally, a wave of panic, has the same Latin root. See again the definition of the French adjective 'vague' that opens chapter 4.) The word 'hysteresis' is rooted through the ancient Greek *hysteros*, meaning 'late' or 'lagging behind' or 'coming after,' to the Sanskrit *ûttaras*, meaning 'uterus.' The Greek term for 'uterus,' the feminine form *hystera*, also derives from the Sanskrit word. Various theories have been offered as to the connection between these seemingly disparate strands of meaning ('late' or 'behind,' and 'uterus'). Thomas Morgan writes:

> Despite the common etymological base (in the Sanskrit *ûttaras*) of this *hysteros* and *hystera* (womb), the *Greek-English Lexicon* does not say why the womb is so called.... From Zeitlin ... suggests that *hystera* may draw on *hysteros* to name the second, or later, sex; John Belton[,] ... noting that one meaning of *hysteros* is 'afterbirth,' proposes that this later stage of delivery may have been thought to have been the womb itself (*hystera*), a new one of which was supposed to grow back. (1994, 54)

Mark Adair explains that the word 'uterus'

> shares a common Sanskrit origin (*uttaras*) with the adjective *hysteros*, of which one meaning is 'placed behind.' The *hystera* is behind, that is, caudal (toward the tail) to all of the other massy internal organs. (1995, 158)

Especially relevant to our present interests is the fact that the ancients conceived of the uterus as an organ, indeed a creature, that *wandered* throughout the body, thereby causing the symptoms of hysteria. In the *Timaeus* Plato writes,

> In women...[the] womb, a living creature within them with a desire for child-bearing, if it be left long unfruitful beyond the due season, is vexed and aggrieved, and wandering throughout the body and blocking the channels of the breath, by forbidding respiration brings the sufferer to extreme distress and causes all manner of disorders.

Indeed the notion that female hysteria was caused by a 'wandering womb' persisted in European academic medicine into the Middle Ages.

Unsurprisingly, I have not seen mention of an etymological tie between 'vague' and 'hysteretic' in the scholarly literature, so I rest nothing on it. But it would be nice to think that they are distant relatives. Hysteresis is nothing if not the wandering of a system's shifting point between two discrete states.

5.6. THE TRUTH ABOUT TOLERANCE

If the major premises of both versions of the sorites paradox are false, as we believe, why do they seem true? In chapter 4 I claimed that the multi-range semantic theory points toward one possible reason why the major premise of the semantic paradox seems true. We confuse (b), which is true, with (a), which is false:

(a) The increments between adjacent items in a sorites series for vague predicate 'Φ' are sufficiently small as to leave the application of 'Φ' unaffected. In other words, the increments are sufficiently small as to make any differential application of 'Φ' as between them *impermissible*.

(b) The increments between adjacent items in a sorites series for vague predicate 'Φ' are sufficiently small as to make any differential application of 'Φ' as between them *arbitrary*.

In fact, I think the latter confusion also accounts in part for the plausibility of the major premise of the dynamic paradox. But a second reason—the principal one, I think—for the seeming truth of the major premises of both versions of the puzzle comes to light in Part III of the experiment.

In Part III we presented subjects with consecutive pairs of neighboring patches: #1/#2, #2/#3, #3/#4, and so on.[19] The task was to classify each patch in a pair singly, as cued by a black dot. (See Figure 5.7 on p. 148.) The task was performed in the same five conditions as before (though in Part III subjects ran each condition only once). We predicted that subjects would virtually always put both members of a pair in the same category. Presumably, in order to do that, they would have to shift categories between consecutive pairs, and the shared patch in those pairs would have to be categorized differently in its two pairings. Our results confirmed this prediction, as shown in Figure 5.14. For example, in the B[r] condition the subject shifted categories from *blue* to *borderline* between the pairs #22/#21 and #21/#20. The shared patch, #21, was classified as blue in the former pair and as borderline in the latter. (Notice that hysteresis occurred also in this pairwise presentation, in the G[r] condition.)

How does this finding help to explain the intuitive appeal of the major premises of the sorites paradoxes? Consider that those premises only ever make reference to two neighboring items in a sorites series. Therefore it seems plausible that when we go to evaluate those

stm	BG		GB		Rn		B[r]				G[r]				stm
1	-	-	-	-	-	-	-	-	-	-	-	-	-	-	1
2	-	-	-	-	-	-	-	-	-	-	-	-	-	-	2
3	-	-	-	-	-	-	-	-	-	-	-	-	-	-	3
4	-	-	G	-	G	-	-	-	-	-	-	-	-	-	4
5	-	G	G	G	G	G	-	-	-	-	G	-	-	-	5
6	G	G	G	G	G	G	-	-	-	-	G	G	-	-	6
7	G	G	G	G	G	G	-	-	-	-	G	G	-	-	7
8	G	G	G	G	G	G	-	-	-	-	G	G	-	-	8
9	G	G	G	G	G	G	-	-	-	-	G	G	-	-	9
10	G	G	G	G	G	G	-	-	-	-	G	G	G	-	10
11	G	G	G	G	G	G	-	-	-	-	G	G	b	G	11
12	G	G	G	G	G	G	-	-	-	-	G	G	b	b	12
13	G	G	G	G	G	G	-	-	-	-	G	G	b	b	13
14	G	G	b	G	b	G	-	-	-	-	G	G	b	b	14
15	G	G	b	b	b	b	-	-	-	-	b	G	-	b	15
16	G	G	b	b	b	b	-	-	-	-	-	b	-	-	16
17	G	G	b	b	b	b	-	-	-	-	-	-	-	-	17
18	G	b	b	b	b	b	-	-	-	-	-	-	-	-	18
19	b	b	B	b	B	b	-	-	-	-	-	-	-	-	19
20	b	b	B	B	B	B	-	b	-	-	-	-	-	-	20
21	b	b	B	B	B	B	b	B	-	B	-	-	-	-	21
22	b	B	B	B	B	B	B	B	B	-	-	-	-	-	22
23	B	B	B	B	B	B	B	B	-	-	-	-	-	-	23
24	B	B	B	B	B	B	B	B	-	-	-	-	-	-	24
25	B	B	B	B	B	B	B	B	-	-	-	-	-	-	25
26	B	B	B	B	B	B	B	B	-	-	-	-	-	-	26
27	B	B	B	B	B	B	B	B	-	-	-	-	-	-	27
28	B	B	B	B	B	B	B	B	-	-	-	-	-	-	28
29	B	B	B	B	B	B	B	B	-	-	-	-	-	-	29
30	B	B	B	B	B	B	B	B	-	-	-	-	-	-	30
31	B	B	B	B	B	B	B	B	-	-	-	-	-	-	31
32	B	B	B	B	B	B	B	B	-	-	-	-	-	-	32
33	B	B	B	B	B	B	B	B	-	-	-	-	-	-	33
34	B	B	B	B	-	B	B	-	-	-	-	-	-	-	34
35	B	-	-	B	-	-	-	-	-	-	-	-	-	-	35
36	-	-	-	-	-	-	-	-	-	-	-	-	-	-	36
37	-	-	-	-	-	-	-	-	-	-	-	-	-	-	37

BG = stimuli presented in order (straight through) from blue to green
GB = stimuli presented in order (straight through) from green to blue
Rn = stimuli presented in random order
B[r] = reversal condition starting at blue
G[r] = reversal condition starting at green

Figure 5.14. Data from one subject for Part III of the experiment (pairwise condition). The two members of each pair were always categorized identically. For example, in the G[r] reversal condition, the subject started with the pair #5/#6 and categorized both patches as green. He then continued with green until the pair #14/#15, shifting to borderline at #15/#16. Hence the shared patch #15 was classified as green in the #14/#15 pair and as borderline in the #15/#16 pair. In addition, after reversing direction, the subject exhibited hysteresis, continuing to categorize the pairs as borderline until arriving back at the pair #10/#11, where he shifted back to green. See www.oup.com/us/raffman for color illustrations.

premises, when we reflect on their truth value, we think about only two neighboring items *pairwise*, together at the same time as it were, and mentally compare them. The results of Part III of the experiment suggest that when we do this, we always find ourselves inclined to place both items in the same category. This, I think, is the truth about tolerance: The tolerance of a vague word is a feature of its competent use with respect to incrementally different items considered pairwise—not a feature of its semantics strictly speaking. Perhaps we can say that tolerance is a pragmatic feature of vague words, embodying the commonsense precept that, all else being equal, like things should be treated alike. Maybe there is even a pragmatic rule something like this:

(Tol) For any vague expression 'Φ,' speaker S, and items x and y considered pairwise: If x and y differ incrementally on a dimension decisive of the application of 'Φ,' then if S classifies x as Φ, S should also classify y as Φ.

No paradox is spawned by Tol, since the minor premise and conclusion of the dynamic sorites refer to items considered individually. (And, of course, the minor premise and conclusion of the semantic sorites make no reference at all to how items are or should be classified by competent speakers.)

5.7. LOOKING BACK: RULES, REASONS, AND THE GOVERNING VIEW

Many philosophers think that reference to the causal psychological mechanisms involved in language production and comprehension cannot enter into a proper understanding or theoretical account of competent linguistic practice. For example, Louise Antony explains that, in Dummett's eyes,

> causal accounts of the mechanisms by which a speaker's lan-
> guage operates are simply irrelevant to an understanding of the
> speaker's implicit grasp of the nature of linguistic practice. Any
> move toward examination of the causal bases of linguistic behav-
> ior *necessarily* involves a shift from intentional to non-intentional
> terms of description—causal accounts of language use are thus,
> for him, always incommensurable with rationalistic accounts,
> and cannot be viewed as elaborations or supplementations of
> them. (1997, 198)

It is one thing to discount the significance of causal mechanisms for the semantics of vague words and quite another to discount their significance for a theory of competent use (the "practice"). According to the multiple range theory of vagueness, reference to underlying causal mechanisms provides more even than "elaboration" or "supplementation" of an account of use: As far as vague words are concerned, an account of competent linguistic practice just is in part a causal-mechanical story. It must be a partly causal-mechanical story because brute causal mechanism is what makes possible the arbitrariness essential to competent use. Brute causal mechanism is what enables competent speakers to classify incrementally different items differentially. It's not that incrementally different items cannot be classified differently, but rather that any such differential classification must be made *arbitrarily*, by a kind of psycholinguistic coin toss, if you will. And we can meet the latter requirement only if no rule specifies a particular stopping place in a sorites series. Stopping places must be determined mechanically. I said earlier that the idea of a rule dictating that we stop at no particular place may seem oxymoronic, but it is of the essence of vagueness.

Echoing Dummett, Sainsbury writes that

> any attempt to describe boundarylessness in…psychological or neurophysiological terms will…miss the normative features.…No such facts will begin to capture such aspects of the use of the word 'red' as the mandatoriness of its application in some central cases, the freedom available for borderlines, and such rules as that anything at least as red as a red thing is not merely likely to be called 'red' but ought to be so called. (1990, 263)

Sainsbury may be right about the mandatoriness of application in central cases, and the rule he mentions is correct if restricted to pairwise judgments; but he is wrong about the freedom available for borderlines (variable items, on our view).[20] In fact, I suspect that the *only* way to capture that freedom is to understand our classifications of variable items as the result of brute mechanical operations; here, freedom is arbitrariness. In addition, the smoothing effect of the psychological mechanism of hysteresis in our applications of vague words explains how a competent speaker is able to shift categories without disturbing the seamlessness of a sorites series. In the case of vague words, it is only by understanding certain aspects of the underlying machinery that we begin to understand how their semantics may be implemented in their competent use.

These remarks about the role of mechanism in a theory of vagueness bring us back, at last, to the governing view of competent language use (section 1.6). Recall that this traditional view consists of two theses (Wright, 1987): (i) competent language use is entirely rule-governed, and (ii) the rules in question are discoverable by means of various processes of rational (e.g., philosophical) self-reflection, independently of empirical investigation. Wright contends that the governing view is incoherent because those reflective processes deliver inconsistent rules—namely, a rule that says, for example, that if two items look the same in hue, then either both are blue or neither is, and a rule that says that items that look like patch #30 are green. In contrast, I suggest that, on the one hand, the first thesis of the governing view is too stringent; while on the other hand, Wright misstates the first of the two rules he cites. In fact, *most* (not all) of our competent use of vague words is governed by at least two fully consistent rules: first, a rule that any differential categorization of incrementally different items, in particular any stopping place in a sorites series, must be arbitrary, and second, Tol, a rule that incrementally different items should be categorized identically when considered pairwise. As far as I can see, these rules were discovered by the sorts of reflective procedures endorsed in the second thesis of the governing view. Tol may have required empirical testing for its confirmation, but not for its initial discovery. Moreover, given that I just stated these rules in ordinary English, we speakers can have propositional, personal-level knowledge of them, contrary to what Wright concludes.

At the same time, competent use of a vague expression cannot be wholly rule-governed; the first thesis of the governing view is incorrect. In a certain range of cases—what we have called the 'variable' cases—the rules give out; use floats free of its semantic moorings, and the application of a vague word is, from the viewpoint of semantics, anomalous. This is the point at which mechanism enters the practice. Thus competent use is not fully determined by the semantic theory. It is not the job of a semantic theory to fully describe, a fortiori to fully prescribe, the competent use of a vague word—not even relative to a given context or V-index.

This is not to say that, with respect to the variable cases at issue, our applications of vague words are irrational or unintelligible. It's not as if we are breaking rules, or attempting to follow inconsistent rules, as some theorists have suggested (e.g., Horgan 1995b). Recognizing that brute psychology must finally take over, Wright explains that the "(crazy) idea that competence [with a vague predicate] somehow accordingly involves *disrespecting* the rules is an artifact of a misplaced adherence to…an incoherent over-rationalisation of our practices" (2007, 20). (By 'over-rationalisation' Wright presumably means something like 'over-estimation of the scope of the rules of application for a vague word.'[21]) Moreover, the "purely mechanical" hysteresis observed in our experiment is a pattern or regularity in our unruly use of vague words that makes it more, rather than less, intelligible—even rational. Use wanders, but not incoherently. As Wright observes, recalling Wittgenstein, "not everything judged rationally is judged for reasons" (2007, 20).[22] Brute mechanism is what enables us to shift from one predicate to another without installing a sharp boundary in a sorites series and what enables our stopping places to be nonlegislative. Generally speaking, brute mechanism is what enables our discrete language to make contact with a seamless world.

APPENDIX

The following are some additional sentences for evaluation according to the multi-range semantics.

How do we evaluate the sentence

(S8) On December 15, 1684, J. S. Bach was bald

if we want to take account of the vagueness of both the predicate 'bald' and the name 'J. S. Bach'? (Recall that we take the vagueness of a proper name to be simply the vagueness of 'person' or 'individual'; see chapter 1, note 25.) Suppose that we are working with the V-index ⟨ developmental stage; conceptus; humans ⟩ for 'J. S. Bach'. Bach was born on March 21, 1685; so we can suppose that on December 15, 1684, his mother was in roughly her sixth month of pregnancy. Did the individual J. S. Bach exist on that date? The semantic tree for 'J. S. Bach' contains branches individuated by the name's ranges of application, where the latter are defined over an ordering of developmental stages beginning with, say, J. S. Bach at age ten on March 21, 1695, and proceeding by one-day increments back to Bach's conceptus on, say, June 21, 1684. The ranges of the name will be various segments of that ordering, each beginning with the ten-year-old and ending on a different day (see Figure A1). We can say that Bach existed relative to each branch whose V-extension contains the stage associated with December 15, 1684—here, the branches ending at October 14, November 3, and December 12, 1684. We can say that Bach existed relative to each branch whose V-extension contains the stage associated with December 15, 1684—here, the branches ending at October 14, November 3, and December 12, 1684.

Next, suppose that our V-index for 'bald' is ⟨ number of hairs; hairy; humans ⟩. To evaluate S8, we generate the Cartesian product of the set of branches in the 'J. S. Bach' tree and the set of branches in the 'bald' tree. There will be no siblings. S8 will be true relative to pairs that are such that the December 15, 1684, stage is in the V-extension of the 'J. S. Bach' branch and the number of hairs possessed by that stage is in the V-extension of the 'bald' branch.

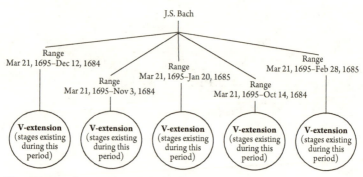

Figure A1. Part of a semantic tree for the name 'J. S. Bach'.

Sometimes a V-index will employ a vague predicate (other than the contrastive term) whose own ranges of application are relevant to the evaluation of a sentence. Consider for instance the sentence

(S9) Warren is generous compared to rich Americans

relative to the V-index ⟨percentage of salary donated to charity; <u>average</u>; rich Americans, 2001⟩. Whether S9 is true will depend partly upon what counts as being rich for an American, and 'rich' is vague. (Maybe 'American' is too, but set that aside.) Suppose we are using 'rich' relative to the V-index ⟨salary; <u>upper middle income</u>; Americans, 2001⟩ and working with the salaries from $250,000 to $50,000. Different ranges of 'rich' will contain different salaries, and a person will be rich relative to each semantic branch whose range of application includes her salary. The point is that the evaluation of S9 may depend upon which range of application of 'rich' is being employed. To reflect this dependence, we need to get the application of 'generous' to interact in the right way with the ranges of application of 'rich'.

A first pass at representing this interaction is shown in Figure A2. First we generate a semantic tree for 'rich' with the specified V-index. Then we have each branch from the latter tree generating a 'generous' tree. The fact that each 'generous' tree grows out of a branch from the 'rich' tree partly determines which branches grow in the 'generous' trees. Warren is generous relative a given 'generous' branch only if he donates a percentage of his salary that belongs to the range of application of 'generous' on that branch, i.e., only if his percentage is large compared to the percentage that rich Americans donate, where what counts as a rich American is specified by the relevant branch of 'rich'.

S10 implicates two sets of trees:

(S10) All violinists are musicians.

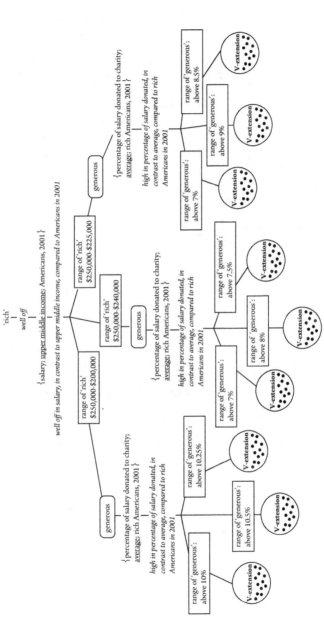

Figure A2. Part of a semantic tree for evaluating the sentence 'Warren is generous compared to rich Americans' relative to the V-index {salary; upper middle income; Americans, 2001} for 'rich' and the V-index {percentage of salary donated to charity; average; rich Americans, 2001} for 'generous'.

Unlike 'tall' and 'short', or 'rich' and 'middle income,' the predicates 'violinist' and 'musician' are not incompatibles; their relationship is more like that of species to genus or determinate to determinable. Nevertheless, the same evaluation procedure can be applied. Since S10 is presumably meant to hold for all relevant V-indices, it is evaluated relative to the permissible selected pairs of branches from the Cartesian product of the set of all branches from all trees for 'violinist' and the set of all branches from all trees for 'musician'. ('Violinist' and 'musician' could share for example the V-index { percentage of income derived from the relevant activity; <u>bus driver</u>; Russians in 1950}.) S10 will be true relative to every such pair in which every person who belongs to the V-extension of the 'violinist' branch also belongs to the V-extension of the 'musician' branch—namely, every permissible selected pair at every world.

S11 is another necessarily true sentence:

(S11) Anyone who is tall in contrast to average is neither short in contrast to average nor short in contrast to tall.

S11 implicates three sets of semantic trees: the set of all trees for 'tall in contrast to average', the set of all trees for 'short in contrast to average', and the set of all trees for 'short in contrast to tall.' Presumably all three predicates are to be relativized to the same V-index ({ height; 0; jockeys}, for one). Therefore, from the Cartesian product of the three sets of branches, we select those triples in which all three branches contain the same V-index. We then evaluate S11 relative to each permissible selected triple. S11 will turn out to be true relative to every permissible selected triple of branches at every world.

S12 implicates two semantic trees for 'black' whose V-indices differ in their respect coordinates:

(S12) Mimi's fur is black in contrast to brown and in contrast to grey.

Suppose the operative V-indices are { hue; 0; cat fur} and { whiteness; 0; cat fur}, respectively. Since these V-indices are not siblings, S12 will be evaluated relative to every pair of branches from the Cartesian product of the two sets of branches from the two trees. As far as 'black' is concerned, S12 will be true relative to those pairs of branches in which Mimi's fur belongs to both V-extensions, and false otherwise.

As far as I can see, the predicate in S13 is neither vague nor V-index-sensitive:

(S13) Joe is tall relative to branch b in semantic tree t.

Suppose that 'b' and 't' refer to the leftmost branch in Figure 4.8 on page 115. It is difficult to see how the predicate 'tall relative to branch b, etc.' could permit arbitrarily variable application. If that's right, then it does not have multiple ranges of application and is not vague. S13 is true only if Joe's height is contained in the range of application on branch b in tree t.

NOTES

Chapter 1

1. Nonlinguistic symbols too can be indeterminate in a way that differs from being vague. Consider for example a stick figure: ⚦ Is the represented person male or female? dressed or undressed? bald or hairy? There is no fact of the matter, but the figure seems nonspecific rather than vague.
2. I insert the hyphen in 'not-Φ' only to avoid scope ambiguities. This practice can cause confusions of its own, though, so let me emphasize that 'not-Φ' just means whatever 'not Φ' means.
3. Some theorists of vagueness think that soriticality follows from (or even consists in) possession of borderline cases; for example, Andrei Marmor contends that

> when a word, W, is vague, there are bound to be borderline cases of W's application to objects . . . about which there is no saying whether W applies or not. In other words, if W is vague then we are bound to have a sorites sequence. (2012, 3)

   I think the connection cannot be that tight, for reasons that will emerge.
4. See, for example,. Dummett 1975. See also Dominic Hyde's entry on the sorites paradox in the *Stanford Encyclopedia of Philosophy* (2011) for an illuminating overview of different formulations of the puzzle. Presumably an adequate solution will resolve all of them.
5. The term 'boundaryless' comes from Sainsbury 1990.

NOTES

6. Machina's theory is truth-functional; Edgington's is not. Halldén (1949), Zadeh (1965, 1975), Cook (2002), and Smith (2008) are some others who have defended multivalued approaches to vagueness.
7. Truth *simpliciter* or 'super-truth' is ordinary truth, for the supervaluationist. Strictly speaking, precisifications precisify whole languages, not just individual predicates. But we can be informal here.
8. Kamp (1981), Horgan (1995b), and Soames (2002) are some others who have defended contextualist accounts of vagueness; see also Pinkal (1983, 1995) and Manor (1995). Kamp is widely regarded as the originator of this approach. Akerman (2012) provides helpful discussion.
9. Williamson allows that God may know the locations of the sharp boundaries of a vague word (1994, 212). The opening passage from Genesis seems to leave the matter up in the air.
10. As you might expect, the four families of theories sketched here have spawned all sorts of hybrids. For instance, Kamp (1975) combines supervaluational and degree-theoretic elements, and Graff (2000) puts contextualism together with epistemicism. Perhaps we should also distinguish a small family of pragmatic approaches to vagueness and the sorites; see e.g. Lewis (1979), Burns (1991), and Van Kerkhove (2003). Burns follows Lewis in defending a pragmatic theory that is supposed to be classical. I do not fully understand this approach, but my impression is that insofar as it acknowledges the possibility of borderline cases, it collapses into supervaluationism (see Keefe 2000, chapter 6, for discussion). Unger (1979) retains a classical logic and semantics for vague words but at the cost of claiming that they are referentially vacuous.
11. Specifically, scalar adjectives; see for example Jason Stanley's discussion of Graff's view (2005a, 170).
12. Incomprehensibly, some have assumed a great deal more than that. After reviewing the four families of theories discussed above, Keefe writes,

> I do not think that there is any hope for as yet undiscovered alternatives differing radically from [these theories]. So although I may not have eliminated, or provided comparisons with, every possible account of vagueness, I maintain that I have dealt with all those with any plausibility. (2000, 152)

13. For now I will go along with the usual practice of speaking interchangeably of *having blurred boundaries* and *lacking sharp boundaries*, but there will be reasons to distinguish the two; see chapter 4, section 4.6.
14. Actually Ebbs distinguishes between 'weak' and 'strong' senses of 'sharp boundary.' The one defined here is the weak sense; see Ebbs (2001, 306).
15. In chapter 3 I will be more specific about what I mean by a 'context.' For now I use the term in a relaxed way to refer to factors like comparison class and contrastive category. In particular I do not intend any of the technical senses of the

notion employed in Raffman (1994, 1996) or Shapiro (2007). As will become clear, I am not advancing a contextualist theory of vagueness.

16. An informal version of the paradox, called the "forced march" or "dynamic" sorites, is framed in terms of classifications made by a competent speaker who proceeds step by step along a sorites series. I will make a lot of this version of the puzzle in chapter 5 in connection with the competent *use* of vague words, as distinct from their semantics strictly speaking.

17. The anti-extension of 'Φ' is just the extension of 'not Φ'.

18. Kennedy (1999) makes the same observation but for different reasons.

19. For linguists: A Google search for the expression 'more medium than' yielded 501 results, of which the vast majority did not contain comparative uses of 'medium.' Some examples:

His legacy is **more medium than** message.

Notley is **more medium than** poet.

For good aeration, don't use **more medium than** 20% of the total flask volume.

One apparently comparative use was:

[A] speed of 0.1 (pu) is **more medium than** a speed of 0.5 (pu).

But plausibly the writer here means that a speed of 0.1 is *closer to being* medium, or is a *better example* of a medium speed, than a speed of 0.5. A Google search for 'less medium than' yielded seventeen results. Only one seemed to contain a comparative form of 'medium':

[I like a] filet or top sirloin... done medium though maybe a little **less medium than** the ribeye.

But here the writer probably means that she wants the top sirloin cooked to a point farther from medium (i.e., more rare, less well done) than the ribeye. (Unlike 'medium,' the predicates 'rare' and 'well done' are gradable.) Again this doesn't seem to be a comparative use of 'medium.'

More plausible uses can be found for 'very medium'. For example, at www. tripadvisor.com, we find a review referring to "a noisy and very medium quality restaurant".

To my ear, though, these uses of 'medium' don't sound genuinely comparative. A "very medium quality" restaurant is very clearly or very consistently medium as opposed to good. Of course these examples don't show conclusively that 'medium' isn't gradable, but they are suggestive.

20. Thanks to Phil Serchuk for this objection.

21. Here I am grateful to Terry Horgan for discussion.

22. See Shapiro (2007, 4) for relevant discussion.

23. An anonymous referee for Oxford University Press wonders whether 'vague' is polysemous, that is, whether there are different kinds of vagueness—one consisting in soriticality, one in possession of borderlines, one in gradability, and

so on. Of course I cannot rule out this possibility, but prima facie the existence of a single theory that accounts for all of the cases at issue would be reason to think that a single phenomenon is at work. My aim, like that of most theorists of vagueness, is to provide such a theory.

24. Whereas Wright recoils from this conflict, Horgan (1995b) embraces it.

25. There is disagreement as to whether indexicals and demonstratives are vague; see for example Ellis (2004) and Gert (2008). Ordinary proper names are also sometimes said to be vague. Russell offers the following charming example, which seems to suggest as much:

> Mr. Ebenezer Wilkes Smith was born, and being born is a gradual process. It would seem natural to suppose that the name was not attributable before birth; if so, there was doubt, while birth was taking place, whether the name was attributable. . . . If . . . the name was attributable before birth, . . . no one can decide how long before birth the name became attributable. . . . There must gradually come a stage . . . when the name [becomes] attributable, but no one can say precisely when this stage has been reached. (1999, 63)

However, consider that the issue in Russell's example is not whether the organism in question was Ebenezer Wilkes Smith as opposed to somebody else, but whether it was Ebenezer Wilkes Smith as opposed to no one at all. This suggests that what's actually vague is not the name itself but rather the underlying concept 'person' or 'individual,' upon which the application of the name 'EWS' depends. For present purposes, then, I will suppose that proper names per se are not vague. (This needn't mean that they are precise; maybe they are neither vague nor precise. See my remarks about 'true' on p. 128.) What turns on this point is the question of whether all vague words are context-sensitive; arguably, proper names are not context-sensitive. Names shared by multiple objects or individuals, such as 'John Smith' and 'Mary Jones,' can seem to be context-sensitive since contextual information may be needed to determine which John Smith or Mary Jones we are talking about. But we could eliminate the context-sensitivity by, say, using subscripts to give everyone a unique name.

26. One might think that 'tolerance' is a term of art and that Wright can define it however he likes. However, I believe that Wright means not to introduce a stipulative definition but rather to pick out a natural linguistic phenomenon he observes—namely, whatever feature vague words have that makes them appear to generate a sorites paradox—and whose nature he seeks to elucidate by defining 'tolerance' as he does. Similarly, a scientist might introduce a name for an observed natural phenomenon and propose an initial, defeasible definition of it. There is the possibility of discovering that the phenomenon has a nature different from the one initially envisioned. I believe that my analysis of 'tolerance' gets closer to the true nature of the phenomenon than Wright's definition does.

The predicate 'borderline' is sometimes defined and employed by theorists of vagueness as a term of art. For instance, degree theorists may define a borderline case as an item of which 'x is Φ' is true to some degree intermediate between zero and 1; and supervaluationists suppose that a borderline case is an item of which 'x is Φ' is neither true on all complete admissible precisifications nor false on all. (Presumably the latter analyses are meant to be at least coextensive with the ordinary meaning of 'borderline'—whatever exactly that may be.) In contrast, my goal is to provide an analysis that comes as close as possible to the sense of the term 'borderline' in ordinary English (i.e., to what ordinary speakers have in mind).

27. There is no shortage of controversy as to what linguistic competence consists in. For example, is it a form of tacit propositional knowledge of linguistic rules? Does it require knowledge of a semantic theory of the language? Is it causally efficacious in the production of linguistic behavior? (See e.g. Matthews 2003 for a helpful discussion.) As I indicated with respect to the governing view, the theory proposed here will provide support for the idea that competent speakers have propositional knowledge of certain rules governing the use of vague words, but we need a theory-neutral conception of competence to start with. I think we can say simply that a competent speaker is one whose use of a language comports largely with the rules governing that use; similarly, *mutatis mutandis*, for competence with a particular term. (Competence is not infallibility, of course.) In some instances it may suffice to say that a competent speaker is someone who speaks and understands English (for example). However the term is defined, I'm pretty sure that I am a competent speaker, and so are you.

Chapter 2

1. From Snell's obituary by Charles Champlin in *The Los Angeles Times:* http:// articles.latimes.com/1987-07-09/entertainment/ca-2867_1_rubber-stamp.

   Much (though not all) of the material in this chapter has appeared previously in 2005a and 2009. I thank the *Philosophical Review* and Oxford University Press for permission.

2. See Keefe and Smith (1997, 1–57) for a guide to different versions of the standard analysis of borderline cases. Contrary to the usual practice, I do not suppose that a semantic conception of borderline cases just is a version of the standard analysis that interprets the definiteness operator semantically (as in the text above). I emphasize this point because the view I will propose is genuinely semantic but does not employ a definiteness operator.

3. Given my definition of 'Φ-ordering,' I do not say that an ordering on a relevant dimension, for example height, is a height-ordering. A height-ordering would be an ordering from an item that has a height to an item that does not. Rather, a tall-ordering on the decisive dimension of height is an ordering *of*

heights—in other words an ordering of items all of which have a height. Similarly, our blue-ordering is an ordering of hues and our rich-ordering an ordering of salaries.

4. Endicott introduces the apt expression 'extravagantly vague' to characterize legal predicates that are multidimensionally vague (2011, 24–25).

5. I say 'may be' because presumably other dimensions, not discussed here, would need to be considered as well.

6. Two points are worth keeping in mind. First, a Φ-ordering differs from a sorites series for 'Φ' in that a sorites series must contain only finitely many items, and each item must be incrementally different from the next. A Φ-ordering that defines borderline cases for 'Φ' needn't satisfy either of these conditions. Second, the existence or possibility of a Φ-ordering does not show that 'Φ' is gradable: A Φ-ordering is just a linear ordering of values on a dimension decisive of the application of 'Φ.' So, for example, a medium-ordering would be an ordering of shirt sizes, or cooking temperatures, or heights. I suppose we could even say that a 6-foot-ordering is an ordering of heights progressing from six feet to any other height. (See again the penultimate paragraph of section 1.3.)

7. Here especially I am indebted to Terry Horgan for helpful discussion.

8. The symbol '*' is not used here as a functor. 'Blue*' is a variable that stands in for the various incompatibles of 'blue,' namely, 'green,' 'blue green,' 'red,' 'pink,' etc.; 'rich*' stands in for 'middle income,' 'upper middle income,' 'poor,' etc.

9. See for example Barsalou (1983) for evidence of the robustness of what he calls 'ad hoc categories.' His examples are predicates like 'things to take on a camping trip' and 'places to look for antique desks' and 'ways to escape being killed by the mafia.'

10. However, I do claim that *vagueness* is defined in terms of the permissibility of variable classifications; see chapter 4.

11. I should note, though, that Shapiro's is meant to be a stipulative definition of 'borderline' as a term of art, whereas Wright's target (like mine), if I understand him, is the ordinary meaning of the word 'borderline' in English.

12. Thanks to John Collins for requesting this clarification.

13. It is an interesting question why 'rich' should have borderline cases while 'not-rich' does not. The heterogeneous character of the extension of 'not-rich,' even within a given not-rich-ordering, is surely significant. (Several audience members have asked how my view accommodates tall [towering] borderline cases. The answer is that there are no such cases, no matter how 'borderline' is defined, since all towering things are tall.)

14. McGee and McLaughlin (1994) could have supposed that Tarmin had enough canine characteristics to ensure that 'dog' and 'wolf' were the only extant predicates in the running, as it were—but not that she was either a dog or a wolf.

If she was neither definitely a dog nor definitely a wolf, as they claim, then she was neither a dog nor a wolf, and a new category was needed; see chapter 4, note 26.

15. I use 'blue green' to name the hue category between *blue* and *green*, 'blue blue green' for the hue between *blue* and *blue green*, and so on. 'Blue green' and other incompatibles of 'blue' are to be distinguished from predicates like 'ultramarine' and 'indigo,' which name determinates, not incompatibles, of blue. (Ultramarine and indigo are presumably incompatibles of each other, not of blue.) I take it the proposed disjunction would not include any determinates. I thank Rob Koons and Nicholas Asher for discussion of this point.

A bit of trivia illustrates that terms like 'blue green' may be in use in ordinary language. A hue called 'blue green' was introduced into the Crayola crayon box in 1949, in addition to the hues blue and green, and to the best of my knowledge remains in the box of 120 hues available today. Also included are orange yellow, yellow orange, red orange, and red violet. The box included a further distinct hue called 'orange red' from 1949 until 1990.

16. Here one is reminded of the passage from Dummett (1997) cited above, pp. 33–34.

17. After completing this work, I learned that Haim Gaifman makes a similar proposal in his 2010, 35–37.

18. For that matter, if an indefinite hierarchy of borderline cases were required for blurred boundaries, then there would be sharp cut-offs in a sorites series. No one who thinks that vagueness is semantic will go along with that.

19. Sainsbury (1997) blames the reappearance of sharp boundaries on the appeal to sets. But it is important to appreciate that virtually all theories of vagueness arrive ultimately at some tripartite classification or other (which may or may not result in, or reflect, sharp boundaries). Most theories must confront the fact that, on pain of incoherence, there can be no borderline cases between the items of which 'x is Φ' is true and the items of which 'x is Φ' is untrue, where by 'untrue' I mean *anything other than true*. Even Sainsbury himself, who aims to abolish boundaries altogether by conceiving of satisfaction of a vague predicate on the model of attraction to a magnetic pole, allows that 'some objects cluster firmly to one pole, some to another, and some, though sensitive to the forces, join no cluster' (1997, 258). I owe this observation about Sainsbury to Jack Arnold.

20. Again, unlike some other theorists, I do not define borderline cases in terms of permissible variability of classification. Rather, anything that can competently be classified as borderline, that is, as not-Φ and as not-Φ^*, can also competently be classified as Φ and as Φ^*; cf. p. 41.

21. I have avoided talk of our *knowing* that a borderline case is not-Φ and not-Φ^*. This is not because I think that any facts about borderline cases are hidden from us but rather because certain features of the semantics of vague predicates call

into question whether our "access" to borderline cases is properly called 'knowledge.' See pp. 100–101.

22. For illustration and discussion of the agonies see, for example, Wright 1987, 228–234; Heck 1993; Keefe 2000, 26–36, 208–211; Fara 2003.

23. Here and throughout I use the term 'average' in its informal sense of 'in the middle' or 'typical,' not its mathematical sense.

24. Though I don't fully understand her sophisticated view, I believe that Susanne Bobzien (2013) has made a structurally analogous proposal in terms of contradictories, employing the standard analysis of 'borderline' rather than an incompatibilist one.

Chapter 3

1. The idea that one or another type of linguistic expression contains a (perhaps hidden) indexical element is popular these days. It has been adapted to secondary quality terms (e.g., Soames 1998), moral terms (e.g., Dreier 1990), and epistemic operators (e.g., DeRose 1992), among others.

2. I am grateful to Trevor Teitel for extensive commentary on this chapter in particular.

3. More fully: "The character of 'I' [is] represented by the function… that assigns to each context that content which is represented by the constant function from possible worlds to the agent of the context" (Kaplan 1978, 403).

4. A context may also include, as needed, an addressee (the referent of 'you'), a class of which the speaker is a member (the referent of 'we'), a place distinct from the location of the speaker (the referent of 'there'), and so forth. Although Kaplan's treatment of indexicals has its critics (e.g., Lewis 1980, Reimer 1991, Salmon 2002, Caplan 2003, Schiffer 2005, King 2012), many philosophers of language accept some version of it. See Braun 2007 for an extremely helpful survey of the issues.

5. Strictly speaking, Kaplan's theory concerns not utterances but rather what he calls 'occurrences' of a word or sentence in a given context, or 'sentences-in-a-context.' For example, it is in the first instance an occurrence of 'I will be queen,' in a context whose speaker is Elizabeth, that expresses the content *that Elizabeth will be queen,* and the occurrence can be understood and evaluated whether or not she actually utters the sentence.

6. See Dever (2004) for criticism of the usual view that the character of an indexical expression is autonomous from the content.

7. I have been talking as if the notion of stable content is uncontroversial, but the nature, even the existence, of such an element of meaning is disputed. For example, is it fully propositional, that is (roughly), is it truth-evaluable as it stands? If not, what sort of content is it, and what sort of supplementation or enrichment

does it need? Can the distinction between stable and context-relative contents be drawn within semantics, or does it straddle the semantics/pragmatics divide (wherever that is)? (Preyer and Peter 2005 provides a good overview of the issues.) Joining these debates would take us off on a tangent, so I am going to be as frugal as I can and simply help myself to a pair of suppositions that should be adequate for constructing a theory of sense for vague words. I will suppose (i) that a context-sensitive vague predicate has a stable content of the sort I have described and (ii) that contextual factors operate on that stable content to yield richer, context-relative contents. If either (i) or (ii) is faulty, my theory of sense will need to be revised, but as I have said, this will not affect the theory of vagueness.

8. See, for example, Soames (2002), Stanley (2005b), and Raffman (2005b) for relevant discussion.

9. Often the conversation preceding an utterance, or even the expressions contained in the utterance itself, make the relevant factors explicit. For instance, the sentence 'Federer is a brilliant tennis player,' which uses the predicate 'brilliant' attributively, specifies its own comparison class. See, for example, Szabo (2001) in this connection.

10. The contrastive or opposed category need not be an incompatible. For example, one might say that Federer is a player in contrast to a coach; but one could be both.

11. For doubts about the role of comparison classes altogether, see Kyburg and Morreau (2000).

12. I don't mean that speakers must have contrastive categories or comparison classes and so on consciously in mind when they apply vague terms—though pragmatic considerations may sometimes require that they make those contextual factors explicit. See above.

13. See also Reimer (1991, 1992), Recanati (2000), Bach (2006), King (2012) for relevant discussion.

14. See also Caplan (2003) in this regard.

15. See Cohen (forthcoming) for an illuminating survey of responses to the apparent "impurities" in certain uses of "pure" indexicals.

16. 'Sole' may be too strong. For example, King (2012) writes: "An object o is the value of an occurrence of a demonstrative just in case the speaker intends o to be the value *and the speaker successfully reveals her intention*" (2012, 8; emphasis added). Maybe something analogous is required in the case of a vague word.

17. Again, in this connection see, for example, Bach (2006) and King (2012) on indexicals.

18. For allied views, see also Bach (2006) and Schiffer (2005).

19. It may be helpful to distinguish between two kinds of conclusions that a hearer can draw about the meaning of an occurrence of a vague predicate on the basis of pragmatic information supplied by a context. First, that information may help

a hearer to figure out which content of a predicate is expressed, by helping him to decide which V-index the speaker has chosen to use. Second, recovering that information may enable the hearer to ascertain the speaker's broader communicative intentions—for example, to ascertain that when her partner says, "It's late," he means it's time to leave the party and go home.

Chapter 4

1. Again, experimental evidence to support this claim will come in chapter 5.
2. Of course we may sometimes need to negotiate precise boundaries or accommodate another speaker's stopping place for purposes of smooth communication (see, e.g., Lewis 1979, Shapiro 2006, Richard 2008).
3. I thank George Pappas for pressing this question.
4. For convenience I will suppose that the ranges of a vague word 'Φ' are defined over replete Φ-orderings (cf. section 2.2); specifically, I will suppose that a range of application of 'Φ' is a segment of a replete Φ-ordering to whose values 'Φ' can competently be applied. (A replete Φ-ordering, recall, contains all possible values that can be linearly ordered on a decisive dimension between a Φ value and a not-Φ value; for example, a replete ordering of salaries from \$200,000 (rich) to \$50,000 (not-rich) contains all possible salaries that can be linearly ordered between those two amounts.) I say 'for convenience' because, as I noted in chapter 2, the extensions of some vague words may be only partially ordered; hence the values in their ranges of application may be only partially ordered as well. 'Big' and 'nice' were the examples we discussed.
5. It will turn out that having a single extension relative to a given V-index at a given world, corresponding to a single competent way of being applied or a single competent stopping place, is what having sharp boundaries consists in; see section 4.3.
6. But only by philosophers, interestingly—never by linguists or psychologists. I suspect the latter would regard the error-theoretic proposal as perverse.
7. For that matter, such an error theory would seem to entail some form of epistemicism about vagueness.
8. Contrast Shapiro (2007), pages 36–44, for example.
9. The introduction of ranges of application reveals that a further coordinate may be needed in a V-index. Sometimes, in order for a given V-index-relative content of a vague predicate 'Φ' to determine multiple ranges of application, the V-index in question must specify not only a contrastive category but also what I will call a *flanking* category to which 'Φ' is contrasted "on the other side," as it were. For instance, suppose we are using the predicate 'blue' with the V-index $\{$ hue; green; 0 $\}$. A range of application of 'blue' for that V-index is supposed to

contain the blues in a replete linear ordering of hues, relative to that V-index. The V-index tells us that at one end of each range the blues will be flanked by (contrasted to) greens, but what about the other end? Are the blues flanked by reds, or violets, or blue-violets, or what? The answer matters because 'blue' will have different ranges of application when contrasted with 'violet' than when contrasted with 'blue-violet,' for example. Thus in order to specify fully a range of application for 'blue,' we may need to include a coordinate for a flanking category—as in, say, $\{$ hue; <u>green,</u> <u>violet;</u> 0 $\}$. The content determined by the latter V-index will determine ranges of application of 'blue' in which the blues are delimited on one side by greens and on the other side by violets. The V-index $\{$ hue; <u>green,</u> <u>blue-violet;</u> 0 $\}$ will determine ranges in which the blues are delimited on one side by greens and on the other side by blue-violets. (The latter ranges of application will be on average narrower than the former, since blue-violet is nearer to blue than violet is. We could say that the latter V-index sets a higher standard for being blue.) In contrast, the predicate 'tall' cannot have an "upper" flanking category, since any height taller than a tall height is also tall. For present purposes we won't get into trouble if we omit the flanking category coordinate.

10. Intuitively, unlike precisifications, ranges do not undergo completion; ranges are complete ab initio and contain only items (values) that satisfy the predicate.

11. A sorites series for the predicate 'range of application of "Φ"' would be a series of orderings progressing incrementally from one that is a range of application of 'Φ' to one that is not. For instance, a sorites series for the predicate 'range of application of "rich"' relative to Vinny could proceed by $1 increments from the ordering $200,000 to $150,000, which is a range of application of 'rich,' to the ordering $200,000 to $50,000, which is not. And you and I could permissibly vary in our stopping places in that series. (Relative to Vinny, the ordering $200,000 to $50,000 is a rich-ordering but not a range of application of 'rich.' A rich-ordering extends to a not-rich value, whereas a range of 'rich' contains only rich values.)

12. This example was provided by an anonymous referee for Oxford University Press.

13. A referee for Oxford University Press writes, "I guess it would follow, on your view, that 'person' is not vague (or not as vague as one might think) since people who are pro-life and some who are pro-choice give reasons for putting the boundary where they do." But 'person' is vague on my view: Conception is a process—there is no "moment of conception"—and if we made the increments in that process small enough, even the pro-life side would be forced to choose arbitrarily a particular moment as the inception of personhood. To put the point another way, the reasons given by those who "give reasons for putting the boundary where they do" are not reasons to put the boundary at a certain moment in gestation rather than, for example, a nanosecond earlier or later. They are reasons

to put the boundary at conception rather than at birth, for example, or at the quickening rather than at conception. So the provision of reasons in such cases does not call into question the vagueness of the term.

14. We will investigate this idea further in chapter 5, when we consider some pragmatic aspects of vague words.

15. You may wonder whether relativity to ranges of application is itself a form of V-index-relativity, since both ranges and V-indices are, or consist of, factors with which the extensions of vague predicates vary. The two species of relativity are importantly different, however. We will be better positioned to appreciate the difference after I have said more about the *use* of ranges of application in chapter 5.

16. The V-extension of 'not-rich' picked out by a given branch is just the complement of the V-extension of 'rich' on that branch. Remember that, on our incompatibilist understanding of borderline cases, the V-extensions of 'not-rich' will include any borderline cases of 'rich'; and Excluded Middle holds.

17. The Cartesian product of two sets A and B is the set of all ordered pairs of the form (a, b) where a is an element of A and b is an element of B. The Cartesian product of three sets A, B, and C is the set of all ordered triples of the form (a, b, c) where a is an element of A, b an element of B, and c an element of C, and so on.

18. My talk of 'sibling branches' and 'sibling trees' is short for talk about branches and trees that contain sibling V-indices.

19. In this respect, ranges of application have something in common with precisifications. For example, Keefe and Smith explain that

> precisifications must meet certain constraints: in particular, sentences that are unproblematically true (false) before precisification should stay true (false) afterwards. This applies not just to simple predications like 'Arnie is tall,' but also to general statements such as 'anyone taller than a tall person is also tall' and 'no one who is tall is short.' These statements certainly seem to be true. To preserve the first, there can be no acceptable precisification of 'tall' according to which (say) people who are 5'10" are tall but people who are 5'11" are not. [Similarly,] we cannot sharpen 'tall' so that someone of 5'0" counts as tall while simultaneously sharpening 'short' so that someone of that height also counts as short. (1997, 23)

Ranges of application on sibling branches are analogously constrained.

20. If we handle S3 in the manner just described, then we are working with non-lexical predicates. And we cannot say that the stable content shared by the various V-index-relative contents of 'rich in contrast to middle income'— for example, the V-index-relative contents *rich in contrast to middle income, compared to Americans aged forty to sixty in 2001*, and *rich in contrast to middle income, compared to Russians in the early 20th century*—is roughly the

dictionary definition of 'rich in contrast to middle income.' This shouldn't present a problem, however. What's important is that the V-index-relative contents just cited share the stable content *rich in contrast to middle income*, and we can suppose that the latter is (somehow) composed of the stable contents of its parts.

21. Multidimensional vagueness *may* result in a kind of essential contestedness, but I am not sure of this; see Waldron 2002 for illuminating discussion and, again, section 4.3.

22. Of course, something could be tall relative to one index and short relative to another.

23. See again Figure 5.6 on page 148. The distinction between central and non-central (peripheral?) blues is not the distinction between clear and borderline cases. A central blue is just a shade of blue relatively near to pure or unique blue. The most central blue in a set of shades of blue, for example in a sorites series, is the 'bluest' one, namely, the one that is most similar to pure or unique blue.

24. Of course, applying 'Φ' to the first item in a sorites series but not to the second would be incorrect, in addition to arbitrary.

25. Wright considers but then dismisses the idea that an expression could lack sharp boundaries without being soritical:

> the antiquity of the paradox bears witness to how easy it is to interpret [lack of sharp boundaries] as involving the possession by these predicates of a principle of reapplication through marginal change. But is this a correct interpretation? If 'heap,' for example, lacks sharp boundaries, then certainly we are not equipped to single out any particular transition from n to n–1 grains of salt as being the decisive step in changing a heap into a non-heap; no one such step is decisive. But that is not to say that such a step always *preserves* application of the predicate. Would it not be better to assimilate the situation to that in which borderline states fail to agree upon a common frontier? Their failure to reach agreement does not vindicate the notion that e.g. a single pace in the direction of the other country always keeps one in the original country. For they have at least agreed that there is to be a borderline, that *some* such step is to be a decisive one; what they have not agreed is where. If we regard [vague] predicates...in the terms of this model, we shall conclude that their vagueness is purely a reflection of our intellectual laziness. (1999, 157)

The present discussion suggests that an appeal to laziness isn't the only way to explain how a term lacking sharp boundaries could fail to be soritical.

26. In the case of a creature like McGee and McLaughlin's Tarmin (cf. p. 35), who is supposed to be neither definitely a dog nor definitely a wolf, presumably the scientists would conclude that Tarmin is neither a dog nor a wolf but rather an

instance of a newly discovered species. They cannot conclude either that she is a dog or that she is a wolf, for if she is a dog (wolf), she is definitely a dog (wolf).

Notice that natural kind terms don't even *seem* soritical: Why think that incrementally different creatures in a progression from dog to wolf, or incrementally different plants in a progression from strawberry to raspberry, must belong to the same species? For what it's worth, natural kind predicates don't appear to be gradable, either. For example, the early stages in a dog/wolf ordering do not have a greater amount of doghood than the later stages. An earlier stage may be closer to being a dog, or more similar to a dog, but not *more of a dog*. Here it is worth remembering that association with a linear ordering of values on a decisive dimension is not sufficient for either gradability or vagueness; for example, the precise expression '5 feet 8 inches tall' is associated with a linear ordering on the decisive dimension of height.

27. See Shapiro (2007, 10–11, e.g.) for illuminating development of the notion of open texture in the context of a theory of vagueness.

28. I foreshadowed this distinction in chapter 1, note 13.

29. Actually Fine uses the expression 'true$_T$' in this passage, not 'true' *simpliciter*, because he distinguishes between truth in a precisification (truth$_T$) and truth in all (admissible) precisifications (super-truth). On the multi-range theory, ordinary truth, which is relative to a range of application, is understood in a way that is closer to Fine's truth$_T$ (cf. p. 103)

30. There is controversy as to whether 'true' is best regarded as a predicate or as an operator, among other things (see, e.g., Künne 2003, Mulligan 2010, and Moltmann forthcoming for discussion). We can remain neutral on that question here.

31. A range of application of 'Φ' is a competent way of applying 'Φ'; so if 'range of application of "Φ"' is not vague, neither is 'competent way of applying "Φ."' (For example, 'competent way of applying "prime number"' is precise.) In contrast, 'competent' in 'competent speaker' is presumably vague; in the latter use, the vagueness of 'competent' does not derive from the vagueness of another term. Similarly, compare 'mandates application of "Φ"' and 'mandates punishment,' for example.

32. In section 2.4 I suggested some logically innocuous conceptions of indeterminacy that might apply to borderline cases and variable items.

Chapter 5

1. Here I enlist an idea introduced in Kamp (1975, 1981) and later developed in the contextualist frameworks of Raffman (1994, 1995), Graff (2000), and Shapiro (2007). My use of it here is quite different from the contextualists'.

2. Hysteresis is a hallmark of dynamical systems: "hysteresis occurs when a phase transition in one direction...does not occur at the same value of the control

parameter as a transition in the opposite direction" (Vallacher and Nowak [1994, 120]).

3. The duration of the vowel and the pause are lengthened at the phrase boundary in P(KB). Here Raczaszek et al. (1999) cite Scott (1982).

4. Donald Hubin points out that we can think of the switching of a cell phone signal among different towers in a similar way (personal communication).

5. http://karting.4cycle.com/archive/index.php?t-183077.html

6. Since the term 'subpersonal' is so often misused, let me clarify. Subpersonal states or processes are states or processes of parts of persons rather than of persons. So, for example, edge detection is a subpersonal process: Edge detection is something your edge detectors do, not something *you* do. *You* do not perform Fourier analysis on acoustic wave forms; subpersonal mechanisms in your auditory system do. Because subpersonal processes are not conscious, 'subpersonal' is often taken, wrongly, to mean 'unconscious.' But many unconscious states and processes are personal. For example, *you*— not merely some subpersonal parts of you—have an unconscious wish to kill your father and marry your mother, and *you* have repressed memories. To my knowledge, the first use of the term 'subpersonal' occurs in Dennett (1978).

7. 331 Ovalwood Hall, 1760 University Drive, Mansfield, OH 44906; Lindsey.43@osu.edu.

8. College of Optometry, The Ohio State University, Fry Hall, 338 W 10th Avenue, Columbus, OH 43210-1240, USA; brown.112@osu.edu.

9. See, for example, Hardin (1988) and Raffman (1995) for discussion and references.

10. Consecutive stimuli differed in hue by less than the just noticeable difference (jnd) of our most sensitive subject. We had determined that smallest jnd in an earlier study.

11. See again the entry from *The Oxford English Dictionary* that heads this chapter.

12. Also, this expert subject had not participated in the earlier study to establish our subjects' smallest jnd, so he may have been able to detect the difference in hue between adjacent stimuli and hence to detect the reversal of direction.

13. We can also plausibly rule out at least one kind of response bias, since we found no correlation between starting place and initial shifting place within conditions. (Recall that the starting patch varied at random among the different conditions.) Among other things, later starting patches were not correlated with later shifting patches.

14. As I indicated, we cannot at present think of a way of testing our hypothesis with stimuli other than perceptual values varying along a single continuous dimension. We would be delighted to learn otherwise. (Kalmus's [1979] conclusion that the enhanced contrast he observed was cortical rather than retinal tends to

support the idea that the hysteresis we observed was judgmental, i.e., involved categorization.)

15. In a 1977 paper in *Urban Studies*, P. B. Goodwin of London's Department of Planning and Transportation proposed that the phenomenon of magnetic hysteresis may provide a model of commuters' decisions whether to travel to work by bus or by car. (See the following diagram, simplified from Goodwin [1977, 96].) The x-axis ('G') represents the difference between the cost of travel by the two modes (car being more expensive), while the y-axis ('P_i') represents the probability that an individual will take the bus.

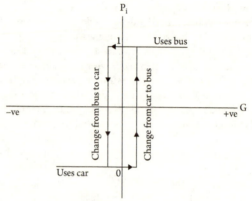

P_i = probability of using bus
G = difference in cost between car and bus (+ or −)

P_i = probability of using bus
G = difference in cost between car and bus (+ or −)
For our purposes, the important feature of the diagram is that a shift from car to bus occurs at a greater differential cost than does a shift from bus back to car. For example, if an individual switches from car to bus when the cost differential is £10, and then the differential increases to £15, she will not revert to her car when the differential drops to just below £10. Rather, further reduction in the differential price of taking the car will be required.

16. Contra Shapiro (2007), for instance.

17. An anonymous referee asks whether the notion that multiple ranges of application are determined by each sense or content of a vague word amounts to a form of *nonindexical contextualism* (e.g., MacFarlane [2007]). Roughly, nonindexical contextualism holds that the extension, not the content, of a context-sensitive word is what varies with context. Despite a certain structural similarity, I think my view is not plausibly understood in this way; most important, the multiplicity of V-extensions of a vague word does not result from any sensitivity to context (V-index). In principle a vague word need not be contextually sensitive at all.

18. The *vagus nerve*, the longest of the cranial nerves, is so named because it "wanders" through the organs in the neck, thorax, and abdomen.
19. Unfortunately, scheduling constraints were such that we were able to run only three subjects in Part III of the experiment.
20. Notice that that freedom is the only "normative feature" of 'red,' mentioned here by Sainsbury, that pertains essentially to its vagueness.
21. Although Wright recognizes that competent use of a vague predicate is not fully rule-governed, so far as I am aware he does not provide a theory that explains that fact.
22. The relevant Wittgenstein is the last sentence of section 289 of *Philosophical Investigations* (1958).

BIBLIOGRAPHY

Abbey, R., 2005. "Is Liberalism Now an Essentially Contested Concept?" *New Political Science* 27.4: 461–480.

Ackerman, F., 1994. "Roots and Consequences of Vagueness." *Philosophical Perspectives* 8: 129–136.

Akerman, J., 2009. "Contextualist Theories of Vagueness." *Philosophy Compass* 7: 470–480.

Adair, M., 1995. "Plato's View of the 'Wandering Uterus.'" *The Classical Journal* 91.2: 153–163.

Antony, Louise M., 1997. "Meaning and Semantic Knowledge." *Aristotelian Society* 71.1 (Suppl.): 177–207.

Bach, K., 2006. "What does it take to refer?" In E. Lepore and B. Smith (eds.), *Oxford Handbook of Philosophy of Language*, Oxford: Oxford University Press, pp. 516–554.

Ball, L., 2008. "Hysteresis in Unemployment." http://www.bos.frb.org/phillips2008/papers/Ball.pdf.

Barker, C., 2002. "The Dynamics of Vagueness." *Linguistics and Philosophy* 25: 1–36.

Barnes, E., 2010. "Ontic Vagueness: A Guide for the Perplexed." *Noûs* 44.4: 601–627.

Barsalou, L., 1983. "Ad Hoc Categories." *Memory and Cognition* 11.3: 211–227.

Bianchi, C., 2001. "Context of Utterance and Intended Context." In V. Akman et al. (eds.), *Context 2001*, LNAI 2116, pp. 73–86. Berlin: Springer-Verlag.

Bobzien, S., 2013. "Higher-Order Vagueness and Borderline Nestings—A Persistent Confusion." *Analytic Philosophy* 54.1: 1–43.

Borg, E., 2006. "Pragmatic Determinants of What Is Said." In K. Brown (ed.), *Encyclopedia of Language and Linguistics*, 2d ed., pp. 737–740. Oxford: Elsevier.

Braun, D., 2012. "Indexicals", *The Stanford Encyclopedia of Philosophy* (Summer 2012 Edition), Edward N. Zalta (ed.), URL = <http://plato.stanford.edu/archives/sum2012/entries/indexicals/>.

Bueno, O., and Colyvan, M., 2012. "Just What Is Vagueness?" *Ratio* 25.1: 19–33.

Burns, L., 1991. *Vagueness: An Investigation into Natural Languages and the Sorites Paradox.* Dordrecht, The Netherlands: Kluwer.

Burns, L. 1995. "Something to do with Vagueness." In T. Horgan (ed.), *Special Issue: Spindel Supplement: Vagueness. The Southern Journal of Philosophy* 33(Suppl.): 23–48.

Caplan, B., 2003. "Putting Things in Contexts." *Philosophical Review* 112.2: 191–214.

Cohen, J., forthcoming. "Indexicality and the Answering Machine Paradox." *Philosophy Compass.* Permalink: http://philosophy-compass.com/2013/02/01/coming-s oon-indexicality-and-the-answering-machine-paradox-by-dr-jonathan-cohen/

Cook, R., 2002. "Vagueness and Mathematical Precision." *Mind* 111: 227–247.

Côté, S. D., Rooney, T. P., Tremblay, J.-P., Dussault, C., and Waller, D. M., 2004. "Ecological Impacts of Deer Overabundance." *Annual Review of Ecology, Evolution, and Systematics* 35: 113–147.

Cresswell, M. J., 1972. "The World Is Everything That Is the Case." *Australasian Journal of Philosophy* 50: 1–13.

Dennett, D., 1978. *Brainstorms.* Cambridge: MIT Press.

Dixit, A., 1992. "Investment and Hysteresis." *The Journal of Economic Perspectives* 6.1: 107–132.

Dreier, J., 1990. "Internalism and Speaker Relativism." *Ethics* 101.1: 6–26.

Dummett, M., 1975. "Wang's Paradox." *Synthèse* 30: 301–324.

Dummett, M., 1978. *Truth and Other Enigmas.* Cambridge, MA: Harvard University Press.

Ebbs, G., 2001. "Vagueness, Sharp Boundaries, and Supervenience Conditions." *Synthèse* 127: 303–323.

Edgington, D., 1997. "Vagueness by Degrees." In R. Keefe and P. Smith (eds.), *Vagueness: A Reader,* pp. 294–316. Cambridge, MA: MIT Press.

Ellis, J., 2004. "Context, Indexicals, and the Sorites." *Analysis* 64.4: 362–364.

Endicott, T., 2000. *Vagueness in Law.* Oxford: Oxford University Press.

Endicott, T., 2011. "The Value of Vagueness." In A. Marmor and S. Soames (eds.), *The Philosophical Foundations of Language in the Law,* p. 14. Oxford: Oxford University Press.

Falk, A., and Zimmermann, F., 2013. "A Taste for Consistency and Survey Response Behavior." *CESifo Economic Studies* 59.1: 181–913.

Fara, D. G., 2003. "Gap Principles, Penumbral Consequence, and Infinitely Higher-Order Vagueness." In J. C. Beall (ed.), *Liars and Heaps: New Essays on Paradox,* pp. 195–222. Oxford: Oxford University Press.

Fine, K., 1975. "Vagueness, Truth, and Logic." *Synthèse* 30: 301–324.

Fodor, J., and Lepore, E., 2004. "Out of Context." *American Philosophical Association Proceedings* 28, 4: 3–20.

Frege, G., 1903. *Grundgesetze der Arithmetik.* Vol. I, *Begriffschriftlich Abgeleitet.* Jena, Germany: Hermann Pohle.

Gaifman, H., 2010. "Vagueness, Tolerance, and Contextual Logic". *Synthese* 174: 5–46.

Gallie, W. B., 1956. "Essentially Contested Concepts." *Proceedings of the Aristotelian Society* 56: 167–198.

Gert, J., 2008. "Vague Terms, Indexicals, and Vague Indexicals." *Philosophical Studies* 140.3: 437–445.

Goodwin, P.B., 1977. "Habit and Hysteresis in Mode Choice." *Urban Studies* 14: 95–98.

Graff, D., 2000. "Shifting Sands: An Interest-Relative Theory of Vagueness." *Philosophical Topics* 28.1: 45–81.

Greenough, P., 2003. "Vagueness: A Minimal Theory." *Mind* 112.446: 235–281.

Halldén, S., 1949. *The Logic of Nonsense.* Uppsala, Sweden: Uppsala Universitets Årsskrift.

Hardin, C. L. 1988. "Phenomenal Colors and Sorites." *Nous* 22: 213–234.

Hawley, K., 2002. "Vagueness and Existence." *Proceedings of the Aristotelian Society*, 52.2: 125–140.

Heck, R. G. 1993. "A Note on the Logic of (Higher-Order) Vagueness." *Analysis* 53: 201–208.

Horgan, T., 1994. "Robust Vagueness and the Forced-March Sorites Paradox." *Philosophical Perspectives* 8: 159–188.

Horgan, T., 1995b. "Transvaluationism: A Dionysian Approach to Vagueness." In T. Horgan (ed.), *Special Issue: Spindel Supplement: Vagueness. The Southern Journal of Philosophy* 33(Suppl.): 97–125.

Hyde, D., 2011. "Sorites Paradox." In E. N. Zalta (ed.), *The Stanford Encyclopedia of Philosophy.* Stanford, CA: Stanford University Press. http://plato.stanford.edu/archives/win2011/entries/sorites-paradox/.

Kalmus, H., 1979. "Dependence of Colour Naming and Monochromator Setting on the Direction of Preceding Changes in Wavelength." *British Journal of Physiological Optics* 33.2: 1–9.

Kamp, H., 1975. "Two Theories about Adjectives." In E. Keenan (ed.), *Formal Semantics for Natural Language*, pp. 123–155. Cambridge, UK: Cambridge University Press.

Kamp, H., 1981. "The Paradox of the Heap." In U. Mönnich (ed.), *Aspects of Philosophical Logic*, pp. 225–277. Dordrecht, The Netherlands: Reidel.

Kaplan, D., 1978. "On the Logic of Demonstratives." In Peter French et al. (eds.), *Contemporary Perspectives in the Philosophy of Language*, pp. 401–412. Minneapolis: University of Minnesota.

Kaplan, D., 1989. "Demonstratives." In J. Almog, J. Perry, and H. Wettstein (eds.), *Themes from Kaplan*, pp. 481–563. Oxford: Oxford University Press.

Kaplan, D., 1989. "Afterthoughts." In J. Almog, J. Perry, and H. Wettstein (eds.), *Themes from Kaplan*, pp. 567–614. Oxford: Oxford University Press.

Keefe, R., 2000. *Theories of Vagueness.* Cambridge, UK: Cambridge University Press.

Keefe, R., and Smith, P. (eds.), 1997. *Vagueness: A Reader.* Cambridge, MA: MIT Press.

Kennedy, C., 2007. "Vagueness and Grammar: The Semantics of Absolute and Gradable Adjectives." *Linguistics and Philosophy* 30.1: 1–45.

Kennedy, C., and McNally, L., 2005. "Scale Structure and the Semantic Typology of Gradable Predicates." *Language* 81.2: 345–381.

Kim, J., 2008. "Evolutionary Design Principles of Modules that Control Cellular Differentiation: Consequences for Hysteresis and Multistationarity." *Bioinformatics* 24.13: 1516–1522.

King, J., 2012. "Speaker Intentions in Context." *Nous* 47.3: 1–19.

Klein, E., 1980. "A Semantics for Positive and Comparative Adjectives." *Linguistics and Philosophy* 4: 1–45.

Künne, W., 2003. *Conceptions of Truth* (Oxford: Oxford University Press).

Kyburg, A., and Morreau, M., 2000. "Fitting Words: Vague Language in Context." *Linguistics and Philosophy* 23: 577–597.

Lewis, D., 1979. "Scorekeeping in a Language Game." *Journal of Philosophical Logic* 8: 339–359.

Lewis, D., 1980. "Index, Context, and Content." In S. Kanger and S. Ohman (eds.) *Philosophy and Grammar*, pp. 79–99. Dordrecht, The Netherlands: Reidel.

Ludlow, P., 1989. "Implicit Comparison Classes." *Linguistics and Philosophy* 12: 519–533.

MacFarlane, J., 2007. "Semantic Minimalism and Nonindexical Contextualism." In G. Preyer and G. Peter (eds.), *Context-Sensitivity and Semantic Minimalism: New Essays on Semantics and Pragmatics*, pp. 240–250. Oxford: Oxford University Press.

Machina, K., 1976. "Truth, Belief, and Vagueness." *Journal of Philosophical Logic* 5: 47–78.

Maddy, P., 2007. *Second Philosophy: A Naturalistic Method*. Oxford: Oxford University Press.

Manor, R., 1995. "Pragmatic Considerations in Semantic Analyses." *Pragmatics and Cognition* 3.2: 225–245.

Marmor, A., 2012. "Varieties of Vagueness in the Law." USC Legal Studies Research Paper 12–18. University of Southern California. http://papers.ssrn.com/sol3/papers.cfm?abstract_id=2039076.

Matthews, R., 2003. "Does Linguistic Competence Require Knowledge of Language?" In A. Barber (ed.), *Epistemology of Language*, pp. 187–216. Oxford: Oxford University Press.

McGee, V., 1990. *Truth, Vagueness, and Paradox*. Indianapolis: Hackett.

McGee, V., and McLaughlin, B., "Distinctions Without a Difference." In T. Horgan (ed.), *Special Issue: Spindel Supplement: Vagueness. The Southern Journal of Philosophy* 33(Suppl.): 203–251.

Moltmann, F., forthcoming. "Truth Predicates in Natural Language." In D. Achourioti, H. Galinon, and J. Martinez (eds.), *Unifying the Philosophy of Truth*. Dordrecht. The Netherlands: Reidel.

Morgan, T. E., 1994. *Men Writing the Feminine: Literature, Theory, and the Questions of Genders*. Albany: State University of New York Press.

Mulligan, K., 2010. "The Truth Predicate vs the Truth Connective: On Taking Connectives Seriously." *Dialectica* 64: 565–584.

Oliva, T. A., Oliver, R. L., and MacMillan, I. C., 1992. "A Catastrophe Model for Developing Service Satisfaction Strategies." *Journal of Marketing* 56.3: 83–95.

Perry, J., 1998. "Indexicals, Contexts and Unarticulated Constituents." In A. Aliseda, R. Gabeek, and D. Westerstahl (eds.), *Computing Natural Language*, pp. 1–11. Stanford, CA: CSLI Publications.

Pinkal, M., 1983. "On the Limits of Lexical Meaning." In R. Bauerle, C. Schwarze, and A. von Stechow (eds.), *Meaning, Use and Interpretation of Language*, pp. 400–422. Berlin: de Gruyter.

Pinkal, M., 1995. *Logic and Lexicon*. Dordrecht, The Netherlands: Kluwer Academic.

Predelli, S., 1998. "Utterance, Interpretation, and the Logic of Indexicals." *Mind and Language*, 13.3: 400–414.

Quinn, W., 1990. "The Puzzle of the Self-Torturer." *Philosophical Studies* 59: 79–90.

Raczaszek, J., Tuller, B., Shapiro, L. P., Case, P., and Kelso, S., 1999. "Categorization of Ambiguous Sentences as a Function of a Changing Prosodic Parameter: A Dynamic Approach." *Journal of Psycholinguistic Research* 28.4: 367–393.

Raffman, D., 1994. "Vagueness Without Paradox." *The Philosophical Review* 103.1: 41–74.

Raffman, D., 1995. "On the Persistence of Phenomenology." In Thomas Metzinger (ed.), *Conscious Experience*, pp. 293–308. Paderborn: Schöningh Verlag.

Raffman, D., 1996. "Vagueness and Context Relativity." *Philosophical Studies* 81: 175–192.

Raffman, D., 2005a. "Borderline Cases and Bivalence." *The Philosophical Review* 114.1: 1–31.

Raffman, D., 2005b. "How to Understand Contextualism About Vagueness: Reply to Stanley." *Analysis* 65.3: 244–248.

Raffman, D., 2009. "Demoting Higher-Order Vagueness." In R. Dietz, S. Morruzzi, and C. Wright (eds.), *Cuts and Clouds*, pp. 535–548. Oxford: Oxford University Press.

Recanati, F., 2001. "Are 'Here' and 'Now' Indexicals?" *Texte* 27: 115–127.

Reimer, M., 1991. "Demonstratives, Demonstrations, and Demonstrata." *Philosophical Studies* 63.2: 187–202.

Robert, P., 1970. *Dictionnaire Alphabetique et Analogique de la Langue Française*. Paris: Société du Nouveau Littré.

Robertson, T., 2000. "On Soames's Solution to the Sorites Paradox." *Analysis* 60.4: 328–334.

Rosenkranz, S., 2003. "Wright on Vagueness and Agnosticism." *Mind* 112.447: 449–464.

Russell, Bertrand, 1923. "Vagueness." *Australasian Journal of Philosophy and Psychology* 1, 84–92.

Sainsbury, M., 1991. "Is There Higher Order Vagueness?" *Philosophical Quarterly* 41: 167–182.

Sainsbury, M., 1997. "Concepts Without Boundaries." In R. Keefe and P. Smith (eds.), *Vagueness: A Reader*, pp. 251–264. Cambridge, MA: MIT Press.

Salmon, N., 2002. "Demonstrating and Necessity." *Philosophical Review* 111.4: 1–20.

Sassoon, G. W., 2007. "Vagueness, Gradability and Typicality: A Comprehensive Semantic Analysis." PhD diss., Tel Aviv University.

Scott, D., 1982. "Duration as a Cue to the Perception of a Phrase Boundary." *Journal of the Acoustical Society of America* 7.4: 996–1006.

Shapiro, S., 2007. *Vagueness in Context*. Oxford: Oxford University Press.

Soames, S., 1998. *Understanding Truth*. Oxford: Oxford University Press.

Soames, S., 2002. "Precis of Understanding Truth and Replies." *Philosophy and Phenomenological Research* 15.2: 429–452.

Sorensen, R., 1988. *Blindspots*. Oxford: Oxford University Press.

Sorensen, R., 2012. "Vagueness." In *The Stanford Encyclopedia of Philosophy* (Summer 2012 edition), Edward N. Zalta (ed.), <http://plato.stanford.edu/archives/sum2012/entries/vagueness/>.

Stanley, J., 2005a. *Knowledge and Practical Interests*. Oxford: Oxford University Press.

Stanley, J., 2005b. "Semantics in Context." In G. Preyer and G. Peter (eds.), *Contextualism*, pp. 221–253. Oxford: Oxford University Press.

Szabo, Z. G., 2001. "Adjectives in Context." In R. Harnish and I. Kenesei (eds.), *Perspectives on Semantics, Pragmatics, and Discourse*, pp. 119–146. Amsterdam: John Benjamins.

Tenenbaum, S., and Raffman, D., 2012. "Vague Projects and the Puzzle of the Self-Torturer." *Ethics* 123.1: 86–112.

Tesser, A., and Achee, J., 1994. "Aggression, Love, Conformity, and Other Social Psychological Catastrophes." In R. Vallacher and A. Nowak (eds.), *Dynamical Systems in Social Psychology*, pp. 96–108. New York: Academic Press.

Tye, M., 1994. "Sorites Paradoxes and the Semantics of Vagueness." *Philosophical Perspectives* 8: 189–206.

Tye, M., 1996. "Fuzzy Realism and the Problem of the Many." *Philosophical Studies* 81.2–3: 215–225.

Unger, P., 1979. "There Are No Ordinary Things." *Synthèse* 41: 117–154.

Van Deemter, K., 2006. "Generating Referring Expressions That Involve Gradable Properties." *Computational Linguistics* 32.2: 195–222.

Van Deemter, K., 2010. *Not Exactly: In Praise of Vagueness*. Oxford: Oxford University Press.

Van der Maas, H., Kolstein, R., and van der Pligt, J., 2003. "Sudden Transitions in Attitudes." *Sociological Methods Research* 32: 125–152.

Van der Maas, H., Jansen, B., and Raijmakers, M., 2004. "Developmental Patterns in Proportional Reasoning." In A. Demetriou and A. Raftopoulos (eds.), *Cognitive*

Developmental Change: Theories, Models, and Measurement, pp. 118–156. Cambridge, UK: Cambridge University Press.

Varzi, A., 2005. "The Vagueness of 'Vague': Rejoinder to Hull." *Mind* 114.455: 695–702.

Voorhoeve, A., and Binmore, K., 2006. "Transitivity, the Sorites Paradox, and Similarity-Based Decision-Making." *Erkenntnis* 64: 101–114.

Unger, P., 1979 "There Are No Ordinary Things." *Synthèse* 41.2:117–154.

Waismann, F., 1945. "Verifiability." In *Proceedings of the Aristotelian Society* 19(Suppl.): 119–150.

Waldron, J., 1994. "Vagueness in Law and Language: Some Philosophical Issues." *California Law Review* 82: 509–525.

Waldron, J., 2002. "Is the Rule of Law an Essentially Contested Concept (in Florida)?" *Law and Philosophy* 21. 2: 137–164.

Walker, M., Wan, X., Kirsch, G., and Rosenbaum, D. S., 2003. "Hysteresis Effect Implicates Calcium Cycling as a Mechanism of Repolarization Alternans." *American Heart Association, Basic Science Reports* 108: 2704–2709.

Williamson, T., 1994. *Vagueness.* London: Routledge.

Wittgenstein, L., 1958. *Philosophical Investigations.* 3d ed. Oxford: Basil Blackwell.

Wright, C., 1975. "On the Coherence of Vague Predicates." *Synthèse* 30.3–4: 325–365.

Wright, C., 1976. "Language Mastery and the Sorites Paradox." In G. Evans and J. McDowell (eds.), *Truth and Meaning,* pp. 223–247. Oxford: Clarendon Press.

Wright, C., 1987. "Further Reflections on the Sorites Paradox." *Philosophical Topics* 15: 227–290.

Wright, C., 1988. "Realism, Anti-Realism, Irrealism, Quasi-Realism." In P. A. French, T. E. Uehling, and H. K. Wettstein (eds.), *Midwest Studies in Philosophy* 12: 25–49.

Wright, C., 1992. "Is Higher Order Vagueness Coherent?" *Analysis* 52: 129–139.

Wright, C., 1994. "The Epistemic Conception of Vagueness." In T. Horgan (ed.), *Special Issue: Spindel Supplement: Vagueness. The Southern Journal of Philosophy* 33(Suppl.): 133–160.

Wright, C., 2007. "Wang's Paradox." In R. E. Auxier and L. E. Hahn (eds.), *Library of Living Philosophers,* vol. 31, pp. 415–444. Chicago: Open Court Publishing.

Zadeh, L. A., 1965. "Fuzzy Sets." *Information and Control* 8: 338–353.

Zadeh, L. A., 1975. "Fuzzy Logic and Approximate Reasoning." *Synthèse* 30: 407–428.

INDEX

abortion, 5, 107, 157, 159–60
Achee, J., 143, 158
Ackerman, F., 6
Adair, M., 171
Akerman, J., 188
ambiguity, 2, 107, 109
Antony, L., 176
arbitrariness, vii, 15–16, 22–24, 36, 57, 92, 94, 101, 105–8, 117, 123–34, 138, 145, 154, 164, 173, 178, 185, 197, 199

Bach, K., 195
Ball, L., 143
Barker, C., 73
Barnes, E., 2
Barsalou, L., 192
Bianchi, C., 85–86
Binmore, K., 6
bivalence, 10–13, 24, 26, 108, 129
board game, 164–9
Bobzien, S., 194
borderline cases, 4–10, 12–14, 16, 20, 23–24, chapter 2 passim, 93–95, 101, 103, 108–9, 127, 129–30, 132, 136–9, 143–6, 149–153, 162, 164, 166–7, 169, 173–4, 177, 187–194, 198–200
  higher-order, 12, 32–33, 46–52, 54, 60–61, 63–64, 66–67, 69–71
  fractal, 52–3, 66, 71

boundaries, 2, 4, 6–7, 9–10, 12–17, 33–34, 47–49, 53–56, 70, 72, 95, 98–99, 102, 105, 107–8, 122–4, 128, 131, 134, 138–9, 154, 162, 177, 179, 187–8, 193, 196–7, 199, 200
boundarylessness, 6, 124, 127, 187
Brown, A., 146ff, 201
Bueno, O., 4, 19
Burns, L., 25, 28, 35, 47, 188

Caplan, B., 194–5
classical logic, 10–13, 26, 33, 38, 41, 44, 57, 70, 188
Cohen, J., 195
Colyvan, M., 4, 19
competence, linguistic, 191
content, stable, 78–9, 81, 87, 89, 91, 103–5, 107, 109, 111–12, 118, 120, 194–5, 19
  context-relative, 78–9, 81–82, 84–89, 91–92, 97, 99, 101, 103–5, 111–12, 118, 120–30, 195–8, 202
context, intended, vs. context of utterance, 84, 86–88
context-sensitivity, xi, 9, 19–21, 72–5, 79–80, 84, 89–91, 97, 103–5, 110, 112–13, 116, 119, 130, 184, 190, 193, 195, 202
contextualism, xii, 9–11, 19, 24, 73, 90, 92, 188, 200, 202
Cook, R., 188

last permissible stopping place   — sorites worry about sharp cutoff
↳ or: at what point would you disagree with   PP. 106, 105
someone who says that x$ is rich
relative to v-index r   122
- At what $-amount is the "genuine disagreement"
possible ?

(b) is false!

if we call   #29 Green, calling #30 Blue is not arbitrary
it is mandatory!

P101 Justification and arbitrariness

↳ a more subtle worry:
A speaker's use does not determine the applicability — i.e. you don't
101   get to be automatically right by being a competent speaker and saying
x is F.

169   But, the range of application gets picked by making the judgment, not
prior to it

There is a tension here: A competent speaker that happens to judge an x as F
outside of any permissible range of application of F is wrong — and presumably we can
tell some story why that happened. But, independently of how you got there, once
you land past the line you're right.

P169: Story/proposal

Dartboard, bullseye : It's like you're throwing a dart at a wall,
and if you land within a certain area you get
to draw the bullseye around the dart.
But if you land outside, you don't get to.

More on justification: P94 - What makes justification trivial?

You judge #15 to be blue because it seems blue. Seemings provide
some justification, so the judgment is justified.

de re / de dicto :   About patch #18 Subject from table 5.8 believes
                     that it is blue and that it is green. And both beliefs are
                     justified. So?

Question on truth →
    Is patch # 17 blue, green? What is true?
    If it is only true relative to a r.o.a., then why can't we be justified
    and know that it is so?

Moreover :

    I classify patch # 30 as blue because it strikes me as bl.
                    # 17   "

    Is one more justified than the other?   / Other truth:
                                                   / The semantics are set.
Nb: "Genuine disagreement is impossible" 94   / If they are also transparent, then
    Cf. Dressgate   / can we be justified in believing
                                                   / that items are within some permissible
                                                     r.o.a. and not in others?

Sharp cutoffs for borderline

    | |
G #1   B#30
    the end of 'permissible ranges of application'
    for Green
    that is vague, ok - but now we got a 'most permissive use of permissible range of application
                                      of green'

Sorites for 'mandates blue'

   ⌐ OK, very good.

   How to solve this?

Justification — contrastivism   Q: How do we get from vague sentences
                                       to propositions?

P. 96 — 'set' as a non-technical term. But! What is the metaphysical status
    of a R.o.a.?

        ⌐ V-index determines 'competent ways of applying'

V-extensions: Objects Instantiating the ranges of application   97

Re: Raffman's response to sharp words
  — competent speakers will even Include / disagree about the endpoints
Contra p. 99 — all agree that's not the case.

Propositions & propositional attitudes

  hysteresis and de re / de dicto

  ⌐ Hysteresis is possible only if we only form de re attitudes,
    not de dicto attitudes.   de re

It is not irrational to believe about patch #15 that it is Blue and that it is not blue.
     "   — "   that patch #15 is and is not blue. ← de dicto

Solution to suspend judgment: Contraries!

not: About patch #15 not blue and not not blue

but!   not blue and not green!

Hm, we don't

?

When part of a propositional attitude of someone,
than there is a fact of the matter which range of applications they are using. (Ok for sentences, too)

But that is not the case for free-standing propositions.